The Prefaces to the Waverley Novels

Sir Walter Scott

The Prefaces
to the
Waverley Novels

Edited by
Mark A. Weinstein

UNIVERSITY OF NEBRASKA PRESS
Lincoln and London

Publishers on the Plains

UNP

Library of Congress Cataloging in Publication Data

Scott, Walter, Sir, bart., 1771–1832.
   The prefaces to the Waverley novels.

   Includes bibliographical references.
   1.   Scott, Walter, Sir, bart., 1771–1832.   Waverley novels.   2.   Prefaces.
I.   Weinstein, Mark A.   II.   Title.
PR5303.W4   823'.7   78–2710
ISBN 0–8032–4700–1

823.7
S431pr

To my dear son,
JONATHAN DAVID

CONTENTS

A Preface to the Prefaces   ix

Part I. *THE EARLY HISTORY*

Waverley (1814): A Postscript Which Should Have
   Been a Preface   3
Waverley (1814): Introductory   7
Introduction to *The Antiquary* (1816)   11
Review of *Tales of My Landlord* (1817)   13
Ivanhoe (1820): Dedicatory Epistle   29
Introductory Epistle to *The Fortunes of Nigel* (1822)   40
Prefatory Letter to *Peveril of the Peak* (1822)   58
Introduction to *Chronicles of the Canongate* (1827)   70

Part II. *THE LATE HISTORY: THE INTRODUCTIONS
    TO THE "MAGNUM OPUS" (1829–32)*

Advertisement   83
General Preface   86
Guy Mannering   103
Rob Roy   115
The Heart of Mid-Lothian   117
The Bride of Lammermoor   122
A Legend of Montrose   128
Ivanhoe   136

The Monastery   147

The Abbot   163

Kenilworth   170

The Pirate   172

The Fortunes of Nigel   177

Peveril of the Peak   184

Quentin Durward   191

St. Ronan's Well   200

Redgauntlet   205

The Betrothed   215

The Talisman   219

Woodstock   224

Chronicles of the Canongate   228

The Fair Maid of Perth   233

Anne of Geierstein   236

Count Robert of Paris   239

Castle Dangerous   245

Notes   251

A Preface to the Prefaces

I

"In the hands of Scott the preface suddenly acquired a dignity and interest which it had never before possessed, and which it has never since attained," wrote M. H. Macartney in 1905.[1] Although Henry James was soon to challenge this supremacy, Scott's prefaces, besides providing delightful reading, remain one of the most important series of revelations that a writer has ever made about his own work.

Scott actually wrote two kinds of preface. The first prefaces appeared upon initial publication of several of his novels: they are witty, ironic, oblique, and written behind various masks. These were Balzac's favorites: "See how he dashes the jesting personages of his preface on the critics! Like splendid hunting-dogs they rush at their quarry and, with a single snap of the jaws, bite the said aristarchs to the bone. These ingenious prefaces, without gall yet *malicieux*, ironical with good nature, in which reason shines, resplendent as Molière could make it, these prefaces are masterpieces to studious minds which have preserved the taste for atticism."[2] The final prefaces were written for the "Magnum Opus" during the last years of Scott's life: they are more straightforward, documentary, reminiscent, and personal. These were Saintsbury's favorites: "These introductions, written before the final inroad had been made on his powers by the united strength of physical and moral misfortune, animated at once by the last glow of those powers, and by the indefinable charm of a fond retrospection, displaying every faculty in autumn luxuriance, are so delightful that they sometimes seem to be the very cream and essence of his literary work in prose. Indeed, I have always wondered why they have not been published separately as a History of the Waverley Novels by their author."[3]

II

It is a commonplace that Scott is his own best critic,[4] but it would be equally true to say that he is his own severest critic. Scott the critic often wrote at the expense of Scott the novelist, and unwary readers have continued to echo his own belittlements. Nevertheless, as Mary Lascelles suggests, Scott is one who "to deprecate censorious judgement and satisfy the critic within" will "seem to make toies of the utmost he can do." In his self-criticism, as in much of his literary career, there is a challenging "strain of negligence, caprice, even mischief."[5] His best prefaces deserve the same kind of close reading and measured response that his best novels are now receiving. For even when he seems to be depreciating most his own achievement, he usually provides the materials for his own defense.

The famous review of the *Tales of My Landlord* in the *Quarterly* (1817) offers an early paradigm. The entire article is a masterpiece of deviousness, with three different writers contributing to the anonymous review.[6] Scott, of course, controls the whole and writes the opening overview of the Waverley Novels. In it, he anticipates the major criticisms that have since been leveled against his work. But he also answers those objections, although, when pressed, he drops his defense. For example, he first protests against the loose construction of the narratives and the "slovenly indifference" of the author. But he adds:

> There may be something of system in it however: for we have remarked, that with an attention which amounts even to affectation, he has avoided the common language of narrative, and thrown his story, as much as possible, into a dramatic shape. In many cases this has added greatly to the effect, by keeping both the actors and action continually before the reader, and placing him, in some measure, in the situation of the audience at a theatre, who are compelled to gather the meaning of the scene from what the dramatis personae say to each other, and not from any explanation addressed immediately to themselves.

A Preface to the Prefaces

It was this same dramatic evolution of her stories that Scott found so refreshing and praiseworthy in Jane Austen. Although Scott's own novels may seem heavily freighted with narration and description to the modern reader, they are far more dramatic than the works of most of his predecessors and contemporaries. The popular Gothics of Mrs. Radcliffe and the historical pageants of Jane Porter give the Waverley Novels a relatively streamlined appearance. After making this defense, however, Scott typically drops it and ends ironically: "But though the author gain this advantage, and thereby compel the reader to think of the personages of the novel and not of the writer, yet the practice, especially pushed to the extent we have noticed, is a principal cause of the flimsiness and incoherent texture of which his greatest admirers are compelled to complain. Few can wish his success more sincerely than we do, and yet without more attention on his own part, we have great doubts of its continuance."

Next, Scott anticipates the second major objection that has always been made against his novels: "the total want of interest which the reader attaches to the character of the hero" and the similarities among the heroes of the different novels, all of them "very amiable and very insipid sort of young men" who are "never actors, but always acted upon." Thus, Thackeray could claim that the hero of the Waverley Novels was the sort of young man every mother wanted her daughter to marry.[7] But Scott answers this objection by reference to his whole narrative strategy. Such heroes are "foreigners to whom every thing in Scotland is strange,—a circumstance which serves as his apology for entering into many minute details which are reflectively, as it were, addressed to the reader through the medium of the hero. While he is going into explanations and details which, addressed directly to the reader, might appear tiresome and unnecessary, he gives interest to them by exhibiting the effect which they produce upon the principal person of his drama, and at the same time obtains a patient hearing for what might otherwise be passed over without attention." Scott always seems willing to sacrifice lesser virtues for the achievement of his major artistic purposes. Again, however, after defending his practice, he accepts the original criticism, or does he? "But if he gains this advantage, it is by sacrificing the character of the hero. No one can be interesting to the reader who is not himself a prime agent in the scene. This is understood even by the worthy citizen and his wife, who are introduced as prolocutors in Fletcher's Knight of the Burning Pestle. When they are asked what the principal person of the drama shall do?—the answer is prompt and ready—'Marry, let him come forth and kill a giant.' There is a good deal of tact in the request." Is this serious criticism or high comedy? What is the tone of Scott's close: "Every hero in poetry, in fictitious narrative, ought to come forth and do or say something or other which no other person could have done or said; make some sacrifice, surmount some difficulty, and become interesting to us otherwise than by his mere appearance on the scene, the passive tool of the other characters"?

Throughout his sections of the review, Scott plays both the brash plaintiff and the sly defendant. He mingles praise and blame with astonishing rapidity and irony. On the one hand, he blames the romancer for having "cruelly falsified history"; on the other, he depreciates the novelist's imagination because of his dependence upon fact. But despite the impishness of the review, Scott reveals himself to be a novelist who has thought seriously about the practice of his profession, and he challenges the reader to do the same.

III

Flaubert's surprising judgment that among English writers only Scott does *not* "want plan"[8] gains support from the evidence of the prefaces. Scott was not merely Fancy's child, warbling his native wood-notes wild, but a developing artificer. He learned from his early mistakes. Although *Waverley* contains grand things, it is the work of a beginner: the dilatory start, the overlong descriptions, the short chapters, the manipulation of the hero's movements up and down the country. Scott himself admitted that "the mode in which I conducted the story scarcely deserved the success which the romance afterwards attained. The tale of *Waverley* was put together with so little care that I cannot boast of having sketched any distinct plan of the work. . . . And though I have been in other instances a sinner in this sort, I do not recollect any of these novels in which I have transgressed so widely as in the first of the series." In the preface to the next novel, *Guy Mannering*, Scott revealed how his original conception got away from him. In the introduction to *The Antiquary*, Scott regretted that he could not unite the "two requisites of a good Novel": the minute description of manners and the arrangement of "an artificial and combined narrative." But the novels of the following golden period—*Old Mortality, Rob Roy, The Heart of Mid-Lothian, The Bride of Lammermoor*—do not draw the censure of Scott the critic. He dwells not on his artistic successes, but only on his failures. Thus, he analyzes in detail the reasons for his first major failure, *The Monastery*, and anyone reading this preface must realize that here is a novelist who carefully considers his craft. In his next novel, *The Abbot*, he determines to recoup the loss of his reputation by paying careful "attention to such principles of composition as I conceived were best suited to the historical novel."

In the general preface to the "Magnum Opus," Scott advertises that he will explain the nature of his original materials. Although many other matters are discussed in the prefaces, the revelation of his sources remains a constant concern. Scott's sources are interesting short stories in themselves, but when compared with the novels, they emphasize that he is a master constructor. It is not the sources, but Scott's use of them that is remarkable. Wherever he borrows, he overpays. From the original two-page letter of Mrs. Goldie, for example, he builds up the complex four-volume structure of *The Heart of Mid-Lothian*. He even changes several of the scant details with which he began. Preface after preface supplies evidence of the same imaginative process. A character or a combination of circumstances or a trait of manners in the boundless field of history stimulates Scott's imagination to create a palace of art that bears little or no relation to the original sketch.

The most modest of artists, Scott reproved his critics only once. He regretted that they saw in Norna of *The Pirate* a mere copy of Meg Merrilies; he goes into unusual detail to point out the significant differences between the two characters. It was important to Scott that individuals within the same genus be distinguished: he makes careful discriminations between Dandie Dinmont and Hobbie Elliot and among Smollett's sea characters. Scott would have been uncomfortable with two of the most influential studies of his works, Georg Lukács's "Scott and the Classical Form of the Historical Novel" and Alexander Welsh's *The Hero of the Waverley Novels*.[9] Both critics see broad recurrent patterns where Scott emphasizes minute particulars; both lump together where Scott individualizes. But perhaps this is merely a local manifestation of the perennial, ironic confrontation between critic and artist.

Scott is the practicing artist who had to develop his own critical position out of his personal experiences. His criticism remains primarily practical rather than theoretical. But David Masson, a nineteenth-century critic, set a generous precedent when he reconsidered his initial verdict that Scott had no theoretical side at all: "Is it that, after all, there was a speculative faculty in Scott which he had not worked? From the shrewdness and sagacity of some of his critical prefaces to his novels, where he discusses principles of literature without seeming to call them such, I am sometimes tempted to believe the latter."[10] For example, from at least the time of his essay upon *Gulliver's Travels* (1814) to the last years of his life when he wrote the final prefaces, Scott was intrigued by the relation between life and art. He was tempted by the successful examples of Smollett and Lesage to believe that fiction should imitate the inconsequence, incoherence, and improbability of human life, and that artistry itself worked against verisimilitude. But he concluded that "though such an unconnected course of adventures is what most frequently occurs in nature, yet the province of the romance writer being artificial, there is more required from him than a mere compliance with the simplicity of reality." The finer model is that of Fielding, especially in *Tom Jones*: "The more closely and happily the story is combined, and the more natural and felicitous the catastrophe, the nearer such a composition will approach the perfection of the novelist's art; nor can an author neglect this branch of his profession without incurring proportional censure." It is a high ideal for a novelist. It is an ideal that Scott admittedly did not always attain. But perhaps, as Flaubert suggests, in his greatest works Scott did achieve that "perfection of the novelist's art."

IV

Like the preface to the second edition of *Lyrical Ballads*, Scott's prefaces reveal that he was consciously encouraging a literary-moral revolution. In this respect, they correct the clichés of literary tradition and the caricature by Mark Twain. Perceiving

A Preface to the Prefaces

time as an ever flowing stream, Scott faces forward to the democratic future although he draws his materials out of the aristocratic past. In the introduction to *The Antiquary* (1816), he reviews his first three novels:

> I have, in the two last narratives especially, sought my principal personages in the class of society who are the last to feel the influence of that general polish which assimilates to each other the manners of different nations. Among the same class I have placed some of the scenes in which I have endeavoured to illustrate the operation of the higher and more violent passions; both because the lower orders are less restrained by the habit of suppressing their feelings, and because I agree with my friend Wordsworth that they seldom fail to express them in the strongest and most powerful language.

Scott sketches "the outline of Dominie Sampson's real story, in which there is neither romantic incident nor sentimental passion; but which, perhaps, from the rectitude and simplicity of character which it displays, may interest the heart and fill the eye of the reader as irresistably as if it respected distresses of a more dignified or refined character." He sees in the prototype of Jeanie Deans a "pleasing and interesting sketch of high principle and steady affection" and develops from it "a theme affording such a pleasing view of the moral dignity of virtue, though unaided by birth, beauty, or talent." Later, while presenting a male counterpart of Jeanie, Scott emphasizes that he is creating a new kind of fictional hero and heroine:

> Having, in the tale of the *Heart of Midlothian*, succeeded in some degree in awakening an interest in behalf of one devoid of those accomplishments which belong to a heroine almost by right, I was next tempted to choose a hero upon the same unpromising plan; and as worth of character, goodness of heart, and rectitude of principle were necessary to one who laid no claim to high birth, romantic sensibility, or any of the usual accomplishments of those who strut through the pages of this sort of composition, I made free with the name of a person [George Heriot] who has left the most magnificent proofs of his benevolence and charity that the capital of Scotland has to display.

Rather than glorifying "the sham chivalries of a brainless and worthless long-vanished society,"[11] Scott anticipates a central mode of Victorian fiction.

The final words of the final preface are Godscroft's verses on Sir James Douglas. But for one who loves Scott, they provide the perfect close:

Good Sir Walter Scott, who wise, and wight, and worthy was,
Was never overglad in no winning, nor yet oversad for no tineing;
Good fortune and evil chance he weighed both in one balance.

Note on the Text

Following the suggestion of Ian Jack that "it might have served as a preface to the whole series of the Waverley Romances,"[12] I begin with the last chapter of *Waverley*, "A Postscript Which Should Have Been a Preface." In it, Scott describes the inspiration behind his finest novels. I then move back to the first chapter of *Waverley*, "Introductory," in which Scott explains his fundamental strategy in historical fiction. In the next two selections, the introduction to *The Antiquary* and the review of *Tales of My Landlord*, Scott comments on his earliest novels. Assuming various personae in the prefaces to *Ivanhoe, Nigel*, and *Peveril*, Scott discusses the historical novel in general and his own practice in particular. Finally, in the introduction to the *Chronicles of the Canongate*, Scott sheds all disguises and speaks about his own works in his own name. This last of the early prefaces anticipates—in both style and content—the later prefaces written for the "Magnum Opus," of which a large selection is included here.

I have used the Dryburgh Edition (1892–94) as my copy text. It was based upon Scott's own annotated copy for the "Magnum Opus" and remains the most authoritative text available. I have made several corrections but only when supported by the evidence of Scott's own manuscripts and proof sheets. For the review of *Tales of My Landlord*, I have used the original text, warts and all, from the *Quarterly Review*.[13]

I have retained most of the notes from the Dryburgh edition, especially those of Scott and David Laing; bracketed footnotes were supplied by an anonymous editor of the Dryburgh edition. I have dropped a few footnotes that I judge to be inconsequential. A full line of points in the text is used to indicate my own deletions. My own notes appear at the end of the book.

A Preface to the Prefaces

I especially thank the following: the National Library of Scotland, for permission to see the manuscript of *Waverley*, the proof sheets of *Ivanhoe* and *The Fortunes of Nigel*, and the manuscript and proof sheets of *Count Robert of Paris*; Mr. D. S. Goodes, Walpole Librarian, King's School, Canterbury, for permission to see the manuscript of *The Fortunes of Nigel*; the Pierpont Morgan Library, for permission to see the manuscript of *Peveril of the Peak*; the Cornell University Library, for permission to see the proof sheets of *Peveril of the Peak*; the New York Public Library and the British Museum, for permission to see their Scott collections; and Mrs. Maxwell-Scott, for permission to print the hitherto unpublished preface to *Count Robert of Paris*.

Part I

THE EARLY HISTORY

WAVERLEY (1814)

A Postscript Which Should Have Been a Preface

Our journey is now finished, gentle reader; and if your patience has accompanied me through these sheets, the contract is, on your part, strictly fulfilled. Yet, like the driver who has received his full hire, I still linger near you, and make, with becoming diffidence, a trifling additional claim upon your bounty and good nature. You are as free, however, to shut the volume of the one petitioner, as to close your door in the face of the other.

This should have been a prefatory chapter, but for two reasons: First, that most novel readers, as my own conscience reminds me, are apt to be guilty of the sin of omission respecting that same matter of prefaces; Secondly, that it is a general custom with that class of students to begin with the last chapter of a work; so that, after all, these remarks, being introduced last in order, have still the best chance to be read in their proper place.

There is no European nation which, within the course of half a century or little more, has undergone so complete a change as this kingdom of Scotland. The effects of the insurrection of 1745,—the destruction of the patriarchal power of the Highland chiefs,—the abolition of the heritable jurisdictions[1] of the Low-land nobility and barons,—the total eradication of the Jacobite party, which, averse to intermingle with the English, or adopt their customs, long continued to pride themselves upon main-taining ancient Scottish manners and customs,—commenced this innovation. The gradual influx of wealth and extension of com-merce have since united to render the present people of Scotland a class of beings as different from their grandfathers as the existing English are from those of Queen Elizabeth's time. The political and economical effects of these changes have been traced by Lord Selkirk with great precision and accuracy.[2] But the change, though steadily and rapidly progressive, has, nevertheless, been gradual; and like those who drift down the stream of a deep and smooth river, we are not aware of the progress we have made until we fix our eye on the now distant point from which we have been drifted. Such of the present generation as can recollect the last twenty or twenty-five years of the eighteenth century will be fully sensible of the truth of this statement; especially if their acquaintance and connexions lay among those who, in my younger time, were facetiously called 'folks of the old leaven,' who still cherished a lingering, though hopeless, attachment to the house of Stuart. This race has now almost entirely vanished from the land, and with it, doubtless, much absurd political prejudice; but also many living examples of singular and disinterested attachment to the principles of loyalty which they received from their fathers, and of old Scottish faith, hospitality, worth, and honour.

It was my accidental lot, though not born a Highlander (which may be an apology for much bad Gaelic), to reside during my childhood and youth among persons of the above description; and now, for the purpose of preserving some idea of the ancient manners of which I have witnessed the almost total extinction, I have embodied in imaginary scenes, and ascribed to fictitious characters, a part of the incidents which I then received from those who were actors in them. Indeed, the most romantic parts of this narrative are precisely those which have a foundation in fact. The exchange of mutual protection between a Highland gentleman and an officer of rank in the king's service, together with the spirited manner in which the latter asserted his right to return the favour he had received, is literally true. The accident by a musket shot, and the heroic reply imputed to Flora, relate to a lady of rank not long deceased. And scarce a gentleman who was 'in hiding' after the battle of Culloden but could tell a tale of strange concealments and of wild and hair's-breadth 'scapes as extraordinary as any which I have ascribed to my heroes. Of this, the escape of Charles Edward himself, as the most prominent, is the most striking example. The accounts of the battle of Preston and skirmish at Clifton are taken from the narrative of intelligent eye-witnesses, and corrected from the *History of the Rebellion* by the late venerable author of *Douglas*.[3] The Lowland Scottish gentlemen and the subordinate characters are not given as individual portraits, but are drawn from the general habits of the period, of which I have witnessed some remnants in my younger days, and partly gathered from tradition.

It has been my object to describe these persons, not by a caricatured and exaggerated use of the national dialect, but by their habits, manners, and feelings, so as in some distant degree to emulate the admirable Irish portraits drawn by Miss Edgeworth,[4] so different from the 'Teagues' and 'dear joys' who so long, with the most perfect family resemblance to each other, occupied the drama and the novel.

I feel no confidence, however, in the manner in which I have executed my purpose. Indeed, so little was I satisfied with my production, that I laid it aside in an unfinished state, and only found it again by mere accident among other waste papers in an old cabinet, the drawers of which I was rummaging in order to accommodate a friend with some fishing-tackle, after it had been mislaid for several years. Two works upon similar subjects, by female authors whose genius is highly creditable to their country, have appeared in the interval; I mean Mrs. Hamilton's *Glenburnie*[5] and the late account of *Highland Superstitions*.[6] But the first is confined to the rural habits of Scotland, of which it has given a picture with striking and impressive fidelity; and the traditional records of the respectable and ingenious Mrs. Grant of Laggan are of a nature distinct from the fictitious narrative which I have here attempted.

I would willingly persuade myself that the preceding work will not be found altogether uninteresting. To elder persons it will recall scenes and characters familiar to their youth; and to the rising generation the tale may present some idea of the manners of their forefathers.

Yet I heartily wish that the task of tracing the evanescent manners of his own country had employed the pen of the only man in Scotland who could have done it justice—of him so eminently distinguished in elegant literature, and whose sketches of Colonel Caustic and Umphraville are perfectly blended with the finer traits of national character.[7] I should in that case have had more pleasure as a reader than I shall ever feel in the pride of a successful author, should these sheets confer upon me that envied distinction. And as I have inverted the usual arrangement, placing these remarks at the end of the work to which they refer, I will venture on a second violation of form, by closing the whole with a Dedication—

THESE VOLUMES

BEING RESPECTFULLY INSCRIBED

TO

OUR SCOTTISH ADDISON,

HENRY MACKENZIE,

BY

AN UNKNOWN ADMIRER

OF

HIS GENIUS.

WAVERLEY (1814)

Introductory

The title of this work has not been chosen without the grave and solid deliberation which matters of importance demand from the prudent. Even its first, or general denomination, was the result of no common research or selection, although, according to the example of my predecessors, I had only to seize upon the most sounding and euphonic surname that English history or topography affords, and elect it at once as the title of my work and the name of my hero. But, alas! what could my readers have expected from the chivalrous epithets of Howard, Mordaunt, Mortimer, or Stanley, or from the softer and more sentimental sounds of Belmour, Belville, Belfield, and Belgrave, but pages of inanity, similar to those which have been so christened for half a century past? I must modestly admit I am too diffident of my own merit to place it in unnecessary opposition to preconceived associations; I have, therefore, like a maiden knight with his white shield, assumed for my hero, WAVERLEY, an uncontaminated name, bearing with its sound little of good or evil, excepting what the reader shall hereafter be pleased to affix to it. But my second or supplemental title was a matter of much more difficult election, since that, short as it is, may be held as pledging the author to some special mode of laying his scene, drawing his characters, and managing his adventures. Had I, for example, announced in my frontispiece, 'Waverley, a Tale of other Days,' must not every novel-reader have anticipated a castle scarce less than that of

Udolpho,[1] of which the eastern wing had long been uninhabited, and the keys either lost, or consigned to the care of some aged butler or housekeeper, whose trembling steps, about the middle of the second volume, were doomed to guide the hero, or heroine, to the ruinous precincts? Would not the owl have shrieked and the cricket cried in my very title-page? and could it have been possible for me, with a moderate attention to decorum, to introduce any scene more lively than might be produced by the jocularity of a clownish but faithful valet, or the garrulous narrative of the heroine's *fille-de-chambre*, when rehearsing the stories of blood and horror which she had heard in the servants' hall? Again, had my title borne, 'Waverley, a Romance from the German,' what head so obtuse as not to image forth a profligate abbot, an oppressive duke, a secret and mysterious association of Rosycrucians and Illuminati,[2] with all their properties of black cowls, caverns, daggers, electrical machines, trap-doors, and dark-lanterns? Or if I had rather chosen to call my work a 'Sentimental Tale,' would it not have been a sufficient presage of a heroine with a profusion of auburn hair, and a harp, the soft solace of her solitary hours, which she fortunately finds always the means of transporting from castle to cottage, although she herself be sometimes obliged to jump out of a two-pair-of-stairs window, and is more than once bewildered on her journey, alone and on foot, without any guide but a blowzy peasant girl, whose jargon she hardly can understand? Or again, if my Waverley had been entitled 'A Tale of the Times,' wouldst thou not, gentle reader, have demanded from me a dashing sketch of the fashionable world, a few anecdotes of private scandal thinly veiled, and if lusciously painted, so much the better? a heroine from Grosvenor Square, and a hero from the Barouche Club or the Four-in-Hand, with a set of subordinate characters from the *élégantes* of Queen Anne Street East, or the dashing heroes of the Bow-Street Office?[3] I could proceed in proving the importance of a title-page, and displaying at the same time my own intimate knowledge of the particular ingredients necessary to the composition of romances and novels of various descriptions;—but it is enough, and I scorn to tyrannise longer over the impatience of my reader, who is doubtless already anxious to know the choice made by an author so profoundly versed in the different branches of his art.

By fixing, then, the date of my story Sixty Years before this present 1st November 1805, I would have my readers understand, that they will meet in the following pages neither a romance of chivalry nor a tale of modern manners; that my hero will neither have iron on his shoulders, as of yore, nor on the heels of his boots, as is the present fashion of Bond Street;[4] and that my damsels will neither be clothed 'in purple and in pall,'[5] like the Lady Alice of an old Ballad, nor reduced to the primitive nakedness of a modern fashionable at a rout. From this my choice of an era the understanding critic may farther presage that the object of my tale is more a description of men than manners. A tale of manners, to be interesting, must either refer to antiquity so great as to have become venerable, or it must bear a vivid reflection of those scenes which are passing daily before our eyes, and are interesting from their novelty. Thus the coat-of-mail of our ancestors, and the triple-furred pelisse of our modern beaux, may, though for very different reasons, be equally fit for the array of a fictitious character; but who, meaning the costume of his hero to be impressive, would willingly attire him in the court dress of George the Second's reign, with its no collar, large sleeves, and low pocket-holes? The same may be urged, with equal truth, of the Gothic hall, which, with its darkened and tinted windows, its elevated and gloomy roof, and massive oaken table garnished with boar's-head and rosemary, pheasants and peacocks, cranes and cygnets, has an excellent effect in fictitious description. Much may also be gained by a lively display of a modern fête, such as we have daily recorded in that part of a newspaper entitled the Mirror of Fashion, if we contrast these, or either of them, with the splendid formality of an entertainment given Sixty Years since; and thus it will be readily seen how much the painter of antique or of fashionable manners gains over him who delineates those of the last generation.

Considering the disadvantages inseparable from this part of my subject, I must be understood to have resolved to avoid them as much as possible, by throwing the force of my narrative upon the characters and passions of the actors;—those passions common to men in all stages of society, and which have alike agitated the human heart, whether it throbbed under the steel corslet of the fifteenth century, the brocaded coat of the eighteenth, or the blue frock and white dimity waistcoat of the present day.* Upon these passions it is no doubt true that the state of manners and laws casts a necessary colouring; but the bearings, to use the language of heraldry, remain the same, though the tincture may be not only different, but opposed in strong contradistinction. The wrath of our ancestors, for example, was coloured *gules*; it broke forth in acts of open and sanguinary violence against the objects of its fury. Our malignant feelings, which must seek gratification through more indirect channels, and undermine the obstacles which they cannot openly bear down, may be rather said to be tinctured *sable*. But the deep-ruling impulse is the same in both cases; and the proud peer, who can now only ruin his neighbour according to law, by protracted suits, is the genuine descendant of the baron who wrapped the castle of his competitor in flames, and knocked him on the head as he endeavoured to escape from the conflagration. It is from the great book of Nature, the same through a thousand editions, whether of black-letter, or wire-wove and hot-pressed, that I have venturously essayed to read a chapter to the public. Some favourable opportunities of contrast have been afforded me by the state of society in the northern part of the island at the period of my history, and may serve at once to vary and to illustrate the moral lessons, which I would willingly consider as the most important part of my plan; although I am sensible how short these will fall of their aim if I shall be found unable to mix them with amusement—a task not quite so easy in this critical generation as it was 'Sixty Years since.'

---

*Alas! that attire, respectable and gentlemanlike in 1805, or thereabouts, is now as antiquated as the Author of Waverley has himself become since that period! The reader of fashion will please to fill up the costume with an embroidered waistcoat of purple velvet or silk, and a coat of whatever colour he pleases.

Introduction to

THE ANTIQUARY (1816)

The present Work completes a series of fictitious narratives intended to illustrate the manners of Scotland at three different periods. *Waverley* embraced the age of our fathers, *Guy Mannering* that of our own youth, and the *Antiquary* refers to the last ten years of the eighteenth century. I have, in the two last narratives especially, sought my principal personages in the class of society who are the last to feel the influence of that general polish which assimilates to each other the manners of different nations. Among the same class I have placed some of the scenes in which I have endeavoured to illustrate the operation of the higher and more violent passions; both because the lower orders are less restrained by the habit of suppressing their feelings, and because I agree with my friend Wordsworth that they seldom fail to express them in the strongest and most powerful language.[1] This is, I think, peculiarly the case with the peasantry of my own country, a class with whom I have long been familiar. The antique force and simplicity of their language, often tinctured with the Oriental eloquence of Scripture, in the mouths of those of an elevated understanding, give pathos to their grief and dignity to their resentment.

I have been more solicitious to describe manners minutely than to arrange in any case an artificial and combined narrative, and have but to regret that I felt myself unable to unite these two requisites of a good Novel.

The knavery of the Adept in the following sheets may appear forced and improbable; but we have had very late instances of the force of superstitious credulity to a much greater extent, and the reader may be assured that this part of the narrative is founded on a fact of actual occurrence.

I have now only to express my gratitude to the public for the distinguished reception which they have given to works that have little more than some truth of colouring to recommend them, and to take my respectful leave, as one who is not likely again to solicit their favour.

Review of

TALES OF MY LANDLORD (1817)

These Tales belong obviously to a class of novels which we have already had occasion repeatedly to notice, and which have attracted the attention of the public in no common degree,—we mean Waverley, Guy Mannering, and the Antiquary, and we have little hesitation to pronounce them either entirely, or in a great measure, the work of the same author. Why he should industriously endeavour to elude observation by taking leave of us in one character, and then suddenly popping out upon us in another, we cannot pretend to guess without knowing more of his personal reasons for preserving so strict an incognito than has hitherto reached us. We can, however, conceive many reasons for a writer observing this sort of mystery; not to mention that it has certainly had its effect in keeping up the interest which his works have excited.

We do not know if the imagination of our author will sink in the opinion of the public when deprived of that degree of invention which we have been hitherto disposed to ascribe to him; but we are certain that it ought to increase the value of his portraits, that human beings have actually sate for them. These coincidences between fiction and reality are perhaps the very circumstances to which the success of these novels is in a great measure to be attributed: for, without depreciating the merit of the artist, every spectator at once recognizes in those scenes and faces which are copied from nature an air of distinct reality, which is not attached to fancy-pieces however happily conceived and elaborately executed. By what sort of freemasonry, if we may use the term, the mind arrives at this conviction, we do not pretend to guess, but every one must have felt that he instinctively and almost insensibly recognizes in painting, poetry, or other works of imagination, that which is copied from existing nature, and that he forthwith clings to it with that kindred interest which thinks nothing which is human indifferent to humanity.[1] Before therefore we proceed to analyse the work immediately before us, we beg leave briefly to notice a few circumstances connected with its predecessors.

Our author has told us it was his object to present a succession of scenes and characters connected with Scotland in its past and present state, and we must own that his stories are so slightly constructed as to remind us of the showman's thread with which he draws up his pictures and presents them successively to the eye of the spectator. He seems seriously to have proceeded on Mr. Bays's maxim—'What the deuce is a plot good for, but to bring in fine things?'[2]—Probability and perspicuity of narrative are sacrificed with the utmost indifference to the desire of producing effect; and provided the author can but contrive to 'surprize and elevate,' he appears to think that he has done his duty to the public. Against this slovenly indifference we have already remonstrated, and we again enter our protest. It is in justice to the author himself that we do so, because, whatever merit individual scenes and passages may possess, (and none have been more ready than ourselves to offer our applause,) it is clear that their effect would be greatly enhanced by being disposed in a clear and continued narrative. We are the more earnest in this matter, because it seems that the author errs chiefly from carelessness. There may be something of system in it however: for we have remarked, that with an attention which amounts even to affectation, he has avoided the common language of narrative, and thrown his story, as much as possible, into a dramatic shape. In many cases this has added greatly to the effect, by keeping both the actors and action continually before the reader, and placing him, in some measure, in the situation of the audience at a theatre, who are compelled to gather the meaning of the scene from what the dramatis personae say to each other, and not from any explanation addressed immediately to themselves. But though the author gain this advantage, and thereby compel the reader to think of the personages of the novel and not of the writer, yet the practice, especially pushed to the extent we have noticed, is a principal cause of the flimsiness and incoherent texture of which his greatest admirers are compelled to complain. Few can wish his success more sincerely than we do, and yet without more attention on his own part, we have great doubts of its continuance.

In addition to the loose and incoherent style of the narration, another leading fault in these novels is the total want of interest which the reader attaches to the character of the hero. Waverley, Brown, or Bertram in Guy Mannering, and Lovel in the Antiquary, are all brethren of a family; very amiable and very insipid sort of young men. We think we can perceive that this error is also in some degree occasioned by the dramatic principle upon which the author frames his plots. His chief characters are never actors, but always acted upon by the spur of circumstances, and have their fates uniformly determined by the agency of the subordinate persons. This arises from the author having usually represented them as foreigners to whom every thing in Scotland is strange,—a circumstance which serves as his apology for entering into many minute details which are reflectively, as it were, addressed to the reader through the medium of the hero. While he is going into explanations and details which, addressed directly to the reader, might appear tiresome and unnecessary, he gives interest to them by exhibiting the effect which they produce upon the principal person of his drama, and at the same time obtains a patient hearing for what might otherwise be passed over without attention. But if he gains this advantage, it is by sacrificing the character of the hero. No one can be interesting to the reader who is not himself a prime agent in the scene. This is understood even by the worthy citizen and his wife, who are introduced as prolocutors in Fletcher's Knight of the Burning Pestle. When they are asked what the principal person of the drama shall do?—the answer is prompt and ready—'Marry, let him come forth and kill a giant.'[3] There is a good deal of tact in the request. Every hero in poetry, in fictitious narrative, ought to come forth and do or say something or other which no other person could have done or said; make some sacrifice, surmount some difficulty, and become interesting to us otherwise than by his mere appearance on the scene, the passive tool of the other characters.

The insipidity of this author's heroes may be also in part referred to the readiness with which he twists and turns his story to produce some immediate and perhaps temporary effect. This could hardly be done without representing the principal character either as inconsistent or flexible in his principles. The ease with which Waverley adopts and afterwards forsakes the Jacobite party in 1745 is a good example of what we mean. Had he been painted as a steady character, his conduct would have been improbable. The author was aware of this; and yet, unwilling to relinquish an opportunity of introducing the interior of the Chevalier's military court, the circumstances of the battle of Preston-pans, and so forth, he hesitates not to sacrifice poor Waverley, and to represent him as a reed blown about at the pleasure of every breeze: a less careless writer would probably have taken some pains to gain the end proposed in a more artful and ingenious manner. But our author was hasty, and has paid the penalty of his haste.

We have hinted that we are disposed to question the originality of these novels in point of invention, and that in doing so, we do not consider ourselves as derogating from the merit of the author, to whom, on the contrary, we give the praise due to one who has collected and brought out with accuracy and effect, incidents and manners which might otherwise have slept in oblivion. We proceed to our proofs.*

The mutual protection afforded by Waverley and Talbot to each other, upon which the whole plot depends, is founded upon one of those anecdotes, which soften the features even of civil war, and as it is equally honourable to the memory of both parties, we have no hesitation to give their names at length. When the Highlanders upon the morning of the battle of Preston made

---

*It will be readily conceived that the curious MSS. and other information of which we have availed ourselves were not accessible to us in this country; but we have been assiduous in our inquiries; and are happy enough to possess a correspondent whose researches on the spot have been indefatigable, and whose kind, and ready communications have anticipated all our wishes.

their memorable attack, a battery of four field pieces was stormed and carried by the Camerons and the Stewarts of Appine. The late Alexander Stuart of Invernahyle was one of the foremost in the charge, and observed an officer of the King's forces, who, scorning to join the flight of all around, remained with his sword in his hand, as if determined to the very last to defend the post assigned to him. The Highland gentleman commanded him to surrender, and received for a reply a thrust which he caught in his target. The officer was now defenceless, and the battle-axe of a gigantic Highlander (the miller of Invernahyle's mill) was uplifted to dash his brains out, when Mr. Stuart with difficulty prevailed on him to surrender. He took charge of his enemy's property, protected his person, and finally obtained him liberty on his parole. The officer proved to be Colonel Allan Whiteford, of Ballochmyle, in Ayrshire, a man of high character and influence, and warmly attached to the house of Hanover; yet such was the confidence existing between these two honourable men, though of different political principles, that while the civil war was raging, and straggling officers from the Highland army were executed without mercy,* Invernahyle hesitated not to pay his late captive a visit as he went back to the Highlands to raise fresh recruits, when he spent a few days among Colonel Whiteford's whig friends as pleasantly and good humouredly as if all had been at peace around him. After the battle of Culloden it was Colonel Whiteford's turn to strain every nerve to obtain Mr. Stuart's pardon. He went to the Lord Justice Clerk, to the Lord Advocate, and to all the officers of state, and each application was answered by the production of a list in which Invernahyle (as the good old gentleman was wont to express it) appeared 'marked with the sign of the beast!' At length Colonel Whiteford went to the Duke of Cumberland.[4] From him also he received a positive refusal. He then limited his request for the present, to a protection for Stuart's house, wife, children, and property. This was also refused by the Duke: on which Colonel Whiteford, taking his commission from his bosom, laid it on the table before his Royal Highness, and asked permission to retire from the service of a sovereign who did not know how to spare a vanquished enemy.

---

*As was the case with MacDonald of Kinloch-moidart.

The Duke was struck, and even affected. He bade the Colonel take up his commission, and granted the protection he required with so much earnestness. It was issued just in time to save the house, corn and cattle, at Invernahyle, from the troops who were engaged in laying waste what it was the fashion to call 'the country of the enemy.' A small encampment of soldiers was formed on Invernahyle's property, which they spared while plundering the country around, and searching in every direction for the leaders of the insurrection, and for Stuart in particular. He was much nearer them than they suspected; for hidden in a cave, (like the Baron of Bradwardine,) he lay for many days within hearing of the sentinels, as they called their watch-word. His food was brought to him by one of his daughters, a child of eight years old, whom Mrs. Stuart was under the necessity of entrusting with this commission, for her own motions and those of all her inmates were closely watched. With ingenuity beyond her years the child used to stray about among the soldiers, who were rather kind to her, and watch the moment when she was unobserved to steal into the thicket, when she deposited whatever small store of provisions she had in charge, at some marked spot, where her father might find it. Invernahyle supported life for several weeks, by means of these precarious supplies, and as he had been wounded in the battle of Culloden, the hardships which he endured were aggravated by great bodily pain. After the soldiers had removed their quarters he had another remarkable escape. As he now ventured to the house at night and left it in the morning, he was espied during the dawn by a party of the enemy who fired at and pursued him. The fugitive being fortunate enough to escape their search, they returned to the house and charged the family with harbouring one of the proscribed traitors. An old woman had presence of mind enough to maintain that the man they had seen was the shepherd. 'Why did he not stop when we called to him?' said the soldiers. 'He is as deaf, poor man, as a peat-stack,' answered the ready-witted domestic. 'Let him be sent for directly.'—The real shepherd accordingly was brought from the hill, and as there was time to tutor him by the way, he was as deaf when he made his appearance as was necessary to sustain his character. Stuart of Invernahyle was afterwards pardoned under

18

the act of indemnity. 'I knew him well,' says our correspondent,[5] 'and have often had these circumstances from his own mouth. He was a noble specimen of the old Highlander, far descended, gallant, courteous and brave even to chivalry. He had been *out* in 1715 and 1745, was an active partaker in all the stirring scenes which passed in the Highlands, betwixt these memorable aeras, and was remarkable, among other exploits, for having fought a duel with the broad sword with the celebrated Rob Roy Mac-Gregor, at the Clachan of Balquidder. He chanced to be in Edinburgh when Paul Jones came into the Firth of Forth, and though then an old man, I saw him in arms, and heard him exult (to use his own words) in the prospect of "drawing his claymore once more before he died." '

The traditions and manners of the Scotch were so blended with superstitious practices and fears, that the author of these novels seems to have deemed it incumbent on him, to transfer many more such incidents to his novels, than seem either probable or natural to an English reader. It may be some apology that his story would have lost the national cast, which it was chiefly his object to preserve, had this been otherwise. There are few families of antiquity in Scotland, which do not possess some strange legends, told only under promise of secrecy, and with an air of mystery; in developing which, the influence of the powers of darkness is referred to. The truth probably is, that the agency of witches and demons was often made to account for the sudden disappearance of individuals and similar incidents, too apt to arise out of the evil dispositions of humanity, in a land where revenge was long held honourable—where private feuds and civil broils disturbed the inhabitants for ages—and where justice was but weakly and irregularly executed. Mr. Law, a conscientious but credulous clergyman of the Kirk of Scotland, who lived in the seventeenth century, has left behind him a very curious manuscript, in which, with the political events of that distracted period, he has intermingled the various portents and marvellous occurrences which, in common with his age, he ascribed to supernatural agency.[6] The following extract will serve to illustrate the taste of this period for the supernatural. When we read such things recorded by men of sense and education, (and Mr. Law was

deficient in neither,) we cannot help remembering the times of paganism, when every scene, incident, and action, had its appropriate and presiding deity. It is indeed curious to consider what must have been the sensations of a person, who lived under this peculiar species of hallucination, believing himself beset on all hands by invisible agents; one who was unable to account for the restiveness of a nobleman's carriage horses otherwise than by the immediate effect of witchcraft: and supposed that the *sage femme* of the highest reputation was most likely to devote the infants to the infernal spirits, upon their very entrance into life.
· ·

To the superstitions of the North Britons must be added their peculiar and characteristic amusements; and here we have some atonement to make to the memory of the learned Paulus Pleydell, whose compotatory relaxations, better information now inclines us to think, we mentioned with somewhat too little reverence.[7] Before the new town of Edinburgh (as it is called) was built, its inhabitants lodged, as is the practice of Paris at this day, in large buildings called *lands*, each family occupying a story, and having access to it by a stair common to all the inhabitants. These buildings, when they did not front the high street of the city, composed the sides of little, narrow, unwholesome *closes* or lanes. The miserable and confined accommodation which such habitations afforded, drove *men of business*, as they were called, that is, people belonging to the law, to hold their professional rendez-vouses in taverns, and many lawyers of eminence spent the principal part of their time in some tavern of note, transacted their business there, received the visits of clients with their writers or attornies, and suffered no imputation from so doing. This practice naturally led to habits of conviviality, to which the Scottish lawyers, till of very late years, were rather too much addicted. Few men drank so hard as the counsellors of the old school, and there survived till of late some veterans who supported in that respect the character of their predecessors. To vary the humour of a joyous evening many frolics were resorted to, and the game of *high jinks* was one of the most common.* In fact,

---

*We have learned, with some dismay, that one of the ablest lawyers Scotland ever produced, and who lives to witness (although in retirement) the various changes which have taken place in her courts of judicature, a man who has filled with marked distinction the highest offices of his profession, *tush'd* (pshaw'd)

high jinks was one of the *petits jeux* with which certain circles were wont to while away the time; and though it claims no alliance with modern associations, yet, as it required some shrewdness and dexterity to support the characters assumed for the occasion, it is not difficult to conceive that it might have been as interesting and amusing to the parties engaged in it, as counting the spots of a pack of cards, or treasuring in memory the rotation in which they are thrown on the table. The worst of the game was what that age considered as its principal excellence, namely, that the forfeitures being all commuted for wine, it proved an encouragement to hard drinking, the prevailing vice of the age.

On the subject of Davie Gellatley, the fool of the Baron of Bradwardine's family, we are assured there is ample testimony that a custom, referred to Shakspeare's time in England, had, and in remote provinces of Scotland, has still its counterpart, to this day. We do not mean to say that the professed jester with his bauble and his party-coloured vestment can be found in any family north of the Tweed. Yet such a personage held this respectable office in the family of the Earls of Strathemore within the last century, and his costly holiday dress, garnished with bells of silver, is still preserved in the Castle of Glamis. But we are assured, that to a much later period, and even to this moment, the habits and manners of Scotland have had some tendency to preserve the existence of this singular order of domestics. There are (comparatively speaking) no poor's rates in the country parishes of Scotland, and of course no work-houses to immure either their worn out poor or the 'moping idiot and the madman gay,' whom Crabbe characterizes as the happiest inhabitants of these mansions, because insensible of their misfortunes.[8] It therefore happens almost necessarily in Scotland, that the house of the nearest proprietor of wealth and consequence proves a place of refuge for these outcasts of society; and until the pressure of the times, and the calculating habits which they have necessarily generated had rendered the maintenance of a human being about such a family an object of some consideration, they usually found an asylum there, and enjoyed the degree of comfort of

extremely at the delicacy of our former criticism. And certainly he claims some title to do so, having been in his youth not only a witness of such orgies as are described as proceeding under the auspices of Mr. Pleydell, but himself a distinguished performer.

which their limited intellect rendered them susceptible. Such idiots were usually employed in some simple sort of occasional labour; and if we are not misinformed, the situation of turn-spit was often assigned them, before the modern improvement of the smoke-jack. But, however employed, they usually displayed towards their benefactors a sort of instinctive attachment which was very affecting. We knew one instance in which such a being refused food for many days, pined away, literally broke his heart, and died within the space of a very few weeks after his benefactor's decease. We cannot now pause to deduce the moral inference which might be derived from such instances. It is however evident, that if there was a coarseness of mind in deriving amusement from the follies of these unfortunate beings, a circumstance to the disgrace of which they were totally insensible, their mode of life was, in other respects, calculated to promote such a degree of happiness as their faculties permitted them to enjoy. But besides the amusement which our forefathers received from witnessing their imperfections and extravagancies, there was a more legitimate source of pleasure in the wild wit which they often flung around them with the freedom of Shakspeare's licensed clowns. There are few houses in Scotland of any note or antiquity where the witty sayings of some such character are not occasionally quoted at this very day. The pleasure afforded to our forefathers by such repartees was no doubt heightened by their wanting the habits of more elegant amusement. But in Scotland the practice long continued, and in the house of one of the very first noblemen of that country (a man whose name is never mentioned without reverence) and that within the last twenty years, a jester such as we have mentioned stood at the side-table during dinner, and occasionally amused the guests by his extemporaneous sallies. Imbecillity of this kind was even considered as an apology for intrusion upon the most solemn occasions. All know the peculiar reverence with which the Scottish of every rank attend on funeral ceremonies. Yet within the memory of most of the present generation, an idiot of an appearance equally hideous and absurd, dressed, as if in mockery, in a rusty and ragged black coat, decorated with a cravat and weepers made of white paper in the form of those worn by the deepest mourners, preceded almost every funeral procession in

Edinburgh, as if to turn into ridicule the last rites paid to mortality.

It has been generally supposed that in the case of these as of other successful novels, the most prominent and peculiar characters were sketched from real life. It was only after the death of Smollet [*sic*], that two barbers and a shoemaker contended about the character of Strap,[9] which each asserted was modelled from his own: but even in the lifetime of the present author, there is scarcely a dale in the pastoral districts of the southern counties but arrogates to itself the possession of the original Dandie Dinmont. As for Baillie MacWheeble, a person of the highest eminence in the law perfectly well remembers having received fees from him. We ourselves think we recognize the prototype of Meg Merrilies, on whose wild fidelity so much of the interest of Guy Mannering hinges, in the Jean Gordon of the following extract:*

'Old Jean Gordon of Yetholm, who had great sway among her tribe, was well remembered by old persons of the last generation. She was quite a Meg Merrilies, and possessed the savage virtue of fidelity in the same perfection. Having been often hospitably received at the farmhouse of Lochside near Yetholm, she had carefully abstained from committing any depredations on the farmer's property. But her sons (nine in number) had not, it seems, the same delicacy and stole a brood-sow from their kind entertainer. Jean was so much mortified at this irregularity, and so much ashamed of it, that she absented herself from Lochside for several years. At length, in consequence of some temporary pecuniary necessity, the Goodman of Lochside was obliged to go to Newcastle to get some money to pay his rent. Returning through the mountains of Cheviot he was benighted and lost his way. A light glimmering through the window of a large waste barn, which had survived the farmhouse to which it had once belonged, guided him to a place of shelter, and when he knocked at the door, it was opened by Jean Gordon. Her very remarkable figure, for she was nearly six feet high, and her equally remarkable features and dress, rendered it impossible to mistake her for a moment; and to meet with such a character in so solitary

---

*See a very curious paper intitled 'Notices on the Scottish Gipsies,' in a new publication called the Edinburgh Monthly Magazine.

a place and probably at no great distance from her clan, was a terrible surprize to the poor man whose rent (to lose which would have been ruin to him) was about his person. Jean set up a loud shout of joyful recognition—"Eh Sirs! the winsome Gude-man of Lochside! Light down, light down, for ye maunna gang farther the night and a friend's house sae near." The farmer was obliged to dismount and accept of the gipsy's offer of supper and a bed. There was abundance of provisions in the barn, however it might be come by, and preparations were going on for a plentiful supper, which the farmer, to the great increase of his anxiety, observed was calculated for ten or twelve guests of the same description probably with his landlady. Jean left him in no doubt on the subject. She brought up the story of the stolen sow, and noticed how much pain and vexation it had given her; like other philosophers, she remarked that the world grows worse daily; and like other parents, that the bairns got out of her guiding and neglected the old gipsy regulations which commanded them to respect in their depredations the property of their benefactors. The end of all this was an inquiry what money the farmer had about him, and an urgent request that he would make her his purse-keeper, since the bairns, as she called her sons, would soon return home. The poor farmer made a virtue of necessity, told his story, and surrendered his gold to Jean's custody; she made him put a few shillings in his pocket, observing it would excite suspicion should he be found travelling altogether pennyless. This arrangement being made, the farmer lay down on a sort of *shake-down*, as the Scotch call it, upon some straw, but, as will easily be believed, slept not. About midnight the gang returned with various articles of plunder, and talked over their exploits in language which made the farmer tremble. They were not long in discovering their guest and demanded of Jean whom she had got there? "E'en the winsome Gude-man of Lochside, poor body," replied Jean, "he's been at Newcastle seeking for siller to pay his rent, honest man, but the de'il be lick'd he's been able to gather in, and so he's gaun e'en hame wi' a toom purse and a sair heart." "That may be, Jean," replied one of the banditti, "but we maun ripe* his pouches a bit and see if it be true or no." Jean set up her throat in exclamations against the breach of hospitality, but

---

*Rummage his pockets.

without producing any change of their determination. The farmer soon heard their stifled whispers and light steps by his bedside, and understood they were rummaging his clothes. When they found the money which the foresight of Jean Gordon had made him retain, they held a consultation if they should take it or no, but the smallness of the booty and the vehemence of Jean's remonstrances determined them in the negative. They caroused and went to rest. So soon as day returned, Jean roused her guest, produced his horse which she had accommodated behind the hallan, and guided him for some miles till he was on the high road to Lochside. She then restored his whole property, nor could his earnest entreaties prevail on her to accept so much as a single guinea.

'I have heard the old people at Jedburgh say that all Jean's sons were condemned to die there on the same day. It is said the Jury were equally divided, but that one of their number, a friend to justice, who had slept during the whole discussion, waked suddenly, and gave his casting vote for condemnation in the emphatic words, "Hang them a'."—Jean was present, and only said, "The Lord help the innocent in a day like this." Her own death was accompanied with circumstances of brutal outrage, of which poor Jean was in many respects wholly undeserving. Jean had among other demerits, or merits, as you may chuse to rank it, that of being a staunch jacobite. She chanced to be at Carlisle upon a fair or market day, soon after the year 1746, where she gave vent to her political partiality, to the great offence of the rabble of that city. Being zealous in their loyalty when there was no danger, in proportion to the tameness with which they had surrendered to the Highlanders in 1745, the mob inflicted upon poor Jean no slighter penalty than that of ducking her to death in the Eden. It was an operation of some time, for Jean was a stout woman, and struggling with her murtherers often got her head above water, and while she had voice left continued to exclaim at such intervals, *"Charlie yet, Charlie yet."* When a child, and among the scenes which she frequented, I have often heard these stories, and cried piteously for the fate of poor Jean Gordon, who, with all the vices and irregularities of her degrated tribe and wandering profession, was always mentioned by those who had known her, with a sort of compassionate regret.'[10]

Although these strong resemblances occur so frequently, and with such peculiar force, as almost to impress us with the conviction that the author sketched from nature, and not from fancy alone; yet we hesitate to draw any positive conclusion, sensible that a character dashed off as the representative of a certain class of men will bear, if executed with fidelity to the general outlines, not only that resemblance which he ought to possess as 'knight of the shire,' but also a special affinity to some particular individual. It is scarcely possible it should be otherwise. When Emery appears on the stage as a Yorkshire peasant, with the habit, manner, and dialect peculiar to the character, and which he assumes with so much truth and fidelity, those unacquainted with the province or its inhabitants see merely the abstract idea, the beau ideal of a Yorkshireman.[11] But to those who are intimate with both, the action and manner of the comedian almost necessarily recal the idea of some individual native (altogether unknown probably to the performer) to whom his exterior and manners bear a casual resemblance. We are therefore on the whole inclined to believe, that the incidents are frequently copied from *actual* occurrences, but that the characters are either entirely fictitious, or if any traits have been borrowed from real life, as in the anecdote which we have quoted respecting Invernahyle, they have been carefully disguised and blended with such as are purely imaginary. We now proceed to a more particular examination of the volumes before us.

They are entitled 'Tales of my Landlord:' why so entitled, excepting to introduce a quotation from Don Quixote,[12] it is difficult to conceive: for Tales of my Landlord they are *not*, nor is it indeed easy to say whose tales they ought to be called. There is a proem, as it is termed, supposed to be written by Jedediah Cleishbotham, the schoolmaster and parish clerk of the village of Gandercleugh, in which we are given to understand that these Tales were compiled by his deceased usher, Mr. Peter Pattieson, from the narratives or conversations of such travellers as frequented the Wallace Inn, in that village. Of this proem we shall only say that it is written in the quaint style of that prefixed by Gay to his Pastorals,[13] being, as Johnson terms it, 'such imitation as he could obtain of obsolete language, and by consequence in a style that was never written nor spoken in any age or place.'[14]

Review of *Tales of My Landlord*

The first of the Tales thus ushered in is entitled the 'Black Dwarf.' It contains some striking scenes, but it is even more than usually deficient in the requisites of luminous and interesting narrative, as will appear from the following abridgment.

. . . .

Such is the brief abstract of a tale of which the narrative is unusually artificial.[15] Neither hero nor heroine excites interest of any sort, being just that sort of *pattern* people whom nobody cares a farthing about. The explanation of the dwarf's real circumstances and character, too long delayed from an obvious wish to protract the mystery, is at length huddled up so hastily that, for our parts, we cannot say we are able to comprehend more of the motives of this principal personage than that he was a mad man, and acted like one—an easy and summary mode of settling all difficulties. As for the hurry and military bustle of the conclusion, it is only worthy of the farce of the Miller and his Men, or any other modern melo-drama, ending with a front crouded with soldiers and scene-shifters, and a back scene in a state of conflagration.[16]

We have dealt with this tale very much according to the clown's argument in favour of Master Froth—'Look upon his face, I will be sworn on a book that his face is the worst part about him, and if his face be the worst part about him, how could Master Froth do the constable's wife any harm?'[17] Even so we will take our oaths that the narrative is the worst part of the Black Dwarf, and that if the reader can tolerate it upon the sketch we have given him, he will find the work itself contains passages both of natural pathos and fantastic terror, not unworthy of the author of the scene of Stanie's burial, in the Antiquary, or the wild tone assumed in the character of Meg Merrilies.

The story which occupies the next three volumes is of much deeper interest, both as a tale and from its connexion with historical facts and personages. It is entitled 'Old Mortality,' but should have been called the Tale of Old Mortality, for the personage so named is only quoted as the authority for the incidents. The story is thus given in the introduction:

. . . .

We intended here to conclude this long article, when a strong report reached us of certain transatlantic confessions, which, if genuine, (though of this we know nothing,) assign a different author to these volumes, than the party suspected by our Scottish correspondents.[18] Yet a critic may be excused seizing upon the nearest suspicious person, on the principle happily expressed by Claverhouse, in a letter to the Earl of Linlithgow. He had been, it seems, in search of a gifted weaver, who used to hold forth at conventicles: 'I sent to seek the webster, (weaver) they brought in his *brother* for him: though he maybe cannot preach like his brother, I doubt not but he is as well principled as he, wherefore I thought it would be no great fault to give him the trouble to go jail with the rest.'

IVANHOE (1820)

DEDICATORY EPISTLE
TO
THE REV. DR. DRYASDUST, F.A.S.
Residing in the Castle Gate, York.

Much esteemed and dear sir,

It is scarcely necessary to mention the various and concurring reasons which induce me to place your name at the head of the following work. Yet the chief of these reasons may perhaps be refuted by the imperfections of the performance. Could I have hoped to render it worthy of your patronage, the public would at once have seen the propriety of inscribing a work designed to illustrate the domestic antiquities of England, and particularly of our Saxon forefathers, to the learned author of the Essays upon the Horn of King Ulphas, and on the Lands bestowed by him upon the patrimony of St. Peter.[1] I am conscious, however, that the slight, unsatisfactory, and trivial manner in which the result of my antiquarian researches has been recorded in the following pages takes the work from under that class which bears the proud motto, *Detur digniori*. On the contrary, I fear I shall incur the censure of presumption in placing the venerable name of Dr. Jonas Dryasdust at the head of a publication which the more grave antiquary will perhaps class with the idle novels and romances of the day. I am anxious to vindicate myself from such a charge; for, although I might trust to your friendship for an apology in your eyes, yet I would not willingly stand convicted in those of the public of so grave a crime as my fears lead me to anticipate my being charged with.

I must therefore remind you, that when we first talked over together that class of productions, in one of which the private and family affairs of your learned northern friend, Mr. Oldbuck of Monkbarns, were so unjustifiably exposed to the public, some discussion occurred between us concerning the cause of the popularity these works have attained in this idle age, which, whatever other merit they possess, must be admitted to be hastily written, and in violation of every rule assigned to the epopeia.[2] It seemed then to be your opinion that the charm lay entirely in the art with which the unknown author had availed himself, like a second M'Pherson,[3] of the antiquarian stores which lay scattered around him, supplying his own indolence or poverty of invention by the incidents which had actually taken place in his country at no distant period, by introducing real characters, and scarcely suppressing real names. It was not above sixty or seventy years, you observed, since the whole north of Scotland was under a state of government nearly as simple and as patriarchal as those of our good allies the Mohawks and Iroquois. Admitting that the Author cannot himself be supposed to have witnessed those times, he must have lived, you observed, among persons who had noted and suffered in them; and even within these thirty years, such an infinite change has taken place in the manners of Scotland that men look back upon the habits of society proper to their immediate ancestors as we do on those of the reign of Queen Anne, or even the period of the Revolution. Having thus materials of every kind lying strewed around him, there was little, you observed, to embarrass the Author, but the difficulty of choice. It was no wonder, therefore, that, having begun to work a mine so plentiful, he should have derived from his works fully more credit and profit than the facility of his labours merited.

Admitting (as I could not deny) the general truth of these conclusions, I cannot but think it strange that no attempt has been made to excite an interest for the traditions and manners of Old England, similar to that which has been obtained in behalf of those of our poorer and less celebrated neighbours. The Kendal green, though its date is more ancient, ought surely to be as dear to our feelings as the variegated tartans of the north. The name of Robin Hood, if duly conjured with, should raise a spirit as soon as that of Rob Roy; and the patriots of England deserve no less their renown in our modern circles than the Bruces and Wallaces of Caledonia. If the scenery of the south be less romantic and

sublime than that of the northern mountains, it must be allowed
to possess in the same proportion superior softness and beauty;
and, upon the whole, we feel ourselves entitled to exclaim with
the patriotic Syrian—'Are not Pharphar and Abana, rivers of
Damascus, better than all the rivers of Israel?'[4]

Your objections to such an attempt, my dear Doctor, were, you
may remember, twofold. You insisted upon the advantages which
the Scotsman possessed, from the very recent existence of that
state of society in which his scene was to be laid. Many now alive,
you remarked, well remembered persons who had not only seen
the celebrated Roy M'Gregor, but had feasted, and even fought,
with him. All those minute circumstances belonging to private life
and domestic character, all that gives verisimilitude to a narrative
and individuality to the persons introduced, is still known and
remembered in Scotland; whereas in England civilisation has
been so long complete, that our ideas of our ancestors are only to
be gleaned from musty records and chronicles, the authors of
which seem perversely to have conspired to suppress in their
narratives all interesting details, in order to find room for flowers
of monkish eloquence, or trite reflections upon morals. To match
an English and a Scottish author in the rival task of embodying
and reviving the traditions of their respective countries would be,
you alleged, in the highest degree unequal and unjust. The
Scottish magician, you said, was, like Lucan's witch, at liberty to
walk over the recent field of battle, and to select for the subject of
resuscitation by his sorceries a body whose limbs had recently
quivered with existence, and whose throat had but just uttered
the last note of agony. Such a subject even the powerful Erictho
was compelled to select, as alone capable of being reanimated
even by *her* potent magic—

> Gelidas leto scrutata medullas,
> Pulmonis rigidi stantes sine vulnere fibras
> Invenit, et vocem defunto in corpore quaerit.[5]

The English author, on the other hand, without supposing him
less of a conjuror than the Northern Warlock, can, you observed,
only have the liberty of selecting his subject amidst the dust of
antiquity, where nothing was to be found but dry, sapless,

31

mouldering, and disjointed bones, such as those which filled the valley of Jehoshaphat. You expressed, besides, your apprehension that the unpatriotic prejudices of my countrymen would not allow fair play to such a work as that of which I endeavoured to demonstrate the probable success. And this, you said, was not entirely owing to the more general prejudice in favour of that which is foreign, but that it rested partly upon improbabilities, arising out of the circumstances in which the English reader is placed. If you describe to him a set of wild manners, and a state of primitive society, existing in the Highlands of Scotland, he is much disposed to acquiesce in the truth of what is asserted. And reason good. If he be of the ordinary class of readers, he has either never seen those remote districts at all, or he has wandered through those desolate regions in the course of a summer tour, eating bad dinners, sleeping on truckle beds, stalking from desolation to desolation, and fully prepared to believe the strangest things that could be told him of a people wild and extravagant enough to be attached to scenery so extraordinary. But the same worthy person, when placed in his own snug parlour, and surrounded by all the comforts of an Englishman's fireside, is not half so much disposed to believe that his own ancestors led a very different life from himself; that the shattered tower which now forms a vista from his window once held a baron who would have hung him up at his own door without any form of trial; that the hinds, by whom his little pet farm is managed, a few centuries ago would have been his slaves; and that the complete influence of feudal tyranny once extended over the neighbouring village, where the attorney is now a man of more importance than the lord of the manor.

While I own the force of these objections, I must confess, at the same time, that they do not appear to me to be altogether insurmountable. The scantiness of materials is indeed a formidable difficulty; but no one knows better than Dr. Dryasdust that to those deeply read in antiquity hints concerning the private life of our ancestors lie scattered through the pages of our various historians, bearing, indeed, a slender proportion to the other matters of which they treat, but still, when collected together, sufficient to throw considerable light upon the *vie privée* of our forefathers; indeed, I am convinced that, however I myself may fail in the ensuing attempt, yet, with more labour in collecting, or more skill in using, the materials within his reach, illustrated as they have been by the labours of Dr. Henry, of the late Mr. Strutt, and, above all, of Mr. Sharon Turner, an abler hand would have been successful; and therefore I protest, beforehand, against any argument which may be founded on the failure of the present experiment.[6]

On the other hand, I have already said that, if anything like a true picture of old English manners could be drawn, I would trust to the good-nature and good sense of my countrymen for ensuring its favourable reception.

Having thus replied, to the best of my power, to the first class of your objections, or at least having shown my resolution to overleap the barriers which your prudence has raised, I will be brief in noticing that which is more peculiar to myself. It seemed to be your opinion that the very office of an antiquary, employed in grave, and, as the vulgar will sometimes allege, in toilsome and minute research, must be considered as incapacitating him from successfully compounding a tale of this sort. But permit me to say, my dear Doctor, that this objection is rather formal than substantial. It is true, that such slight compositions might not suit the severer genius of our friend Mr. Oldbuck.[7] Yet Horace Walpole wrote a goblin tale which has thrilled through many a bosom;[8] and George Ellis could transfer all the playful fascination of a humour as delightful as it was uncommon into his *Abridgement of the Ancient Metrical Romances*.[9] So that, however I may have occasion to rue my present audacity, I have at least the most respectable precedents in my favour.

Still, the severer antiquary may think that, by thus intermingling fiction with truth, I am polluting the well of history with modern inventions, and impressing upon the rising generation false ideas of the age which I describe. I cannot but in some sense admit the force of this reasoning, which I yet hope to traverse by the following considerations.

It is true, that I neither can nor do pretend to the observation of complete accuracy, even in matters of outward costume, much less in the more important points of language and manners. But the same motive which prevents my writing the dialogue of the piece in Anglo-Saxon or in Norman-French, and which prohibits my sending forth to the public this essay printed with the types of Caxton or Wynken de Worde,[10] prevents my attempting to confine myself within the limits of the period in which my story is laid. It is necessary, for exciting interest of any kind, that the subject assumed should be, as it were, translated into the manners, as well as the language, of the age we live in. No fascination has ever been attached to Oriental literature equal to that produced by Mr. Galland's first translation of the *Arabian Tales*; in which, retaining on the one hand the splendour of Eastern costume, and on the other the wildness of Eastern fiction, he mixed these with just so much ordinary feeling and expression as rendered them interesting and intelligible, while he abridged the long-winded narratives, curtailed the monotonous reflections, and rejected the endless repetitions of the Arabian original.[11] The tales, therefore, though less purely Oriental than in their first concoction, were eminently better fitted for the European market, and obtained an unrivalled degree of public favour, which they certainly would never have gained had not the manners and style been in some degree familiarised to the feelings and habits of the western reader.

In point of justice, therefore, to the multitudes who will, I trust, devour this book with avidity, I have so far explained our ancient manners in modern language, and so far detailed the characters and sentiments of my persons, that the modern reader will not find himself, I should hope, much trammelled by the repulsive dryness of mere antiquity. In this, I respectfully contend, I have in no respect exceeded the fair license due to the author of a fictitious composition. The late ingenious Mr. Strutt, in his romance of *Queenhoo Hall*,* acted upon another principle; and, in distinguishing between what was ancient and modern, forgot, as it appears to me, that extensive neutral ground, the large proportion, that is, of manners and sentiments which are common to us and to our ancestors, having been handed down unaltered from them to us, or which, arising out of the principles of our common nature, must have existed alike in either state of society. In this manner, a man of talent, and of great antiquarian erudition, limited the popularity of his work by excluding from it everything

---

*The Author had revised this posthumous work of Mr. Strutt. See Appendix to General Preface to the present edition, *Waverley*.

which was not sufficiently obsolete to be altogether forgotten and unintelligible.

The license which I would here vindicate is so necessary to the execution of my plan, that I will crave your patience while I illustrate my argument a little farther.

He who first opens Chaucer, or any other ancient poet, is so much struck with the obsolete spelling, multiplied consonants, and antiquated appearance of the language, that he is apt to lay the work down in despair, as encrusted too deep with the rust of antiquity to permit his judging of its merits or tasting its beauties. But if some intelligent and accomplished friend points out to him that the difficulties by which he is startled are more in appearance than reality, if, by reading aloud to him, or by reducing the ordinary words to the modern orthography, he satisfies his proselyte that only about one-tenth part of the words employed are in fact obsolete, the novice may be easily persuaded to approach the 'well of English undefiled,'[12] with the certainty that a slender degree of patience will enable him to enjoy both the humour and the pathos with which old Geoffrey delighted the age of Cressy and of Poictiers.

To pursue this a little farther. If our neophyte, strong in the new-born love of antiquity, were to undertake to imitate what he had learnt to admire, it must be allowed he would act very injudiciously if he were to select from the glossary the obsolete words which it contains, and employ those, exclusively of all phrases and vocables retained in modern days. This was the error of the unfortunate Chatterton.[13] In order to give his language the appearance of antiquity, he rejected every word that was modern, and produced a dialect entirely different from any that had ever been spoken in Great Britain. He who would imitate an ancient language with success must attend rather to its grammatical character, turn of expression, and mode of arrangement, than labour to collect extraordinary and antiquated terms, which, as I have already averred, do not in ancient authors approach the number of words still in use, though perhaps somewhat altered in sense and spelling, in the proportion of one to ten.

What I have applied to language, is still more justly applicable to sentiments and manners. The passions, the sources from which these must spring in all their modifications, are generally the same in all ranks and conditions, all countries and ages; and it follows as a matter of course that the opinions, habits of thinking, and actions, however influenced by the peculiar state of society, must still, upon the whole, bear a strong resemblance to each other. Our ancestors were not more distinct from us, surely, than Jews are from Christians; they had 'eyes, hands, organs, dimensions, senses, affections, passions'; were 'fed with the same food, hurt with the same weapons, subject to the same diseases, warmed and cooled by the same winter and summer,' as ourselves.[14] The tenor, therefore, of their affections and feelings must have borne the same general proportion to our own.[15]

It follows, therefore, that of the materials which an author has to use in a romance, or fictitious composition, such as I have ventured to attempt, he will find that a great proportion, both of language and manners, is as proper to the present time as to those in which he has laid his time of action. The freedom of choice which this allows him is therefore much greater, and the difficulty of his task much more diminished, than at first appears. To take an illustration from a sister art, the antiquarian details may be said to represent the peculiar features of a landscape under delineation of the pencil. His feudal tower must arise in due majesty; the figures which he introduces must have the costume and character of their age; the piece must represent the peculiar features of the scene which he has chosen for his subject, with all its appropriate elevation of rock, or precipitate descent of cataract. His general colouring, too, must be copied from Nature. The sky must be clouded or serene, according to the climate, and the general tints must be those which prevail in a natural landscape. So far the painter is bound down by the rules of his art to a precise imitation of the features of Nature; but it is not required that he should descend to copy all her more minute features, or represent with absolute exactness the very herbs, flowers, and trees with which the spot is decorated. These, as well as all the more minute points of light and shadow, are attributes proper to scenery in general, natural to each situation, and subject to the artist's disposal, as his taste or pleasure may dictate.

It is true, that this license is confined in either case within legitimate bounds. The painter must introduce no ornament inconsistent with the climate or country of his landscape; he must not plant cypress trees upon Inch Merrin, or Scottish firs among the ruins of Persepolis; and the author lies under a corresponding restraint. However far he may venture in a more full detail of passions and feelings than is to be found in the ancient compositions which he imitates, he must introduce nothing inconsistent with the manners of the age. His knights, squires, grooms, and yeomen may be more fully drawn than in the hard, dry delineations of an ancient illuminated manuscript; but the character and costume of the age must remain inviolate: they must be the same figures, drawn by a better pencil, or, to speak more modestly, executed in an age when the principles of art were better understood. His language must not be exclusively obsolete and unintelligible; but he should admit, if possible, no word or turn of phraseology betraying an origin directly modern. It is one thing to make use of the language and sentiments which are common to ourselves and our forefathers, and it is another to invest them with the sentiments and dialect exclusively proper to their descendants.

This, my dear friend, I have found the most difficult part of my task; and, to speak frankly, I hardly expect to satisfy your less partial judgment, and more extensive knowledge of such subjects, since I have hardly been able to please my own.

I am conscious that I shall be found still more faulty in the tone of keeping and costume, by those who may be disposed rigidly to examine my Tale, with reference to the manners of the exact period in which my actors flourished. It may be, that I have introduced little which can positively be termed modern; but, on the other hand, it is extremely probable that I may have confused the manners of two or three centuries, and introduced, during the reign of Richard the First, circumstances appropriated to a period either considerably earlier or a good deal later than that era. It is my comfort, that errors of this kind will escape the general class of readers, and that I may share in the ill-deserved applause of those architects who, in their modern Gothic, do not hesitate to introduce, without rule or method, ornaments proper to different styles and to different periods of the art. Those whose extensive researches have given them the means of judging my backslidings with more severity will probably be lenient in proportion to their knowledge of the difficulty of my task. My honest and neglected friend, Ingulphus, has furnished me with many a valuable hint; but the light afforded by the Monk of Croydon, and Geoffrey de Vinsauf, is dimmed by such a conglomeration of uninteresting and unintelligible matter, that we gladly fly for relief to the delightful pages of the gallant Froissart, although he flourished at a period so much more remote from the date of my history.[16] If, therefore, my dear friend, you have generosity enough to pardon the presumptuous attempt to frame for myself a minstrel coronet, partly out of the pearls of pure antiquity, and partly from the Bristol stones and paste with which I have endeavoured to imitate them, I am convinced your opinion of the difficulty of the task will reconcile you to the imperfect manner of its execution.

Of my materials I have but little to say. They may be chiefly found in the singular Anglo-Norman MS. which Sir Arthur Wardour preserves with such jealous care in the third drawer of his oaken cabinet, scarcely allowing any one to touch it, and being himself not able to read one syllable of its contents.[17] I should never have got his consent, on my visit to Scotland, to read in those precious pages for so many hours, had I not promised to designate it by some emphatic mode of printing, as **The Wardour Manuscript**; giving it, thereby, an individuality as important as the Bannatyne MS., the Auchinleck MS., and any other monument of the patience of a Gothic scrivener. I have sent, for your private consideration, a list of the contents of this curious piece, which I shall perhaps subjoin, with your approbation, to the third volume of my Tale, in case the printer's devil should continue impatient for copy, when the whole of my narrative has been imposed.

Adieu, my dear friend; I have said enough to explain, if not to vindicate, the attempt which I have made, and which, in spite of your doubts and my own incapacity, I am still willing to believe has not been altogether made in vain.

I hope you are now well recovered from your spring fit of the gout, and shall be happy if the advice of your learned physician should recommend a tour to these parts. Several curiosities have been lately dug up near the wall, as well as at the ancient station of Habitancum. Talking of the latter, I suppose you have long since heard the news that a sulky, churlish boor has destroyed the ancient statue, or rather bas-relief, popularly called Robin of Redesdale. It seems Robin's fame attracted more visitants than was consistent with the growth of the heather, upon a moor worth a shilling an acre. Reverend as you write yourself, be revengeful for once, and pray with me that he may be visited with such a fit of the stone as if he had all the fragments of poor Robin in that region of his viscera where the disease holds its seat. Tell this not in Gath, lest the Scots rejoice that they have at length found a parallel instance among their neighbours to that barbarous deed which demolished Arthur's Oven.[18] But there is no end to lamentation, when we betake ourselves to such subjects. My respectful compliments attend Miss Dryasdust; I endeavoured to match the spectacles agreeable to her commission, during my late journey to London, and hope she has received them safe, and found them satisfactory. I send this by the blind carrier, so that probably it may be some time upon its journey.* The last news which I hear from Edinburgh is, that the gentleman who fills the situation of Secretary to the Society of Antiquaries of Scotland† is the best amateur draftsman in that kingdom, and that much is expected from his skill and zeal in delineating those specimens of national antiquity which are either mouldering under the slow touch of time, or swept away by modern taste, with the same besom of destruction which John Knox used at the Reformation. Once more adieu; *vale tandem, non immemor mei*.[19] Believe me to be,

Reverend, and very dear Sir,
Your most faithful humble Servant,
LAURENCE TEMPLETON.

Toppingwold, near Egremont,
Cumberland, Nov. 17, 1817.

---

*This anticipation proved but too true, as my learned correspondent did not receive my letter until a twelvemonth after it was written. I mention this circumstance, that a gentleman attached to the cause of learning, who now holds the principal control of the post-office, may consider whether, by some mitigation of the present enormous rates, some favour may not be shown to the correspondents of the principal Literary and Antiquarian Societies. I understand, indeed, that this experiment was once tried, but that the mail-coach having broke down under the weight of packages addressed to members of the Society of Antiquaries, it was relinquished as a hazardous experiment. Surely, however, it would be possible to build these vehicles in a form more substantial, stronger in the perch, and broader in the wheels, so as to support the weight of antiquarian learning; when, if they should be found to travel more slowly, they would be not the less agreeable to quiet travellers like myself.—L. T.

†Mr. Skene of Rubislaw is here intimated, to whose taste and skill the Author is indebted for a series of etchings, exhibiting the various localities alluded to in these novels.

39

Introductory Epistle to
THE FORTUNES OF NIGEL (1822)

CAPTAIN CLUTTERBUCK
TO
THE REVEREND DR. DRYASDUST

DEAR SIR,

I readily accept of, and reply to, the civilities with which you have been pleased to honor me in your obliging letter, and entirely agree with your quotation, of '*Quam bonum et quam jucundum!*'[1] We may indeed esteem ourselves as come of the same family, or, according to our country proverb, as being all one man's bairns; and there needed no apology on your part, reverend and dear sir, for demanding of me any information which I may be able to supply respecting the subject of your curiosity. The interview which you allude to took place in the course of last winter, and is so deeply imprinted on my recollection that it requires no effort to collect all its most minute details.

You are aware that the share which I had in introducing the romance called *The Monastery* to public notice has given me a sort of character in the literature of our Scottish metropolis. I no longer stand in the outer shop of our bibliopolists, bargaining for the objects of my curiosity with an unrespective shop-lad, hustled among boys who come to buy Corderies*[2] and copy-books, and servant-girls cheapening a pennyworth of paper, but am cordially welcomed by the bibliopolist himself, with, 'Pray, walk into the back shop, captain. Boy, get a chair for Captain Clutterbuck.

---

*One of the most common school-books of the last century—*Colloquiorum Centuria Selecta Maturini Corderii* (Laing).

40

Introductory Epistle to *The Fortunes of Nigel*

There is the newspaper, captain—to-day's paper'; or, 'Here is the last new work; there is a folder, make free with the leaves'; or, 'Put it in your pocket and carry it home'; or, 'We will make a bookseller of you, sir, you shall have it at trade price.' Or, perhaps, if it is the worthy trader's own publication, his liberality may even extend itself to—'Never mind booking such a trifle to *you*, sir; it is an over-copy. Pray, mention the work to your reading friends.' I say nothing of the snug, well-selected literary party arranged round a turbot, leg of five-year-old mutton, or some such gear, or of the circulation of a quiet bottle of Robert Cockburn's* choicest black—nay, perhaps of his best blue—to quicken our talk about old books, or our plans for new ones. All these are comforts reserved to such as are freemen of the corporation of letters, and I have the advantage of enjoying them in perfection.

But all things change under the sun; and it is with no ordinary feelings of regret that, in my annual visits to the metropolis, I now miss the social and warm-hearted welcome of the quick-witted and kindly friend† who first introduced me to the public, who had more original wit than would have set up a dozen of professed sayers of good things, and more racy humour than have made the fortune of as many more. To this great deprivation has been added, I trust for a time only, the loss of another bibliopolical friend,‡ whose vigorous intellect and liberal ideas have not only rendered his native country the mart of her own literature, but established there a court of letters, which must command respect, even from those most inclined to dissent from many of its canons. The effect of these changes, operated in a great measure by the strong sense and sagacious calculations of an individual who knew how to avail himself, to an unhoped-for extent, of the various kinds of talent which his country produced, will probably appear more clearly to the generation which shall follow the present.

I entered the shop at the Cross, to inquire after the health of my worthy friend, and learned with satisfaction that his residence in the south had abated the rigour of the symptoms of his disorder. Availing myself, then, of the privileges to which I have alluded, I

*Late wine-merchant in Edinburgh (*Laing*).
†Mr. John Ballantyne, bookseller (*Laing*).
‡Mr. Archibald Constable (*Laing*).

strolled onward in that labyrinth of small dark rooms or crypts, to speak our own antiquarian language, which form the extensive back-settlements of that celebrated publishing-house. Yet, as I proceeded from one obscure recess to another, filled, some of them with old volumes, some with such as, from the equality of their rank on the shelves, I suspected to be the less saleable modern books of the concern, I could not help feeling a holy horror creep upon me, when I thought of the risk of intruding on some ecstatic bard giving vent to his poetical fury; or, it might be, on the yet more formidable privacy of a band of critics, in the act of worrying the game which they had just run down. In such a supposed case, I felt by anticipation the horrors of the Highland seers, whom their gift of deuteroscopy compels to witness things unmeet for mortal eye; and who, to use the expression of Collins,

> Heartless, oft, like moody madness, stare,
> To see the phantom train their secret work prepare.[3]

Still, however, the irresistible impulse of an undefined curiosity drove me on through this succession of darksome chambers, till, like the jeweller of Delhi in the house of the magician Bennaskar,[4] I at length reached a vaulted room, dedicated to secrecy and silence, and beheld, seated by a lamp, and employed in reading a blotted *revise*,* the person, or perhaps I should rather say the eidolon, or representative vision, of the AUTHOR OF *WAVERLEY*! You will not be surprised at the filial instinct which enabled me at once to acknowledge the features borne by this venerable apparition, and that I at once bended the knee, with the classical salutation of, *Salve, magne parens!*[5] The vision, however, cut me short by pointing to a seat, intimating at the same time that my presence was not unexpected, and that he had something to say to me.

I sat down with humble obedience, and endeavoured to note the features of him with whom I now found myself so unexpectedly in society. But on this point I can give your reverence no satisfaction; for, besides the obscurity of the apartment, and the fluttered state of my own nerves, I seemed to myself over-

---

*The uninitiated must be informed that a second proof-sheet is so called.

whelmed by a sense of filial awe, which prevented my noting and recording what it is probable the personage before me might most desire to have concealed. Indeed, his figure was so closely veiled and wimpled, either with a mantle, morning-gown, or some such loose garb, that the verses of Spenser might well have been applied—

> Yet, certes, by her face and physnomy,
> Whether she man or woman only were,
> That could not any creature well descry.[6]

I must, however, go on as I have begun, to apply the masculine gender; for, notwithstanding very ingenious reasons, and indeed something like positive evidence, have been offered to prove the Author of *Waverley* to be two ladies of talent, I must abide by the general opinion, that he is of the rougher sex. There are in his writings too many things

> Quae maribus sola tribuunter,[7]

to permit me to entertain any doubt on that subject. I will proceed, in the manner of dialogue, to repeat as nearly as I can what passed betwixt us, only observing that, in the course of the conversation, my timidity imperceptibly gave way under the familiarity of his address; and that, in the concluding part of our dialogue, I perhaps argued with fully as much confidence as was beseeming.

Author of Waverley. I was willing to see you, Captain Clutterbuck, being the person of my family whom I have most regard for, since the death of Jedediah Cleishbotham,[8] and I am afraid I may have done you some wrong in assigning to you *The Monastery* as a portion of my effects. I have some thoughts of making it up to you, by naming you godfather to this yet unborn babe—(he indicated the proof-sheet with his finger). But first, touching *The Monastery*—how says the world? You are abroad and can learn.

Captain Clutterbuck. Hem! hem! The inquiry is delicate. I have not heard any complaints from the publishers.

Author. That is the principal matter; but yet an indifferent work is sometimes towed on by those which have left harbour before it, with the breeze in their poop. What say the critics?

Captain. There is a general—feeling—that the White Lady is no favourite.

43

Author. I think she is a failure myself; but rather in execution than conception. Could I have evoked an *esprit follet,*[9] at the same time fantastic and interesting, capricious and kind; a sort of wildfire of the elements, bound by no fixed laws or motives of action, faithful and fond, yet teasing and uncertain—

Captain. If you will pardon the interruption, sir, I think you are describing a pretty woman.

Author. On my word, I believe I am. I must invest my elementary spirits with a little human flesh and blood: they are too fine-drawn for the present taste of the public.

Captain. They object, too, that the object of your nixie ought to have been more uniformly noble. Her ducking the priest was no Naiad-like amusement.

Author. Ah! they ought to allow for the capriccios of what is, after all, but a better sort of goblin. The bath into which Ariel, the most delicate creation of Shakspeare's imagination, seduces our jolly friend Trinculo, was not of amber or rose-water.[10] But no one shall find me rowing against the stream. I care not who knows it, I write for general amusement; and, though I never will aim at popularity by what I think unworthy means, I will not, on the other hand, be pertinacious in the defence of my own errors against the voice of the public.

Captain. You abandon, then, in the present work (looking, in my turn, towards the proof-sheet), the mystic, and the magical, and the whole system of signs, wonders, and omens? There are no dreams, or presages, or obscure allusions to future events?

Author. Not a Cock Lane scratch, my son—not one bounce on the drum of Tedworth—not so much as the poor tick of a solitary death-watch in the wainscot.[11] All is clear and above board: A Scots metaphysician might believe every word of it.

Captain. And the story is, I hope, natural and probable; commencing strikingly, proceeding naturally, ending happily, like the course of a famed river, which gushes from the mouth of some obscure and romantic grotto; then gliding on, never pausing, never precipitating its course, visiting, as it were, by natural instinct, whatever worthy subjects of interest are presented by the country through which it passes; widening and deepening in interest as it flows on; and at length arriving at the final catastrophe as at some mighty haven, where ships of all kinds strike sail and yard?

Author. Hey! hey! what the deuce is all this? Why, 'tis Ercles's vein,[12] and it would require some one much more like Hercules than I to produce a story which should gush, and glide, and never pause, and visit, and widen, and deepen, and all the rest on't. I should be chin-deep in the grave, man, before I had done with my task; and, in the meanwhile, all the quirks and quiddities which I might have devised for my reader's amusement would lie rotting in my gizzard, like Sancho's suppressed witticisms, when he was under his master's displeasure.[13] There never was a novel written on this plan while the world stood.

Captain. Pardon me—*Tom Jones*.

Author. True, and perhaps *Amelia* also. Fielding had high notions of the dignity of an art which he may be considered as having founded.[14] He challenges a comparison between the Novel and the Epic. Smollett, Le Sage, and others, emancipating themselves from the strictness of the rules he has laid down, have written rather a history of the miscellaneous adventures which befall an individual in the course of life than the plot of a regular and connected epopeia, where every step brings us a point nearer to the final catastrophe. These great masters have been satisfied if they amused the reader upon the road; though the conclusion only arrived because the tale must have an end, just as the traveller alights at the inn because it is evening.[15]

Captain. A very commodious mode of travelling, for the author at least. In short, sir, you are of opinion with Bayes—'What the devil does the plot signify, except to bring in fine things?'[16]

Author. Grant that I were so, and that I should write with sense and spirit a few scenes unlaboured and loosely put together, but which had sufficient interest in them to amuse in one corner the pain of body; in another, to relieve anxiety of mind; in a third place, to unwrinkle a brow bent with the furrows of daily toil; in another, to fill the place of bad thoughts, or to suggest better; in yet another, to induce an idler to study the history of his country; in all, save where the perusal interrupted the discharge of serious duties, to furnish harmless amusement—might not the author of such a work, however inartifically executed, plead for his errors and negligences the excuse of the slave, who, about to be punished for having spread the false report of a victory, saved himself by exclaiming—'Am I to blame, O Athenians, who have given you one happy day?'

Captain. Will your goodness permit me to mention an anecdote of my excellent grandmother?

Author. I see little she can have to do with the subject, Captain Clutterbuck.

Captain. It may come into our dialogue on Bayes's plan. The sagacious old lady—rest her soul!—was a good friend to the church, and could never hear a minister maligned by evil tongues without taking his part warmly. There was one fixed point, however, at which she always abandoned the cause of her reverend *protégé*: it was so soon as she learned he had preached a regular sermon against slanderers and backbiters.

Author. And what is that to the purpose?

Captain. Only that I have heard engineers say that one may betray the weak point to the enemy by too much ostentation of fortifying it.

Author. And, once more I pray, what is that to the purpose?

Captain. Nay, then, without farther metaphor, I am afraid this new production, in which your generosity seems willing to give me some concern, will stand much in need of apology, since you think proper to begin your defence before the case is on trial. The story is hastily huddled up, I will venture a pint of claret.

Author. A pint of port, I suppose you mean?

Captain. I say of claret—good claret of the Monastery. Ah, sir, would you but take the advice of your friends, and try to deserve at least one-half of the public favour you have met with, we might all drink Tokay!

Author. I care not what I drink, so the liquor be wholesome.

Captain. Care for your reputation, then—for your fame.

Author. My fame? I will answer you as a very ingenious, able, and experienced friend, being counsel for the notorious Jem MacCoul,* replied to the opposite side of the bar, when they laid weight on his client's refusing to answer certain queries, which they said any man who had a regard for his reputation would not hesitate to reply to. 'My client,' said he—by the way, Jem was

---

*This character was a native of London, who was tried and convicted in 1820 of robbing a Glasgow bank of £20,000 (*Laing*).

standing behind him at the time, and a rich scene it was—'is so unfortunate as to have no regard for his reputation; and I should deal very uncandidly with the court should I say he had any that was worth his attention.' I am, though from very different reasons, in Jem's happy state of indifference. Let fame follow those who have a substantial shape. A shadow—and an impersonal author is nothing better—can cast no shade.

Captain. You are not now, perhaps, so impersonal as heretofore. These *Letters* to the Member for the University of Oxford—*

Author. Show the wit, genius, and delicacy of the author, which I heartily wish to see engaged on a subject of more importance; and show, besides, that the preservation of my character of incognito has engaged early talent in the discussion of a curious question of evidence. But a cause, however ingeniously pleaded, is not therefore gained. You may remember the neatly-wrought chain of circumstantial evidence, so artificially brought forward to prove Sir Philip Francis's title to the *Letters of Junius,* seemed at first irrefragable; yet the influence of the reasoning has passed away, and Junius, in the general opinion, is as much unknown as ever.[17] But on this subject I will not be soothed or provoked into saying one word more. To say who I am not would be one step towards saying who I am; and as I desire not, any more than a certain justice of peace mentioned by Shenstone,[18] the noise or report such things make in the world, I shall continue to be silent on a subject which, in my opinion, is very undeserving the noise that has been made about it, and still more unworthy of the serious employment of such ingenuity as has been displayed by the young letter-writer.

Captain. But allowing, my dear sir, that you care not for your personal reputation, or for that of any literary person upon whose shoulders your faults may be visited, allow me to say that common gratitude to the public, which has received you so kindly, and to the critics, who have treated you so leniently, ought to induce you to bestow more pains on your story.

Author. I do entreat you, my son, as Dr. Johnson would have said, 'free your mind from cant.'[19] For the critics, they have their business, and I mine; as the nursery proverb goes—

**Letters to Richard Heber, Esq., Member for the University of Oxford, containing Critical Remarks on the Waverley Novels, and an Attempt to ascertain the Author.* By J. L. Adolphus, Lond. 1821 *(Laing).*

The children in Holland take pleasure in making
What the children in England take pleasure in breaking.

I am their humble jackal, too busy in providing food for them to have time for considering whether they swallow or reject it. To the public I stand pretty nearly in the relation of the postman who leaves a packet at the door of an individual. If it contains pleasing intelligence—a billet from a mistress, a letter from an absent son, a remittance from a correspondent supposed to be bankrupt—the letter is acceptably welcome, and read and re-read, folded up, filed, and safely deposited in the bureau. If the contents are disagreeable, if it comes from a dun or from a bore, the correspondent is cursed, the letter is thrown into the fire, and the expense of postage is heartily regretted; while all the time the bearer of the despatches is, in either case, as little thought on as the snow of last Christmas. The utmost extent of kindness between the author and the public which can really exist is, that the world are disposed to be somewhat indulgent to the succeeding works of an original favourite, were it but on account of the habit which the public mind has acquired; while the author very naturally thinks well of their taste who have so liberally applauded *his* productions. But I deny there is any call for gratitude, properly so called, either on one side or the other.

Captain. Respect to yourself, then, ought to teach caution.

Author. Ay, if caution could augment the chance of my success. But, to confess to you the truth, the works and passages in which I have succeeded have uniformly been written with the greatest rapidity; and when I have seen some of these placed in opposition with others, and commended as more highly finished, I could appeal to pen and standish that the parts in which I have come feebly off were by much the more laboured. Besides, I doubt the beneficial effect of too much delay, both on account of the author and the public. A man should strike while the iron is hot, and hoist sail while the wind is fair. If a successful author keep not the stage, another instantly takes his ground. If a writer lie by for ten years ere he produces a second work, he is superseded by others; or, if the age is so poor of genius that this does not happen, his own reputation becomes his greatest obstacle. The public will expect the new work to be ten times better than its predecessor; the author will expect it should be ten times more popular, and 'tis a hundred to ten that both are disappointed.

Captain. This may justify a certain degree of rapidity in publication, but not that which is proverbially said to be no speed. You should take time at least to arrange your story.

Author. That is a sore point with me, my son. Believe me, I have not been fool enough to neglect ordinary precautions. I have repeatedly laid down my future work to scale, divided it into volumes and chapters, and endeavoured to construct a story which I meant should evolve itself gradually and strikingly, maintain suspense, and stimulate curiosity; and which, finally, should terminate in a striking catastrophe. But I think there is a demon who seats himself on the feather of my pen when I begin to write, and leads it astray from the purpose. Characters expand under my hand; incidents are multiplied; the story lingers, while the materials increase; my regular mansion turns out a Gothic anomaly, and the work is closed long before I have attained the point I proposed.

Captain. Resolution and determined forbearance might remedy that evil.

Author. Alas! my dear sir, you do not know the force of paternal affection. When I light on such a character as Bailie Jarvie, or Dalgetty, my imagination brightens, and my conception becomes clearer at every step which I take in his company, although it leads me many a weary mile away from the regular road, and forces me to leap hedge and ditch to get back into the route again. If I resist the temptation, as you advise me, my thoughts become prosy, flat, and dull; I write painfully to myself, and under a consciousness of flagging which makes me flag still more; the sunshine with which fancy had invested the incidents departs from them, and leaves everything dull and gloomy. I am no more the same author I was in my better mood than the dog in a wheel, condemned to go round and round for hours, is like the same dog merrily chasing his own tail, and gambolling in all the frolic of unrestrained freedom. In short, sir, on such occasions I think I am bewitched.

Captain. Nay, sir, if you plead sorcery, there is no more to be said: he must needs go whom the devil drives. And this, I suppose, sir, is the reason why you do not make the theatrical attempt to which you have been so often urged?

Author. It may pass for one good reason for not writing a play, that I cannot form a plot. But the truth is, that the idea adopted by too favourable judges, of my having some aptitude for that department of poetry, has been much founded on those scraps of old plays which, being taken from a source inaccessible to collectors, they have hastily considered the offspring of my mother-wit. Now, the manner in which I became possessed of these fragments is so extraordinary that I cannot help telling it to you.

You must know that, some twenty years since, I went down to visit an old friend in Worcestershire, who had served with me in the—Dragoons.

Captain. Then you *have* served, sir?

Author. I have—or I have not, which signifies the same thing; Captain is a good travelling name. I found my friend's house unexpectedly crowded with guests, and, as usual, was condemned—the mansion being an old one—to the *haunted apartment.* I have, as a great modern said, seen too many ghosts to believe in them, so betook myself seriously to my repose, lulled by the wind rustling among the lime-trees, the branches of which chequered the moonlight which fell on the floor through the diamonded casement, when, behold, a darker shadow interposed itself, and I beheld visibly on the floor of the apartment—

Captain. The White Lady of Avenel, I suppose? You have told the very story before.

Author. No—I beheld a female form, with mob-cap, bib, and apron, sleeves tucked up to the elbow, a dredging-box in the one hand, and in the other a sauce-ladle. I concluded, of course, that it was my friend's cook-maid walking in her sleep; and as I knew he had a value for Sally, who could toss a pancake with any girl in the county, I got up to conduct her safely to the door. But as I approached her, she said, 'Hold, sir! I am not what you take me for'—words which seemed so apposite to the circumstances, that I should not have much minded them, had it not been for the peculiarly hollow sound in which they were uttered. 'Know, then,' she said, in the same unearthly accents, 'that I am the spirit of Betty Barnes.' 'Who hanged herself for love of the stage-coachman,' thought I; 'this is a proper spot of work!' 'Of that unhappy Elizabeth or Betty Barnes, long cook-maid to Mr. Warburton, the painful collector, but ah! the too careless custodier, of the largest collection of ancient plays ever known—of most of which the titles only are left to gladden the Prolegomena of the Variorum Shakspeare.[20] Yes, stranger, it was these ill-fated hands that consigned to grease and conflagration the scores of small quartos, which, did they now exist, would drive the whole Roxburghe Club out of their senses;[21] it was these unhappy pickers and stealers that singed fat fowls and wiped dirty trenchers with the lost works of Beaumont and Fletcher, Massinger, Jonson, Webster—what shall I say? even of Shakespeare himself!'

Like every dramatic antiquary, my ardent curiosity after some play named in the book of the Master of Revels had often been checked by finding the object of my research numbered amongst the holocaust of victims which this unhappy woman had sacrificed to the God of Good Cheer. It is no wonder then, that, like the Hermit of Parnell,

> I broke the bands of fear and madly cried,
> 'You careless jade!' But scarce the words began,
> When Betty brandish'd high her saucing-pan.[22]

'Beware,' she said, 'you do not, by your ill-timed anger, cut off the opportunity I yet have to indemnify the world for the errors of my ignorance. In yonder coal hole, not used for many a year, repose the few greasy and blackened fragments of the elder drama which were not totally destroyed. Do thou then—' Why, what do you stare at, captain! By my soul, it is true; as my friend Major Longbow says, 'What should I tell you a lie for?'[23]

Captain. Lie, sir! Nay, Heaven forbid I should apply the word to a person so veracious. You are only inclined to chase your tail a little this morning, that's all. Had you not better reserve this legend to form an introduction to *Three Recovered Dramas*, or so?

Author. You are quite right; habit's a strange thing, my son. I had forgot whom I was speaking to. Yes, plays for the closet, not for the stage—

Captain. Right, and so you are sure to be acted; for the managers, while thousands of volunteers are desirous of serving them, are wonderfully partial to pressed men.

Author. I am a living witness, having been, like a second Laberius, made a dramatist whether I would or not.[24] I believe my muse would be *Terryfied** into treading the stage, even if I should write a sermon.

Captain. Truly, if you did, I am afraid folks might make a farce of it; and, therefore, should you change your style, I still advise a volume of dramas like Lord Byron's.

Author. No, his lordship is a cut above me: I won't run my horse against his, if I can help myself. But there is my friend Allan has written just such a play as I might write myself, in a very sunny day, and with one of Bramah's extra patent-pens. I cannot make neat work without such appurtenances.

Captain. Do you mean Allan Ramsay?

Author. No, nor Barbara Allan either. I mean Allan Cunningham,[25] who has just published his tragedy of *Sir Marmaduke Maxwell*, full of merry-making and murdering, kissing and cutting of throats, and passages which lead to nothing, and which are very pretty passages for all that. Not a glimpse of probability is there about the plot, but so much animation in particular passages, and such a vein of poetry through the whole, as I dearly wish I could infuse into my *Culinary Remains*, should I ever be tempted to publish them. With a popular impress, people would read and admire the beauties of Allan; as it is, they may perhaps only note his defects—or, what is worse, not note them at all. But never mind them, honest Allan; you are a credit to Caledonia for all that. There are some lyrical effusions of his, too, which you would do well to read, captain. 'It's hame, and it's hame,' is equal to Burns.[26]

Captain. I will take the hint. The club at Kennaquhair are turned fastidious since Catalani visited the Abbey.[27] *My Poortith Cauld* has been received both poorly and coldly, and *The Banks of Bonnie Doon* have been positively coughed down. *Tempora mutantur.*[28]

Author. They cannot stand still, they will change with all of us. What then?

A man's a man for a' that.[29]

But the hour of parting approaches.

---

*A jocular allusion to the Author's friend Daniel Terry, a celebrated comedian, who dramatised more than one of the Waverley Novels, which were brought on the stage with great success. Sir Walter himself might have been seen as a spectator, enjoying the performance as much as any one (*Laing*).

Captain. You are determined to proceed then in your own system? Are you aware that an unworthy motive may be assigned for this rapid succession of publication? You will be supposed to work merely for the lucre of gain.

Author. Supposing that I did permit the great advantages which must be derived from success in literature to join with other motives in inducing me to come more frequently before the public, that emolument is the voluntary tax which the public pays for a certain species of literary amusement; it is extorted from no one, and paid, I presume, by those only who can afford it, and who receive gratification in proportion to the expense. If the capital sum which these volumes have put into circulation be a very large one, has it contributed to my indulgences only? or can I not say to hundreds, from honest Duncan the paper-manufacturer to the most snivelling of the printer's devils, 'Didst thou not share? Hadst thou not fifteen pence?'[30] I profess I think our Modern Athens[31] much obliged to me for having established such an extensive manufacture; and when universal suffrage comes in fashion, I intend to stand for a seat in the House on the interest of all the unwashed artificers connected with literature.

Captain. This would be called the language of a calico-manufacturer.

Author. Cant again, my dear son: there is lime in this sack, too; nothing but sophistication in this world![32] I do say it, in spite of Adam Smith and his followers, that a successful author is a productive labourer, and that his works constitute as effectual a part of the public wealth as that which is created by any other manufacture.[33] If a new commodity, having an actually intrinsic and commercial value, be the result of the operation, why are the author's bales of books to be esteemed a less profitable part of the public stock than the goods of any other manufacturer? I speak with reference to the diffusion of the wealth arising to the public, and the degree of industry which even such a trifling work as the present must stimulate and reward, before the volumes leave the publisher's shop. Without me it could not exist, and to this extent I am a benefactor to the country. As for my own emolument, it is won by my toil, and I account myself answerable to Heaven only for the mode in which I expend it. The candid may hope it is not all dedicated to selfish purposes; and, without much pretensions to merit in him who disburses it, a part may 'wander, heaven-directed, to the poor.'

Captain. Yet it is generally held base to write from the mere motive of gain.

Author. It would be base to do so exclusively, or even to make it a principal motive for literary exertion. Nay, I will venture to say that no work of imagination, proceeding from the mere consideration of a certain sum of copy-money, ever did, or ever will, succeed. So the lawyer who pleads, the soldier who fights, the physician who prescribes, the clergyman—if such there be—who preaches, without any zeal for his profession, or without any sense of its dignity, and merely on account of the fee, pay, or stipend, degrade themselves to the rank of sordid mechanics. Accordingly, in the case of two of the learned faculties at least, their services are considered as unappreciable, and are acknowledged, not by any exact estimate of the services rendered, but by a *honorarium*, or voluntary acknowledgment. But let a client or patient make the experiment of omitting this little ceremony of the *honorarium*, which is *censé* to be a thing entirely out of consideration between them, and mark how the learned gentleman will look upon his case. Cant set apart, it is the same thing with literary emolument. No man of sense, in any rank of life, is, or ought to be, above accepting a just recompense for his time, and a reasonable share of the capital which owes its very existence to his exertions. When Czar Peter wrought in the trenches, he took the pay of a common soldier; and nobles, statesmen, and divines, the most distinguished of their time, have not scorned to square accounts with their bookseller.

Captain. (Sings.)

> O if it were a mean thing,
> The gentles would not use it;
> And if it were ungodly,
> The clergy would refuse it.

Author. You say well. But no man of honour, genius, or spirit would make the mere love of gain the chief, far less the only, purpose of his labours. For myself, I am not displeased to find the game a winning one; yet while I pleased the public, I should probably continue it merely for the pleasure of playing; for I have felt as strongly as most folks that love of composition which is perhaps the strongest of all instincts, driving the author to the pen, the painter to the pallet, often without either the chance of fame or the prospect of reward. Perhaps I have said too much of this. I might, perhaps, with as much truth as most people, exculpate myself from the charge of being either of a greedy or mercenary disposition; but I am not, therefore, hypocrite enough to disclaim the ordinary motives, on account of which the whole world around me is toiling unremittingly, to the sacrifice of ease, comfort, health, and life. I do not affect the disinterestedness of that ingenious association of gentlemen mentioned by Goldsmith, who sold their magazine for sixpence a-piece, merely for their own amusement.[34]

Captain. I have but one thing more to hint. The world say you will run yourself out.

Author. The world say true; and what then? When they dance no longer, I will no longer pipe; and I shall not want flappers enough to remind me of the apoplexy.[35]

Captain. And what will become of us then, your poor family? We shall fall into contempt and oblivion.

Author. Like many a poor fellow, already overwhelmed with the number of his family, I cannot help going on to increase it. ''Tis my vocation, Hal.'[36] Such of you as deserve oblivion—perhaps the whole of you—may be consigned to it. At any rate, you have been read in your day, which is more than can be said of some of your contemporaries of less fortune and more merit. They cannot say but that you *had* the crown. It is always something to have engaged the public attention for seven years. Had I only written *Waverley*, I should have long since been, according to the established phrase, 'the ingenious author of a novel much admired at the time.' I believe, on my soul, that the reputation of *Waverley* is sustained very much by the praises of those who may be inclined to prefer that tale to its successors.

Captain. You are willing, then, to barter future reputation for present popularity?

Author. *Meliora spero.* Horace himself expected not to survive in all his works; I may hope to live in some of mine. *Non omnis moriar.*[37] It is some consolation to reflect that the best authors in all countries have been the most voluminous; and it has often happened that those who have been best received in their own time have also continued to be acceptable to posterity. I do not think so ill of the present generation as to suppose that its present favour necessarily infers future condemnation.

Captain. Were all to act on such principles, the public would be inundated.

Author. Once more, my dear son, beware of cant. You speak as if the public were obliged to read books merely because they are printed; your friends the booksellers would thank you to make the proposition good. The most serious grievance attending such inundations as you talk of is that they make rags dear. The multiplicity of publications does the present age no harm, and may greatly advantage that which is to succeed us.

Captain. I do not see how that is to happen.

Author. The complaints in the time of Elizabeth and James of the alarming fertility of the press were as loud as they are at present; yet look at the shore over which the inundation of that age flowed, and it resembles now the Rich Strand of the *Faëry Queene*—

> Bestrew'd all with rich array,
> Of pearl and precious stones of great assay;
> And all the gravel mix'd with golden ore.[38]

Believe me, that even in the most neglected works of the present age the next may discover treasures.

Captain. Some books will defy all alchemy.

Author. They will be but few in number; since, as for writers who are possessed of no merit at all, unless indeed they publish their works at their own expense, like Sir Richard Blackmore,[39] their power of annoying the public will be soon limited by the difficulty of finding undertaking booksellers.

Captain. You are incorrigible. Are there no bounds to your audacity?

Author. There are the sacred and eternal boundaries of honour and virtue. My course is like the enchanted chamber of Britomart—

> Where as she look'd about, she did behold
> How over that same door was likewise writ,
> *Be Bold—Be Bold*, and everywhere *Be Bold*.
> Whereat she mused, and could not construe it;

> At last she spied at that room's upper end
> Another iron door, on which was writ—
> BE NOT TOO BOLD.[40]

Captain. Well, you must take the risk of proceeding on your own principles.

Author. Do you act on yours, and take care you do not stay idling here till the dinner-hour is over. I will add this work to your patrimony, *valeat quantum.*[41]

Here our dialogue terminated; for a little sooty-faced Apollyon[42] from the Canongate came to demand the proof-sheet on the part of Mr. M'Corkindale;* and I heard Mr. C. rebuking Mr. F. in another compartment of the same labyrinth I have described, for suffering any one to penetrate so far into the *penetralia* of their temple.[43]

I leave it to you to form your own opinion concerning the import of this dialogue, and I cannot but believe I shall meet the wishes of our common parent in prefixing this letter to the work which it concerns.

> I am, reverend and dear Sir,
> Very sincerely and affectionately
> Yours, etc. etc.
> CUTHBERT CLUTTERBUCK.

KENNAQUHAIR, 1*st April* 1822.

---

*This painstaking man was for many years foreman in Ballantyne's printing-office (*Laing*).

Prefatory Letter to

PEVERIL OF THE PEAK (1822)

FROM
THE. REV. DR. DRYASDUST OF YORK
TO
CAPTAIN CLUTTERBUCK,

Residing at Fairy Lodge, near Kennaquhair, N.B.

VERY WORTHY AND DEAR SIR,

To your last letter I might have answered, with the classic, *Haud equidem invideo, miror magis.*[1] For though my converse, from infancy, has been with things of antiquity, yet I love not ghosts or spectres to be commentators thereon; and truly your account of the conversation you held with our great parent, in the crypt, or most intimate recess, of the publishers at Edinburgh, had upon me much the effect of the apparition of Hector's phantom on the hero of the Aeneid—

Obstupui, steteruntque comae.[2]

And, as I said above, I repeat that I wondered at the vision, without envying you the pleasure of seeing our great progenitor. But it seems that he is now permitted to show himself to his family more freely than formerly; or that the old gentleman is turned somewhat garrulous in these latter days; or, in short, not to exhaust your patience with conjectures of the cause, I also have seen the vision of the Author of *Waverley*. I do not mean to take any undue state on myself, when I observe, that this interview was marked with circumstances in some degree more formally complaisant than those which attended your meeting with him in our worthy publisher's; for yours had the appearance of a fortuitious rencontre, whereas mine was preceded by the communication of a large roll of papers, containing a new history, called *Peveril of the Peak*.

58

Prefatory Letter to *Peveril of the Peak*

I no sooner found that this manuscript consisted of a narrative, running to the length of perhaps three hundred and thirty pages in each volume, or thereabouts, than it instantly occurred to me from whom this boon came; and having set myself to peruse the written sheets, I began to entertain strong expectations that I might, peradventure, next see the Author himself.

Again, it seems to me a marked circumstance that, whereas an inner apartment of Mr. Constable's shop was thought a place of sufficient solemnity for your audience, our venerable senior was pleased to afford mine in the recesses of my own lodgings, *intra parietes*,[3] as it were, and without the chance of interruption. I must also remark, that the features, form, and dress of the *eidolon*, as you well term the apparition of our parent, seemed to me more precisely distinct than was vouchsafed to you on the former occasion. Of this hereafter; but Heaven forbid I should glory or set up any claim of superiority over the other descendants of our common parent from such decided marks of his preference. *Laus propria sordet*.[4] I am well satisfied that the honour was bestowed not on my person, but my cloth: that the preference did not elevate Jonas Dryasdust over Clutterbuck, but the doctor of divinity over the captain. *Cedant arma togae*[5]—a maxim never to be forgotten at any time, but especially to be remembered when the soldier is upon half-pay.

But I bethink me that I am keeping you all this while in the porch, and wearying you with long inductions, when you would have me *properare in mediam rem*.[6] As you will, it shall be done; for, as his Grace is wont to say of me wittily, 'No man tells a story so well as Dr. Dryasdust, when he has once got up to the starting-post.' *Jocose hoc*.[7] But to continue.

I had skimmed the cream of the narrative which I had received about a week before, and that with no small cost and pain; for the hand of our parent is become so small and so crabbed that I was obliged to use strong magnifiers. Feeling my eyes a little exhausted towards the close of the second volume, I leaned back in my easy-chair, and began to consider whether several of the objections which have been particularly urged against our father and patron might not be considered as applying, in an especial manner, to the papers I had just perused. 'Here are figments enough,' said I to myself, 'to confuse the march of a whole history—anachronisms enough to overset all chronology! The old gentleman hath broken all bounds: *abiit, evasit, erupit.*'[8]

As these thought passed through my mind, I fell into a fit of musing, which is not uncommon with me after dinner, when I am altogether alone, or have no one with me but my curate. I was awake, however; for I remembered seeing, in the embers of the fire, a representation of a mitre, with the towers of a cathedral in the background; moreover, I recollect gazing for a certain time on the comely countenance of Dr. Whiterose, my uncle by the mother's side—the same who is mentioned in *The Heart of Mid-lothian*[9]—whose portrait, graceful in wig and canonicals, hangs above my mantelpiece. Farther, I remember marking the flowers in the frame of carved oak, and casting my eye on the pistols which hang beneath, being the firearms with which, in the eventful year 1746, my uncle meant to have espoused the cause of Prince Charles Edward; for, indeed, so little did he esteem personal safety in comparison of steady High Church principle, that he waited but the news of the Adventurer's reaching London to hasten to join his standard.

Such a doze as I then enjoyed, I find compatible with indulging the best and deepest cogitations which at any time arise in my mind. I chew the cud of sweet and bitter fancy,[10] in a state betwixt sleeping and waking, which I consider as so highly favourable to philosophy, that I have no doubt some of its most distinguished systems have been composed under its influence. My servant is, therefore, instructed to tread as if upon down; my door-hinges are carefully oiled, and all appliances used to prevent me from being prematurely and harshly called back to the broad waking-day of a laborious world. My custom, in this particular, is so well known, that the very schoolboys cross the alley on tiptoe, betwixt the hours of four and five. My cell is the very dwelling of Morpheus. There is indeed a bawling knave of a broom-man, *quem ego*[11]—But this is matter for the quarter-sessions.

As my head sunk back upon the easy-chair in the philosophical mood which I have just described, and the eyes of my body began to close, in order, doubtless, that those of my understanding might be the more widely opened, I was startled by a knock at the door, of a kind more authoritatively boisterous than is given at that hour by any visitor acquainted with my habits. I started up in my seat, and heard the step of my servant hurrying along the passage, followed by a very heavy and measured pace, which shook the long oak-floored gallery in such a manner as forcibly to arrest my attention. 'A stranger, sir, just arrived from Edinburgh by the north mail, desires to speak with your reverence.' Such were the words with which Jacob threw the door to the wall; and the startled tone in which he pronounced them, although there was nothing particular in the annunciation itself, prepared me for the approach of a visitor of uncommon dignity and importance.

The Author of *Waverley* entered, a bulky and tall man, in a travelling great-coat, which covered a suit of snuff-brown, cut in imitation of that worn by the great Rambler.* His flapped hat—for he disdained the modern frivolities of a travelling-cap—was bound over his head with a large silk handkerchief, so as to protect his ears from cold at once and from the babble of his pleasant companions in the public coach from which he had just alighted. There was somewhat of a sarcastic shrewdness and sense which sat on the heavy penthouse of his shaggy grey eyebrow; his features were in other respects largely shaped, and rather heavy than promising wit or genius; but he had a notable projection of the nose, similar to that line of the Latin poet—

Immodicum surgit pro cuspide rostrum.[12]

A stout walking-stick stayed his hand; a double Barcelona protected his neck; his belly was something prominent, 'but that's not much',[13] his breeches were substantial thick-set, and a pair of top-boots, which were slipped down to ease his sturdy calves, did not conceal his comfortable travelling stockings of lamb's wool, wrought, not on the loom, but on wires, and after the venerable ancient fashion known in Scotland by the name of 'ridge-and-furrow.' His age seemed to be considerably above fifty, but could not amount to threescore, which I observed with pleasure, trusting there may be a good deal of work had out of him yet; especially as a general haleness of appearance—the compass and strength of his voice, the steadiness of his step, the rotundity of his calf, the depth of his 'hem,' and the sonorous emphasis of his sneeze, were all signs of a constitution built for permanence.

---

*Dr. Samuel Johnson, author of *The Rambler* (Laing).

It struck me forcibly, as I gazed on this portly person, that he realized, in my imagination, the Stout Gentleman in No. II., who afforded such subject of varying speculation to our most amusing and elegant Utopian traveller, Master Geoffrey Crayon.[14] Indeed, but for one little trait in the conduct of the said Stout Gentleman—I mean the gallantry towards his landlady, a thing which would greatly derogate from our senior's character—I should be disposed to conclude that Master Crayon had, on that memorable occasion, actually passed his time in the vicinity of the Author of *Waverley*. But our worthy patriarch, be it spoken to his praise, far from cultivating the society of the fair sex, seems, in avoiding the company of womankind, rather to imitate the humour of our friend and relation, Master Jonathan Oldbuck, as I was led to conjecture, from a circumstance which occurred immediately after his entrance.

Having acknowledged his presence with fitting thanks and gratulations, I proposed to my venerated visitor, as the refreshment best suited to the hour of the day, to summon my cousin and housekeeper, Miss Catharine Whiterose, with the tea-equipage; but he rejected my proposal with disdain worthy of the Laird of Monkbarns. 'No scandal-broth,' he exclaimed—'no unidea'd woman's chatter for me. Fill the frothed tankard—slice the fatted rump; I desire no society but yours, and no refreshment but what the cask and the gridiron can supply.'

The beefsteak, and toast, and tankard were speedily got ready; and whether an apparition or a bodily presentation, my visitor displayed dexterity as a trencherman which might have attracted the envy of a hungry hunter after a fox-chase of forty miles. Neither did he fail to make some deep and solemn appeals not only to the tankard aforesaid, but to two decanters of London particular Madeira and old port; the first of which I had extracted from its ripening place of deposition within reach of the genial warmth of the oven; the other, from a deep crypt in mine own ancient cellar, which whilom may have held the vintages of the victors of the world, the arch being composed of Roman brick. I could not help admiring and congratulating the old gentleman upon the vigorous appetite which he displayed for the genial cheer of Old England. 'Sir,' was his reply, 'I must eat as an Englishman to qualify myself for taking my place at one of the

Prefatory Letter to *Peveril of the Peak*

most select companies of right English spirits which ever girdled in and hewed asunder a mountainous sirloin and a generous plum-pudding.'

I inquired, but with all deference and modesty, whither he was bound, and to what distinguished society he applied a description so general. I shall proceed, in humble imitation of your example, to give the subsequent dialogue in a dramatic form, unless when description becomes necessary.

Author of Waverley. To whom should I apply such a description, save to the only society to whom it can be thoroughly applicable— those unerring judges of old books and old wine—the Roxburghe Club of London? Have you not heard that I have been chosen a member of that society of select bibliomaniacs?*[15]

Dryasdust. (Rummaging in his pocket.) I did hear something of it from Captain Clutterbuck, who wrote to me—ay, here is his letter—that such a report was current among the Scottish antiquaries, who were much alarmed lest you should be seduced into the heresy of preferring English Beef to seven-year-old black-faced mutton, Maraschino to whisky, and turtle-soup to cock-a-leekie; in which case, they must needs renounce you as a lost man. 'But,' adds our friend, looking at the letter, his hand is rather of a military description, better used to handle the sword than the pen—'our friend is so much upon the SHUN'—the *shun*, I think it is—'that it must be no light temptation which will withdraw him from his incognito.'

Author. No light temptation, unquestionably; but this is a powerful one, to hob-or-nob with the lords of the literary treasures of Althorpe and Hodnet,† in Madeira negus, brewed by

*The Author has pride in recording that he had the honour to be elected a member of this distinguished association, merely as the Author of *Waverley*, without any other designation; and it was an additional inducement to throw off the masque of an anonymous author, that it gives him a right to occupy the vacant chair at that festive board.

†Althorpe, the seat of the Earls Spencer, in the county of Northampton, contains perhaps the most valuable private collection of early printed books either in England or elsewhere. Full justice has been rendered to this library by the Rev. Dr. Dibdin, in his *Bibliotheca Spenceriana*, and his *Aedes Althorpianae*, forming seven large and handsome volumes, profusely illustrated. Mr. Heber's collection, intended for his seat of Hodnet, in Shropshire, was much less fortunate. The greater portion of his library remained in London, until the entire collection, after his death, was dispersed by auction in the years 1834–1837 (*Laing*).

the classical Dibdin;[16] to share those profound debates which stamp accurately on each 'small volume, dark with tarnished gold,' its collar, not of S. S. but of R. R.;[17] to toast the immortal memory of Caxton, Valdarfar, Pynson, and the other fathers of that great art which has made all, and each of us, what we are.[18] These, my dear son, are temptations to which you see me now in the act of resigning that quiet chimney-corner of life in which, unknowing and unknown—save by means of the hopeful family to which I have given birth—I proposed to wear out the end of life's evening grey.

So saying, our venerable friend took another emphatic touch of the tankard, as if the very expression had suggested that specific remedy against the evils of life recommended in the celebrated response of Johnson's anchorite—

Come, my lad, and drink some beer.[19]

When he had placed on the table the silver tankard, and fetched a deep sigh to collect the respiration which the long draught had interrupted, I could not help echoing it in a note so pathetically compassionate that he fixed his eyes on me with surprise. 'How is this?' said he, somewhat angrily; 'do you, the creature of my will, grudge me my preferment? Have I dedicated to you and your fellows the best hours of my life for these seven years past, and do you presume to grumble or repine because, in those which are to come, I seek for some enjoyment of life in society so congenial to my pursuits?' I humbled myself before the offended senior, and professed my innocence in all that could possibly give him displeasure. He seemed partly appeased, but still bent on me an eye of suspicion, while he questioned me in the words of old Norton, in the ballad of the *Rising in the North Country*.

Author. What wouldst thou have, Francis Norton?
　　　Thou art my youngest son and heir;
　　　Something lies brooding at thy heart—
　　　Whate'er it be, to me declare.

Dryasdust. Craving, then, your paternal forgiveness for my presumption, I only sighed at the possibility of your venturing yourself amongst a body of critics to whom, in the capacity of skilful antiquaries, the investigation of truth is an especial duty, and who may therefore visit with the more severe censure those aberrations which it is so often your pleasure to make from the path of true history.

Author. I understand you. You mean to say these learned persons will have but little toleration for a romance or a fictitious narrative founded upon history?

Dryasdust. Why, sir, I do rather apprehend that their respect for the foundation will be such that they may be apt to quarrel with the inconsistent nature of the superstructure; just as every classical traveller pours forth expressions of sorrow and indignation when, in travelling through Greece, he chances to see a Turkish kiosk rising on the ruins of an ancient temple.

Author. But since we cannot rebuild the temple, a kiosk may be a pretty thing, may it not? Not quite correct in architecture, strictly and classically criticized; but presenting something uncommon to the eye, and something fantastic to the imagination, on which the spectator gazes with pleasure of the same description which arises from the perusal of an Eastern tale.

Dryasdust. I am unable to dispute with you in metaphor, sir; but I must say, in discharge of my conscience, that you stand much censured for adulterating the pure sources of historical knowledge. You approach them, men say, like the drunken yeoman who, once upon a time, polluted the crystal spring which supplied the thirst of his family, with a score of sugar loaves and a hogshead of rum; and thereby converted a simple and wholesome beverage into a stupifying, brutifying, and intoxicating fluid, sweeter, indeed, to the taste than the natural lymph, but, for that very reason, more seductively dangerous.

Author. I allow your metaphor, doctor; but yet, though good punch cannot supply the want of spring water, it is, when modestly used, no *malum in se*;[20] and I should have thought it a shabby thing of the parson of the parish had he helped to drink out the well on Saturday night and preached against the honest, hospitable yeoman on Sunday morning. I should have answered him that the very flavour of the liquor should have put him at once upon his guard; and that, if he had taken a drop over much, he ought to blame his own imprudence more than the hospitality of his entertainer.

Dryasdust. I profess I do not exactly see how this applies.

Author. No; you are one of those numerous disputants who will never follow their metaphor a step farther than it goes their own way. I will explain. A poor fellow, like myself, weary with ransacking his own barren and bounded imagination, looks out for some general subject in the huge and boundless field of history, which holds forth examples of every kind; lights on some personage, or some combination of circumstances, or some striking trait of manners, which he thinks may be advantageously used as the basis of a fictitious narrative; bedizens it with such colouring as his skill suggests, ornaments it with such romantic circumstances as may heighten the general effect, invests it with such shades of character as will best contrast with each other, and thinks, perhaps, he has done some service to the public, if he can present to them a lively fictitious picture, for which the original anecdote or circumstance which he made free to press into his service only furnished a slight sketch. Now I cannot perceive any harm in this. The stores of history are accessible to every one, and are no more exhausted or impoverished by the hints thus borrowed from them than the fountain is drained by the water which we subtract for domestic purposes. And in reply to the sober charge of falsehood against a narrative announced positively to be fictitious, one can only answer by Prior's exclamation—

Odzooks, must one swear to the truth of a song?[21]

Dryasdust. Nay; but I fear me that you are here eluding the charge. Men do not seriously accuse you of misrepresenting history; although I assure you I have seen some grave treatises in which it was thought necessary to contradict your assertions.

Author. That certainly was to point a discharge of artillery against a wreath of morning mist.

Dryasdust. But besides, and especially, it is said that you are in danger of causing history to be neglected, readers being contented with such frothy and superficial knowledge as they acquire from your works, to the effect of inducing them to neglect the severer and more accurate sources of information.

Author. I deny the consequence. On the contrary, I rather hope that I have turned the attention of the public on various points which have received elucidation from writers of more learning and research, in consequence of my novels having attached some

66

interest to them. I might give instances, but I hate vanity—I hate vanity. The history of the divining-rod is well known: it is a slight, valueless twig in itself, but indicates, by its motion, where veins of precious metal are concealed below the earth, which afterwards enrich the adventurers by whom they are laboriously and carefully wrought. I claim no more merit for my historical hints; but this is something.

Dryasdust. We severer antiquaries, sir, may grant that this is true; to wit, that your works may occasionally have put men of solid judgment upon researches which they would not perhaps have otherwise thought of undertaking. But this will leave you still accountable for misleading the young, the indolent, and the giddy, by thrusting into their hands works which, while they have so much the appearance of conveying information as may prove perhaps a salve to their consciences for employing their leisure in the perusal, yet leave their giddy brains contented with the crude, uncertain, and often false statements which your novels abound with.[22]

Author. It would be very unbecoming in me, reverend sir, to accuse a gentleman of your cloth of cant; but, pray, is there not something like it in the pathos with which you enforce these dangers? I aver, on the contrary, that by introducing the busy and the youthful to 'truths severe in fairy fiction dressed,'*[23] I am doing a real service to the more ingenious and the more apt among them; for the love of knowledge wants but a beginning— the least spark will give fire when the train is properly prepared; and having been interested in fictitious adventures, ascribed to an historical period and characters, the reader begins next to be anxious to learn what the facts really were, and how far the novelist has justly represented them.

But even where the mind of the more careless reader remains satisfied with the light perusal he has afforded to a tale of fiction, he will still lay down the book with a degree of knowledge, not

---

*The doctor has denied the Author's title to shelter himself under this quotation; but the Author continues to think himself entitled to all the shelter which, threadbare as it is, it may yet be able to afford him. The truth severe applies not to the narrative itself, but to the moral it conveys, in which the Author has not been thought deficient. The 'fairy fiction' is the conduct of the story which the tale is invented to elucidate.

perhaps of the most accurate kind, but such as he might not otherwise have acquired. Nor is this limited to minds of a low and incurious description; but, on the contrary, comprehends many persons otherwise of high talents, who, nevertheless, either from lack of time or of perseverance, are willing to sit down contented with the slight information which is acquired in such a manner. The great Duke of Marlborough, for example, having quoted in conversation some fact of English history rather inaccurately, was requested to name his authority. 'Shakspeare's historical plays,' answered the conqueror of Blenheim; 'the only English history I ever read in my life.' And a hasty recollection will convince any of us how much better we are acquainted with those parts of English history which that immortal bard has dramatized than with any other portion of British story.

Dryasdust. And you, worthy sir, are ambitious to render a similar service to posterity?

Author. May the saints forefend I should be guilty of such unfounded vanity! I only show what has been done when there were giants in the land. We pigmies of the present day may at least, however, do something; and it is well to keep a pattern before our eyes, though that pattern be inimitable.

Dryasdust. Well, sir, with me you must have your own course; and for reasons well known to you, it is impossible for me to reply to you in argument. But I doubt if all you have said will reconcile the public to the anachronisms of your present volumes. Here you have a Countess of Derby fetched out of her cold grave and saddled with a set of adventures dated twenty years after her death, besides being given up as a Catholic, when she was in fact a zealous Huguenot.

Author. She may sue me for damages, as in the case Dido *versus* Virgil.

Dryasdust. A worse fault is, that your manners are even more incorrect than usual. Your Puritan is faintly traced in comparison to your Cameronian.

Author. I agree to the charge; but although I still consider hypocrisy and enthusiasm as fit food for ridicule and satire, yet I am sensible of the difficulty of holding fanaticism up to laughter or abhorrence without using colouring which may give offence to the sincerely worthy and religious. Many things are lawful which, we are taught, are not convenient; and there are many tones of feeling which are too respectable to be insulted, though we do not altogether sympathize with them.

Dryasdust. Not to mention, my worthy sir, that perhaps you may think the subject exhausted.

Author. The devil take the men of this generation for putting the worst construction on their neighbour's conduct!

So saying, and flinging a testy sort of adieu towards me with his hand, he opened the door and ran hastily downstairs. I started on my feet and rang for my servant, who instantly came. I demanded what had become of the stranger. He denied that any such had been admitted. I pointed to the empty decanters, and he—he—he had the assurance to intimate that such vacancies were sometimes made when I had no better company than my own. I do not know what to make of this doubtful matter, but will certainly imitate your example in placing this dialogue, with my present letter, at the head of *Peveril of the Peak*.

I am, Dear Sir, very much,
Your faithful and obedient Servant,

JONAS DRYASDUST.

Michaelmas Day, 1822,
YORK.

Introduction to

CHRONICLES OF THE CANONGATE (1827)

All who are acquainted with the early history of the Italian stage are aware that *arlechino* is not, in his original conception, a mere worker of marvels with his wooden sword, a jumper in and out of windows, as upon our theatre, but, as his parti-coloured jacket implies, a buffoon or clown, whose mouth, far from being eternally closed, as amongst us, is filled, like that of Touchstone, with quips, and cranks, and witty devices, very often delivered extempore. It is not easy to trace how he became possessed of his black vizard, which was anciently made in the resemblance of the face of a cat; but it seems that the mask was essential to the performance of the character, as will appear from the following theatrical anecdote:—

An actor on the Italian stage permitted at the *foire du St. Germain*, in Paris, was renowned for the wild, venturous, and extravagant wit, the brilliant sallies and fortunate repartees, with which he prodigally seasoned the character of the parti-coloured jester. Some critics, whose good-will towards a favourite performer was stronger than their judgment, took occasion to remonstrate with the successful actor on the subject of the grotesque vizard. They went wilily to their purpose, observing, that his classical and Attic wit, his delicate vein of humour, his happy turn for dialogue, were rendered burlesque and ludicrous by this unmeaning and bizarre disguise, and that those attributes would become far more impressive if aided by the spirit of his eye and the expression of his natural features. The actor's vanity was easily so far engaged as to induce him to make the experiment. He played harlequin barefaced, but was considered on all hands as having made a total failure. He had lost the audacity which a sense of incognito bestowed, and with it all the reckless play of raillery which gave vivacity to his original acting. He cursed his advisers, and resumed his grotesque vizard; but, it is said, without ever being able to regain the careless and successful levity which the consciousness of the disguise had formerly bestowed.

Perhaps the Author of *Waverley* is now about to incur a risk of the same kind, and endanger his popularity by having laid aside his incognito. It is certainly not a voluntary experiment, like that of harlequin; for it was my original intention never to have avowed these works during my lifetime, and the original manuscripts were carefully preserved, though by the care of others rather than mine, with the purpose of supplying the necessary evidence of the truth when the period of announcing it should arrive.* But the affairs of my publishers having unfortunately passed into a management different from their own, I had no right any longer to rely upon secrecy in that quarter; and thus my mask, like my Aunt Dinah's in *Tristram Shandy*, having begun to wax a little threadbare about the chin, it became time to lay it aside with a good grace, unless I desired it should fall in pieces from my face, which was now become likely.

Yet I had not the slightest intention of selecting the time and place in which the disclosure was finally made; nor was there any concert betwixt my learned and respected friend Lord Meadowbank† and myself upon that occasion. It was, as the reader is probably aware, upon the 23d February last [1827], at a public meeting, called for establishing a professional Theatrical Fund in Edinburgh, that the communication took place. Just before we sat down to table, Lord Meadowbank asked me privately whether I was still anxious to preserve my incognito on the subject of what were called the Waverley Novels? I did not immediately see the purpose of his lordship's question, although I certainly might have been led to infer it, and replied that the secret had now of

---

*These manuscripts are at present (August 1831) advertised for public sale, which is an addition, though a small one, to other annoyances.

†One of the Supreme Judges of Scotland, termed Lords of Council and Session.

necessity become known to so many people that I was indifferent on the subject. Lord Meadowbank was thus induced, while doing me the great honour of proposing my health to the meeting, to say something on the subject of these Novels, so strongly connecting them with me as the author, that, by remaining silent, I must have stood convicted, either of the actual paternity, or of the still greater crime of being supposed willing to receive indirectly praise to which I had no just title. I thus found myself suddenly and unexpectedly placed in the confessional, and had only time to recollect that I had been guided thither by a most friendly hand, and could not, perhaps, find a better public opportunity to lay down a disguise which began to resemble that of a detected masquerader. I had therefore the task of avowing myself, to the numerous and respectable company assembled, as the sole and unaided author of these Novels of Waverley, the paternity of which was likely at one time to have formed a controversy of some celebrity, for the ingenuity with which some instructors of the public gave their assurance on the subject was extremely persevering.

I now think it further necessary to say, that, while I take on myself all the merits and demerits attending these compositions, I am bound to acknowledge with gratitude hints of subjects and legends which I have received from various quarters, and have occasionally used as a foundation of my fictitious compositions, or woven up with them in the shape of episodes. I am bound, in particular, to acknowledge the unremitting kindness of Mr. Joseph Train, supervisor of excise at Dumfries, to whose unwearied industry I have been indebted for many curious traditions and points of antiquarian interest.[1] It was Mr. Train who brought to my recollection the history of Old Mortality, although I myself had had a personal interview with that celebrated wanderer so far back as about 1792, when I found him on his usual task. He was then engaged in repairing the gravestones of the Covenanters who had died while imprisoned in the Castle of Dunnottar, to which many of them were committed prisoners at the period of Argyle's rising; their place of confinement is still called the Whigs' Vault. Mr. Train, however, procured for me far more extensive information concerning this singular person, whose name was Paterson, than I had been able to acquire during my own short conversation with him.* He was, as I think I have somewhere already stated, a native of the parish of Closeburn, in Dumfriesshire, and it is believed that domestic affliction, as well as devotional feeling, induced him to commence the wandering mode of life which he pursued for a very long period. It is more than twenty years since Robert Paterson's death, which took place on the highroad near Lockerby, where he was found exhausted and expiring. The white pony, the companion of his pilgrimage, was standing by the side of its dying master, the whole furnishing a scene not unfitted for the pencil. These particulars I had from Mr. Train.

Another debt, which I pay most willingly, I owe to an unknown correspondent, a lady,† who favoured me with the history of the upright and high-principled female whom, in *The Heart of Midlothian*, I have termed Jeanie Deans. The circumstance of her refusing to save her sister's life by an act of perjury, and undertaking a pilgrimage to London to obtain her pardon, are both represented as true by my fair and obliging correspondent; and they led me to consider the possibility of rendering a fictitious personage interesting by mere dignity of mind and rectitude of principle, assisted by unpretending good sense and temper, without any of the beauty, grace, talent, accomplishment, and wit to which a heroine of romance is supposed to have a prescriptive right. If the portrait was received with interest by the public, I am conscious how much it was owing to the truth and force of the original sketch, which I regret that I am unable to present to the public, as it was written with much feeling and spirit.

Old and odd books, and a considerable collection of family legends, formed another quarry, so ample, that it was much more likely that the strength of the labourer should be exhausted than that materials should fail. I may mention, for example's sake, that the terrible catastrophe of *The Bride of Lammermoor* actually occurred in a Scottish family of rank. The female relative, by whom the melancholy tale was communicated to me many years since, was a near connexion of the family in which the event happened, and always told it with an appearance of melancholy

---

*See, for some further particulars, the notes to *Old Mortality*.
†The late Mrs. Goldie.

mystery, which enhanced the interest. She had known, in her youth, the brother who rode before the unhappy victim to the fatal altar, who, though then a mere boy, and occupied almost entirely with the gaiety of his own appearance in the bridal procession, could not but remark that the hand of his sister was moist, and cold as that of a statue. It is unnecessary further to withdraw the veil from this scene of family distress, nor, although it occurred more than a hundred years since, might it be altogether agreeable to the representatives of the families concerned in the narrative.[2] It may be proper to say, that the events alone are imitated; but I had neither the means nor intention of copying the manners, or tracing the characters, of the persons concerned in the real story.

Indeed, I may here state generally, that, although I have deemed historical personages free subjects of delineation, I have never on any occasion violated the respect due to private life. It was indeed impossible that traits proper to persons, both living and dead, with whom I have had intercourse in society, should not have risen to my pen in such works as *Waverley* and those which followed it. But I have always studied to generalise the portraits, so that they should still seem, on the whole, the productions of fancy, though possessing some resemblance to real individuals. Yet I must own my attempts have not in this last particular been uniformly successful. There are men whose characters are so peculiarly marked, that the delineation of some leading and principal feature inevitably places the whole person before you in his individuality. Thus, the character of Jonathan Oldbuck, in *The Antiquary*, was partly founded on that of an old friend of my youth, to whom I am indebted for introducing me to Shakspeare, and other invaluable favours; but I thought I had so completely disguised the likeness that his features could not be recognised by any one now alive. I was mistaken, however, and indeed had endangered what I desired should be considered as a secret; for I afterwards learned that a highly respectable gentleman, one of the few surviving friends of my father,* and an acute critic, had said, upon the appearance of the work, that he was now convinced who was the author of it, as he recognised, in the

---

*James Chalmers, Esq., solicitor-at-law, London, who died during the publication of the Collected Edition of these novels. (Aug. 1831.)

Antiquary of Monkbarns, traces of the character of a very intimate friend of my father's family.[9]

I may here also notice, that the sort of exchange of gallantry which is represented as taking place betwixt the Baron of Bradwardine [*Waverley*] and Colonel Talbot is a literal fact. The real circumstances of the anecdote, alike honourable to Whig and Tory, are these:—

Alexander Stewart of Invernahyle—a name which I cannot write without the warmest recollections of gratitude to the friend of my childhood, who first introduced me to the Highlands, their traditions and their manners—had been engaged actively in the troubles of 1745. As he charged at the battle of Preston with his clan, the Stewarts of Appine, he saw an officer of the opposite army standing alone by a battery of four cannon, of which he discharged three on the advancing Highlanders, and then drew his sword. Invernahyle rushed on him, and required him to surrender. 'Never to rebels!' was the undaunted reply, accompanied with a lounge, which the Highlander received on his target; but instead of using his sword in cutting down his now defenceless antagonist, he employed it in parrying the blow of a Lochaber axe, aimed at the officer by the miller, one of his own followers, a grim-looking old Highlander, whom I remember to have seen. Thus overpowered, Lieutenant-Colonel Allan Whitefoord, a gentleman of rank and consequence, as well as a brave officer, gave up his sword, and with it his purse and watch, which Invernahyle accepted, to save them from his followers. After the affair was over, Mr. Stewart sought out his prisoner, and they were introduced to each other by the celebrated John Roy Stewart, who acquainted Colonel Whitefoord with the quality of his captor, and made him aware of the necessity of receiving back his property, which he was inclined to leave in the hands into which it had fallen. So great became the confidence established betwixt them, that Invernahyle obtained from the Chevalier his prisoner's freedom upon parole; and soon afterwards, having been sent back to the Highlands to raise men, he visited Colonel Whitefoord at his own house, and spent two happy days with him and his Whig friends, without thinking, on either side, of the civil war which was then raging.

When the battle of Culloden put an end to the hopes of Charles

Edward, Invernahyle, wounded and unable to move, was borne from the field by the faithful zeal of his retainers. But, as he had been a distinguished Jacobite, his family and property were exposed to the system of vindictive destruction too generally carried into execution through the country of the insurgents. It was now Colonel Whitefoord's turn to exert himself, and he wearied all the authorities, civil and military, with his solicitations for pardon to the saver of his life, or at least for a protection for his wife and family. His applications were for a long time unsuccessful. 'I was found with the mark of the beast upon me in every list' was Invernahyle's expression. At length Colonel Whitefoord applied to the Duke of Cumberland, and urged his suit with every argument which he could think of. Being still repulsed, he took his commission from his bosom, and, having said something of his own and his family's exertions in the cause of the house of Hanover, begged to resign his situation in their service, since he could not be permitted to show his gratitude to the person to whom he owed his life. The Duke, struck with his earnestness, desired him to take up his commission, and granted the protection required for the family of Invernahyle.

The chieftain himself lay concealed in a cave near his own house, before which a small body of regular soldiers were encamped. He could hear their muster-roll called every morning, and their drums beat to quarters at night, and not a change of the sentinels escaped him. As it was suspected that he was lurking somewhere on the property, his family were closely watched, and compelled to use the utmost precaution in supplying him with food. One of his daughters, a child of eight or ten years old, was employed as the agent least likely to be suspected. She was an instance among others, that a time of danger and difficulty creates a premature sharpness of intellect. She made herself acquainted among the soldiers, till she became so familiar to them that her motions escaped their notice; and her practice was to stroll away into the neighbourhood of the cave, and leave what slender supply of food she carried for that purpose under some remarkable stone, or the root of some tree, where her father might find it as he crept by night from his lurking-place. Times became milder, and my excellent friend was relieved from proscription by the Act of Indemnity. Such is the interesting story which I have rather injured than improved by the manner in which it is told in *Waverley*.

This incident, with several other circumstances illustrating the Tales in question, was communicated by me to my late lamented friend, William Erskine, a Scottish judge, by the title of Lord Kinedder, who afterwards reviewed with far too much partiality the *Tales of my Landlord* for the *Quarterly Review* of January 1817.*[4] In the same article are contained other illustrations of the Novels, with which I supplied my accomplished friend, who took the trouble to write the review. The reader who is desirous of such information will find the original of Meg Merrilies, and I believe of one or two other personages of the same cast of character, in the article referred to.

I may also mention, that the tragic and savage circumstances which are represented as preceding the birth of Allan M'Aulay, in *The Legend of Montrose*, really happened in the family of Stewart of Ardvoirlich. The wager about the candlesticks, whose place was supplied by Highland torch-bearers, was laid and won by one of the MacDonalds of Keppoch.

There can be but little amusement in winnowing out the few grains of truth which are contained in this mass of empty fiction. I may, however, before dismissing the subject, allude to the various localities which have been affixed to some of the scenery introduced into these novels, by which, for example, Wolf's Hope is identified with Fast Castle in Berwickshire, Tillietudlem with Draphane in Clydesdale, and the valley in *The Monastery*, called Glendearg, with the dale of the river Allan, above Lord Somerville's villa, near Melrose. I can only say that, in these and other instances, I had no purpose of describing any particular local spot; and the resemblance must therefore be of that general kind which necessarily exists between scenes of the same character. The iron-bound coast of Scotland affords upon its headlands and promontories fifty such castles as Wolf's Hope; every county has a valley more or less resembling Glendearg; and if castles like Tillietudlem, or mansions like the Baron of Bradwardine's, are

---

*Lord Kinedder died in August 1822. Eheu! (Aug. 1831.)

now less frequently to be met with, it is owing to the rage of indiscriminate destruction, which has removed or ruined so many monuments of antiquity, when they were not protected by their inaccessible situation.*

The scraps of poetry which have been in most cases tacked to the beginning of chapters in these novels are sometimes quoted either from reading or from memory, but, in the general case, are pure invention. I found it too troublesome to turn to the collection of the British poets to discover apposite mottoes, and, in the situation of the theatrical mechanist, who, when the white paper which represented his shower of snow was exhausted, continued the storm by snowing brown, I drew on my memory as long as I could, and, when that failed, eked it out with invention. I believe that, in some cases, where actual names are affixed to the supposed quotations, it would be to little purpose to seek them in the works of the authors referred to. In some cases I have been entertained when Dr. Watts and other graver authors have been ransacked in vain for stanzas for which the novelist alone was responsible.

And now the reader may expect me, while in the confessional, to explain the motives why I have so long persisted in disclaiming the works of which I am now writing. To this it would be difficult to give any other reply save that of Corporal Nym: it was the Author's humour or caprice for the time.[5] I hope it will not be construed into ingratitude to the public, to whose indulgence I have owed my *sang froid* much more than to any merit of my own, if I confess that I am, and have been, more indifferent to success, or to failure, as an author than may be the case with others, who feel more strongly the passion for literary fame, probably because they are justly conscious of a better title to it. It was not until I had attained the age of thirty years that I made any serious attempt at distinguishing myself as an author; and at that period men's hopes, desires, and wishes have usually acquired something of a decisive character, and are not eagerly and easily diverted into a new channel. When I made the discovery—for to me it was one—that by amusing myself with composition, which I felt a

---

*I would particularly intimate the Kaim of Urie, on the eastern coast of Scotland, as having suggested an idea for the tower called Wolf's Crag, which the public more generally identified with the ancient tower of Fast Castle.

delightful occupation, I could also give pleasure to others, and became aware that literary pursuits were likely to engage in future a considerable portion of my time, I felt some alarm that I might acquire those habits of jealousy and fretfulness which have lessened, and even degraded, the character even of great authors, and rendered them, by their petty squabbles and mutual irritability, the laughing-stock of the people of the world. I resolved, therefore, in this respect to guard my breast, perhaps an unfriendly critic may add, my brow, with triple brass,* and as much as possible to avoid resting my thoughts and wishes upon literary success, lest I should endanger my own peace of mind and tranquillity by literary failure. It would argue either stupid apathy or ridiculous affectation to say that I have been insensible to the public applause, when I have been honoured with its testimonies; and still more highly do I prize the invaluable friendships which some temporary popularity has enabled me to form among those of my contemporaries most distinguished by talents and genius, and which I venture to hope now rest upon a basis more firm than the circumstances which gave rise to them. Yet feeling all these advantages as a man ought to do, and must do, I may say, with truth and confidence, that I have, I think, tasted of the intoxicating cup with moderation, and that I have never, either in conversation or correspondence, encouraged discussions respecting my own literary pursuits. On the contrary, I have usually found such topics, even when introduced from motives most flattering to myself, rather embarrassing and disagreeable.

I have now frankly told my motives for concealment, so far as I am conscious of having any, and the public will forgive the egotism of the detail as what is necessarily connected with it. The author, so long and loudly called for, has appeared on the stage and made his obeisance to the audience. Thus far his conduct is a mark of respect. To linger in their presence would be intrusion.

I have only to repeat that I avow myself in print, as formerly in words, the sole and unassisted author of all the novels published as works of the 'Author of *Waverley*.' I do this without shame, for I am unconscious that there is anything in their composition which deserves reproach, either on the score of religion or morality, and

---

*Not altogether impossible when it is considered that I have been at the bar since 1792. (Aug. 1831.)

without any feeling of exultation, because, whatever may have been their temporary success, I am well aware how much their reputation depends upon the caprice of fashion; and I have already mentioned the precarious tenure by which it is held as a reason for displaying no great avidity in grasping at the possession.

I ought to mention, before concluding, that twenty persons, at least, were, either from intimacy or from the confidence which circumstances rendered necessary, participant of this secret; and as there was no instance, to my knowledge, of any one of the number breaking faith, I am the more obliged to them, because the slight and trivial character of the mystery was not qualified to inspire much respect in those entrusted with it. Nevertheless, like Jack the Giant-Killer, I was fully confident in the advantage of my 'coat of darkness,' and had it not been from compulsory circumstances, I would have indeed been very cautious how I parted with it.

As for the work which follows, it was meditated, and in part printed, long before the avowal of the novels took place, and originally commenced with a declaration that it was neither to have introduction nor preface of any kind. This long proem, prefixed to a work intended not to have any, may, however, serve to show how human purposes, in the most trifling as well as the most important affairs, are liable to be controlled by the course of events. Thus, we begin to cross a strong river with our eyes and our resolution fixed on that point of the opposite shore on which we purpose to land; but, gradually giving way to the torrent, are glad, by the aid perhaps of branch or bush, to extricate ourselves at some distant, and perhaps dangerous, landing-place, much farther down the stream than that on which we had fixed our intentions.

Hoping that the courteous reader will afford to a known and familiar acquaintance some portion of the favour which he extended to a disguised candidate for his applause, I beg leave to subscribe myself his obliged humble servant,

WALTER SCOTT.

ABBOTSFORD, *October* 1, 1827.

Part II

THE LATE HISTORY
THE INTRODUCTIONS TO THE
"MAGNUM OPUS" (1829–32)

ADVERTISEMENT

It has been the occasional occupation of the Author of Waverley, for several years past, to revise and correct the voluminous series of Novels which pass under that name, in order that, if they should ever appear as his avowed productions, he might render them in some degree deserving of a continuance of the public favour with which they have been honoured ever since their first appearance. For a long period, however, it seemed likely that the improved and illustrated edition which he meditated would be a posthumous publication. But the course of the events which occasioned the disclosure of the Author's name having, in a great measure, restored to him a sort of parental control over these Works, he is naturally induced to give them to the press in a corrected, and, he hopes, an improved form, while life and health permit the task of revising and illustrating them. Such being his purpose, it is necessary to say a few words on the plan of the proposed Edition.

In stating it to be revised and corrected, it is not to be inferred that any attempt is made to alter the tenor of the stories, the character of the actors, or the spirit of the dialogue. There is no doubt ample room for emendation in all these points,—but where the tree falls it must lie. Any attempt to obviate criticism, however just, by altering a work already in the hands of the public is generally unsuccessful. In the most improbable fiction, the reader still desires some air of *vraisemblance*, and does not relish that the incidents of a tale familiar to him should be altered to suit the taste of critics, or the caprice of the Author himself. This process of feeling is so natural, that it may be observed even in children, who cannot endure that a nursery story should be repeated to them differently from the manner in which it was first told.

But without altering, in the slightest degree, either the story or the mode of telling it, the Author has taken this opportunity to correct errors of the press and slips of the pen. That such should exist cannot be wondered at, when it is considered that the Publishers found it their interest to hurry through the press a succession of the early editions of the various Novels, and that the Author had not the usual opportunity of revision. It is hoped that the present edition will be found free from errors of that accidental kind.

The Author has also ventured to make some emendations of a different character, which, without being such apparent deviations from the original stories as to disturb the reader's old associations, will, he thinks, add something to the spirit of the dialogue, narrative, or description. These consist in occasional pruning where the language is redundant, compression where the style is loose, infusion of vigour where it is languid, the exchange of less forcible for more appropriate epithets—slight alterations in short, like the last touches of an artist, which contribute to heighten and finish the picture, though an inexperienced eye can hardly detect in what they consist.

The General Preface to the new Edition, and the Introductory Notices to each separate work, will contain an account of such circumstances attending the first publication of the Novels and Tales as may appear interesting in themselves, or proper to be communicated to the public. The Author also proposes to publish, on this occasion, the various legends, family traditions, or obscure historical facts which have formed the ground-work of these Novels, and to give some account of the places where the scenes are laid, when these are altogether, or in part, real; as well as a statement of particular incidents founded on fact; together with a more copious Glossary, and Notes explanatory of the ancient customs and popular superstitions referred to in the Romances.

Advertisement

Upon the whole, it is hoped that the Waverley Novels, in their new dress, will not be found to have lost any part of their attractions in consequence of receiving illustrations by the Author, and undergoing his careful revision.

ABBOTSFORD, *January* 1829.

GENERAL PREFACE

—And must I ravel out
My weaved-up follies?
Richard II. Act IV.

Having undertaken to give an Introductory Account of the compositions which are here offered to the public, with Notes and Illustrations, the Author, under whose name they are now for the first time collected, feels that he has the delicate task of speaking more of himself and his personal concerns than may perhaps be either graceful or prudent. In this particular he runs the risk of presenting himself to the public in the relation that the dumb wife in the jest-book held to her husband, when, having spent half of his fortune to obtain the cure of her imperfection, he was willing to have bestowed the other half to restore her to her former condition. But this is a risk inseparable from the task which the Author has undertaken, and he can only promise to be as little of an egotist as the situation will permit. It is perhaps an indifferent sign of a disposition to keep his word, that, having introduced himself in the third person singular, he proceeds in the second paragraph to make use of the first. But it appears to him that the seeming modesty connected with the former mode of writing is overbalanced by the inconvenience of stiffness and affectation which attends it during a narrative of some length, and which may be observed less or more in every work in which the third person is used, from the *Commentaries of Caesar* to the *Autobiography of Alexander the Corrector.**

---

*A name assumed by Alexander Cruden, best known as the author of the *Concordance*. He published *The Adventures of Alexander the Corrector* in 1754 and 1755 (*Laing*).

General Preface

I must refer to a very early period of my life, were I to point out my first achievements as a tale-teller; but I believe some of my old schoolfellows can still bear witness that I had a distinguished character for that talent, at a time when the applause of my companions was my recompense for the disgraces and punishments which the future romance-writer incurred for being idle himself, and keeping others idle, during hours that should have been employed on our tasks. The chief enjoyment of my holidays was to escape with a chosen friend, who had the same taste with myself, and alternately to recite to each other such wild adventures as we were able to devise. We told, each in turn, interminable tales of knight-errantry and battles and enchantments, which were continued from one day to another as opportunity offered, without our ever thinking of bringing them to a conclusion. As we observed a strict secrecy on the subject of this intercourse, it acquired all the character of a concealed pleasure, and we used to select for the scenes of our indulgence long walks through the solitary and romantic environs of Arthur's Seat, Salisbury Crags, Braid Hills, and similar places in the vicinity of Edinburgh; and the recollection of those holidays still forms an oasis in the pilgrimage which I have to look back upon. I have only to add, that my friend* still lives, a prosperous gentleman, but too much occupied with graver business to thank me for indicating him more plainly as a confidant of my childish mystery.

When boyhood advancing into youth required more serious studies and graver cares, a long illness threw me back on the kingdom of fiction, as if it were by a species of fatality. My indisposition arose, in part at least, from my having broken a blood-vessel; and motion and speech were for a long time pronounced positively dangerous. For several weeks I was confined strictly to my bed, during which time I was not allowed to speak above a whisper, to eat more than a spoonful or two of boiled rice, or to have more covering than one thin counterpane. When the reader is informed that I was at this time a growing youth, with the spirits, appetite, and impatience of fifteen, and suffered, of course, greatly under this severe regimen, which the repeated return of my disorder rendered indispensable, he will

---

*John Irving, Writer to the Signet in Edinburgh, died 1850 (*Laing*).

not be surprised that I was abandoned to my own discretion, so far as reading (my almost sole amusement) was concerned, and still less so, that I abused the indulgence which left my time so much at my own disposal.

There was at this time a circulating library in Edinburgh, founded, I believe, by the celebrated Allan Ramsay,[1] which, besides containing a most respectable collection of books of every description, was, as might have been expected, peculiarly rich in works of fiction. It exhibited specimens of every kind, from the romances of chivalry and the ponderous folios of *Cyrus and Cassandra*,[2] down to the most approved works of later times. I was plunged into this great ocean of reading without compass or pilot; and, unless when some one had the charity to play at chess with me, I was allowed to do nothing save read from morning to night. I was, in kindness and pity, which was perhaps erroneous, however natural, permitted to select my subjects of study at my own pleasure, upon the same principle that the humours of children are indulged to keep them out of mischief. As my taste and appetite were gratified in nothing else, I indemnified myself by becoming a glutton of books. Accordingly, I believe I read almost all the romances, old plays, and epic poetry in that formidable collection, and no doubt was unconsciously amassing materials for the task in which it has been my lot to be so much employed.

At the same time I did not in all respects abuse the license permitted me. Familiar acquaintance with the specious miracles of fiction brought with it some degree of satiety, and I began by degrees to seek in histories, memoirs, voyages and travels, and the like, events nearly as wonderful as those which were the work of imagination, with the additional advantage that they were at least in a great measure true. The lapse of nearly two years, during which I was left to the exercise of my own free will, was followed by a temporary residence in the country,[3] where I was again very lonely but for the amusement which I derived from a good though old-fashioned library. The vague and wild use which I made of this advantage I cannot describe better than by referring my reader to the desultory studies of Waverley in a similar situation, the passages concerning whose course of reading were

88

imitated from recollections of my own. It must be understood that the resemblance extends no farther.

Time, as it glided on, brought the blessings of confirmed health and personal strength, to a degree which had never been expected or hoped for. The severe studies necessary to render me fit for my profession occupied the greater part of my time; and the society of my friends and companions, who were about to enter life along with me, filled up the interval with the usual amusements of young men. I was in a situation which rendered serious labour indispensable; for, neither possessing, on the one hand, any of those peculiar advantages which are supposed to favour a hasty advance in the profession of the law, nor being, on the other hand, exposed to unusual obstacles to interrupt my progress, I might reasonably expect to succeed according to the greater or less degree of trouble which I should take to qualify myself as a pleader.

It makes no part of the present story to detail how the success of a few ballads had the effect of changing all the purpose and tenor of my life, and of converting a painstaking lawyer of some years' standing into a follower of literature. It is enough to say, that I had assumed the latter character for several years before I seriously thought of attempting a work of imagination in prose, although one or two of my poetical attempts did not differ from romances otherwise than by being written in verse. But yet I may observe, that about this time (now, alas! thirty years since) I had nourished the ambitious desire of composing a tale of chivalry, which was to be in the style of the *Castle of Otranto*,[4] with plenty of Border characters and supernatural incident. Having found unexpectedly a chapter of this intended work among some old papers, I have subjoined it to this introductory essay, thinking some readers may account as curious the first attempts at romantic composition by an author who has since written so much in that department. And those who complain, not unreasonably, of the profusion of the Tales which have followed *Waverley*, may bless their stars at the narrow escape they have made, by the commencement of the inundation, which had so nearly taken place in the first year of the century, being postponed for fifteen years later.

This particular subject was never resumed, but I did not abandon the idea of fictitious composition in prose, though I determined to give another turn to the style of the work.

My early recollections of the Highland scenery and customs made so favourable an impression in the poem called the *Lady of the Lake*, that I was induced to think of attempting something of the same kind in prose.[5] I had been a good deal in the Highlands at a time when they were much less accessible and much less visited than they have been of late years, and was acquainted with many of the old warriors of 1745, who were like most veterans, easily induced to fight their battles over again for the benefit of a willing listener like myself. It naturally occurred to me that the ancient traditions and high spirit of a people who, living in a civilised age and country, retained so strong a tincture of manners belonging to an early period of society, must afford a subject favourable for romance, if it should not prove a curious tale marred in the telling.

It was with some idea of this kind that, about the year 1805, I threw together about one-third part of the first volume of *Waverley*. It was advertised to be published by the late Mr. John Ballantyne, bookseller in Edinburgh, under the name of *Waverley, or 'tis Fifty Years since*—a title afterwards altered to *'Tis Sixty Years since*, that the actual date of publication might be made to correspond with the period in which the scene was laid. Having proceeded as far, I think, as the seventh chapter, I showed my work to a critical friend, whose opinion was unfavourable;[6] and having then some poetical reputation, I was unwilling to risk the loss of it by attempting a new style of composition. I therefore threw aside the work I had commenced, without either reluctance or remonstrance. I ought to add that, though my ingenious friend's sentence was afterwards reversed on an appeal to the public, it cannot be considered as any imputation on his good taste; for the specimen subjected to his criticism did not extend beyond the departure of the hero for Scotland, and consequently had not entered upon the part of the story which was finally found most interesting.

Be that as it may, this portion of the manuscript was laid aside in the drawers of an old writing-desk, which, on my first coming to reside at Abbotsford in 1811, was placed in a lumber garret and entirely forgotten. Thus, though I sometimes, among other literary avocations, turned my thoughts to the continuation of the romance which I had commenced, yet, as I could not find what I had already written, after searching such repositories as were within my reach, and was too indolent to attempt to write it anew from memory, I as often laid aside all thoughts of that nature.

Two circumstances in particular recalled my recollection of the mislaid manuscript. The first was the extended and well-merited fame of Miss Edgeworth,[7] whose Irish characters have gone so far to make the English familiar with the character of their gay and kind-hearted neighbours of Ireland, that she may be truly said to have done more towards completing the Union than perhaps all the legislative enactments by which it has been followed up.[8]

Without being so presumptuous as to hope to emulate the rich humour, pathetic tenderness, and admirable tact which pervade the works of my accomplished friend, I felt that something might be attempted for my own country, of the same kind with that which Miss Edgeworth so fortunately achieved for Ireland— something which might introduce her natives to those of the sister kingdom in a more favourable light than they had been placed hitherto, and tend to procure sympathy for their virtues and indulgence for their foibles. I thought also, that much of what I wanted in talent might be made up by the intimate acquaintance with the subject which I could lay claim to possess, as having travelled through most parts of Scotland, both Highland and Lowland, having been familiar with the elder as well as more modern race, and having had from my infancy free and unrestrained communication with all ranks of my countrymen, from the Scottish peer to the Scottish ploughman. Such ideas often occurred to me, and constituted an ambitious branch of my theory, however far short I may have fallen of it in practice.

But it was not only the triumphs of Miss Edgeworth which waked in me emulation, and disturbed my indolence. I chanced actually to engage in a work which formed a sort of assay piece, and gave me hope that I might in time become free of the craft of romance-writing, and be esteemed a tolerable workman.

In the year 1807–8 I undertook, at the request of John Murray, Esq., of Albemarle Street,[9] to arrange for publication some posthumous productions of the late Mr. Joseph Strutt, distinguished as an artist and an antiquary, amongst which was an unfinished romance, entitled *Queenhoo Hall*.[10] The scene of the tale was laid in the reign of Henry VI., and the work was written to illustrate the manners, customs, and language of the people of England during that period. The extensive acquaintance which Mr. Strutt had acquired with such subjects in compiling his laborious *Horda Angel-Cynnan*, his *Regal and Ecclesiastical Antiquities*, and his *Essay on the Sports and Pastimes of the People of England* had rendered him familiar with all the antiquarian lore necessary for the purpose of composing the projected romance; and although the manuscript bore the marks of hurry and incoherence natural to the first rough draught of the author, it evinced (in my opinion) considerable powers of imagination.

As the work was unfinished, I deemed it my duty, as editor, to supply such a hasty and inartificial conclusion as could be shaped out from the story, of which Mr. Strutt had laid the foundation. This concluding chapter is also added to the present Introduction, for the reason already mentioned regarding the preceding fragment. It was a step in my advance towards romantic composition; and to preserve the traces of these is in a great measure the object of this Essay.

Queenhoo Hall was not, however, very successful. I thought I was aware of the reason, and supposed that, by rendering his language too ancient, and displaying his antiquarian knowledge too liberally, the ingenious author had raised up an obstacle to his own success. Every work designed for mere amusement must be expressed in language easily comprehended; and when, as is sometimes the case in *Queenhoo Hall*, the author addresses himself exclusively to the antiquary, he must be content to be dismissed by the general reader with the criticism of Mungo, in the *Padlock*, on the Mauritanian music, 'What signifies me hear, if me no understand?'[11]

I conceived it possible to avoid this error; and, by rendering a similar work more light and obvious to general comprehension, to escape the rock on which my predecessor was shipwrecked. But I was, on the other hand, so far discouraged by the indifferent reception of Mr. Strutt's romance as to become satisfied that the manners of the middle ages did not possess the interest which I had conceived; and was led to form the opinion that a romance founded on a Highland story and more modern events would have a better chance of popularity than a tale of chivalry. My thoughts, therefore, returned more than once to the tale which I had actually commenced, and accident at length threw the lost sheets in my way.

I happened to want some fishing-tackle for the use of a guest, when it occurred to me to search the old writing-desk already mentioned, in which I used to keep articles of that nature. I got access to it with some difficulty; and, in looking for lines and flies, the long-lost manuscript presented itself. I immediately set to work to complete it according to my original purpose. And here I must frankly confess that the mode in which I conducted the story scarcely deserved the success which the romance afterwards attained. The tale of *Waverley* was put together with so little care that I cannot boast of having sketched any distinct plan of the work. The whole adventures of Waverley, in his movements up and down the country with the Highland cateran Bean Lean, are managed without much skill. It suited best, however, the road I wanted to travel, and permitted me to introduce some descriptions of scenery and manners, to which the reality gave an interest which the powers of the Author might have otherwise failed to attain for them. And though I have been in other instances a sinner in this sort, I do not recollect any of these novels in which I have transgressed so widely as in the first of the series.

Among other unfounded reports, it has been said that the copyright of *Waverley* was, during the book's progress through the press, offered for sale to various booksellers in London at a very inconsiderable price. This was not the case. Messrs. Constable and Cadell, who published the work, were the only persons acquainted with the contents of the publication, and they offered a large sum for it while in the course of printing, which, however, was declined, the Author not choosing to part with the copyright.[12]

The origin of the story of *Waverley*, and the particular facts on which it is founded, are given in the separate introduction prefixed to that romance in this edition, and require no notice in this place.

Waverley was published in 1814, and, as the title-page was without the name of the author, the work was left to win its way in the world without any of the usual recommendations. Its progress was for some time slow; but after the first two or three months its popularity had increased in a degree which must have satisfied the expectations of the Author, had these been far more sanguine than he ever entertained.

Great anxiety was expressed to learn the name of the author, but on this no authentic information could be attained. My original motive for publishing the work anonymously was the consciousness that it was an experiment on the public taste which might very probably fail, and therefore there was no occasion to take on myself the personal risk of discomfiture. For this purpose considerable precautions were used to preserve secrecy. My old friend and schoolfellow, Mr. James Ballantyne, who printed these Novels, had the exclusive task of corresponding with the Author, who thus had not only the advantage of his professional talents, but also of his critical abilities.[13] The original manuscript, or, as it is technically called, copy, was transcribed under Mr. Ballantyne's eye by confidential persons; nor was there an instance of treachery during the many years in which these precautions were resorted to, although various individuals were employed at different times. Double proof-sheets were regularly printed off. One was forwarded to the Author by Mr. Ballantyne, and the alterations which it received were, by his own hand, copied upon the other proof-sheet for the use of the printers, so that even the corrected proofs of the Author were never seen in the printing office; and thus the curiosity of such eager inquirers as made the most minute investigation was entirely at fault.

But although the cause of concealing the author's name in the first instance, when the reception of *Waverley* was doubtful, was natural enough, it is more difficult, it may be thought, to account for the same desire for secrecy during the subsequent editions, to the amount of betwixt eleven and twelve thousand copies, which followed each other close, and proved the success of the work. I am sorry I can give little satisfaction to queries on this subject. I have already stated elsewhere that I can render little better reason for choosing to remain anonymous than by saying with Shylock, that such was my humour.[14] It will be observed that I had not the usual stimulus for desiring personal reputation, the desire, namely, to float amidst the conversation of men. Of literary fame, whether merited or undeserved, I had already as much as might have contented a mind more ambitious than mine; and in entering into this new contest for reputation I might be said rather to endanger what I had than to have any considerable chance of acquiring more. I was affected, too, by none of those motives which, at an earlier period of life, would doubtless have operated upon me. My friendships were formed, my place in society fixed, my life had attained its middle course. My condition in society was higher perhaps than I deserved, certainly as high as I wished, and there was scarce any degree of literary success which could have greatly altered or improved my personal condition.

I was not, therefore, touched by the spur of ambition, usually stimulating on such occasions; and yet I ought to stand exculpated from the charge of ungracious or unbecoming indifference to public applause. I did not the less feel gratitude for the public favour, although I did not proclaim it; as the lover who wears his mistress's favour in his bosom is as proud, though not so vain, of possessing it as another who displays the token of her grace upon his bonnet. Far from such an ungracious state of mind, I have seldom felt more satisfaction than when, returning from a pleasure voyage, I found *Waverley* in the zenith of popularity, and public curiosity in full cry after the name of the Author. The knowledge that I had the public approbation was like having the property of a hidden treasure, not less gratifying to the owner than if all the world knew that it was his own. Another advantage was connected with the secrecy which I observed. I could appear or retreat from the stage at pleasure, without attracting any personal notice or attention, other than what might be founded on suspicion only. In my own person also, as a successful author in another department of literature, I might have been charged with too frequent intrusions on the public patience; but the Author of *Waverley* was in this respect as impassible to the critic as the Ghost of *Hamlet* to the partizan of Marcellus. Perhaps the curiosity of the public, irritated by the existence of a secret, and kept afloat by the discussions which took place on the subject from time to time, went a good way to maintain an unabated interest in these frequent publications. There was a mystery concerning the author which each new novel was expected to assist in unravelling, although it might in other respects rank lower than its predecessors.

I may perhaps be thought guilty of affectation, should I allege as one reason of my silence a secret dislike to enter on personal discussions concerning my own literary labours. It is in every case a dangerous intercourse for an author to be dwelling continually among those who make his writings a frequent and familiar subject of conversation, but who must necessarily be partial judges of works composed in their own society. The habits of self-importance which are thus acquired by authors are highly injurious to a well-regulated mind; for the cup of flattery, if it does not, like that of Circe, reduce men to the level of beasts, is sure, if eagerly drained, to bring the best and the ablest down to that of fools. This risk was in some degree prevented by the mask which I wore; and my own stores of self-conceit were left to their natural course, without being enhanced by the partiality of friends or adulation of flatterers.

If I am asked further reasons for the conduct I have long observed, I can only resort to the explanation supplied by a critic as friendly as he is intelligent;[15] namely, that the mental organisation of the novelist must be characterised, to speak craniologically, by an extraordinary development of the passion for delitescency![16] I the [sic] rather suspect some natural disposition of this kind; for, from the instant I perceived the extreme curiosity manifested on the subject, I felt a secret satisfaction in baffling it, for which, when its unimportance is considered, I do not well know how to account.

My desire to remain concealed, in the character of the author of these Novels, subjected me occasionally to awkward embarrassments, as it sometimes happened that those who were sufficiently intimate with me would put the question in direct terms. In this case, only one of three courses could be followed. Either I must have surrendered my secret, or have returned an equivocating answer, or, finally, must have stoutly and boldly denied the fact. The first was a sacrifice which I conceive no one had a right to force from me, since I alone was concerned in the matter. The alternative of rendering a doubtful answer must have left me open to the degrading suspicion that I was not unwilling to assume the merit (if there was any) which I dared not absolutely lay claim to; or those who might think more justly of me must have received such an equivocal answer as an indirect avowal. I therefore considered myself entitled, like an accused person put upon trial, to refuse giving my own evidence to my own conviction, and flatly to deny all that could not be proved against me. At the same time I usually qualified my denial by stating that, had I been the author of these works, I would have felt myself quite entitled to protect my secret by refusing my own evidence, when it was asked for to accomplish a discovery of what I desired to conceal.

The real truth is, that I never expected or hoped to disguise my connection with these Novels from any one who lived on terms of intimacy with me. The number of coincidences which necessarily existed between narratives recounted, modes of expression, and opinions broached in these Tales and such as were used by their Author in the intercourse of private life must have been far too great to permit any of my familiar acquaintances to doubt the identity betwixt their friend and the Author of *Waverley*; and I believe they were all morally convinced of it. But while I was myself silent, their belief could not weigh much more with the world than that of others; their opinions and reasoning were liable to be taxed with partiality, or confronted with opposing arguments and opinions; and the question was not so much whether I should be generally acknowledged to be the author, in spite of my own denial, as whether even my own avowal of the works, if such should be made, would be sufficient to put me in undisputed possession of that character.

I have been often asked concerning supposed cases, in which I was said to have been placed on the verge of discovery; but, as I maintained my point with the composure of a lawyer of thirty years' standing, I never recollect being in pain or confusion on the subject. In Captain Medwyn's *Conversations of Lord Byron*[17] the reporter states himself to have asked my noble and highly-gifted friend, 'If he was certain about these novels being Sir Walter Scott's?' To which Lord Byron replied, 'Scott as much as owned himself the Author of *Waverley* to me in Murray's shop. I was talking to him about that novel, and lamented that its author had not carried back the story nearer to the time of the Revolution. Scott, entirely off his guard, replied, "Ay, I might have done so; but—" there he stopped. It was in vain to attempt to correct himself; he looked confused, and relieved his embarrassment by a precipitate retreat.' I have no recollection whatever of this scene taking place, and I should have thought that I was more likely to have laughed than to appear confused, for I certainly never hoped to impose upon Lord Byron in a case of the kind; and from the manner in which he uniformly expressed himself, I knew his opinion was entirely formed, and that any disclamations of mine would only have savoured of affectation. I do not mean to insinuate that the incident did not happen, but only that it could hardly have occurred exactly under the circumstances narrated, without my recollecting something positive on the subject. In another part of the same volume Lord Byron is reported to have expressed a supposition that the cause of my not avowing myself the Author of *Waverley* may have been some surmise that the reigning family would have been displeased with the work. I can only say, it is the last apprehension I should have entertained, as indeed the inscription to these volumes sufficiently proves.[18] The sufferers of that melancholy period have, during the last and present reign, been honoured both with the sympathy and protection of the reigning family, whose magnanimity can well pardon a sigh from others, and bestow one themselves, to the memory of brave opponents, who did nothing in hate, but all in honour.

While those who were in habitual intercourse with the real author had little hesitation in assigning the literary property to him, others, and those critics of no mean rank, employed themselves in investigating with persevering patience any characteristic features which might seem to betray the origin of these Novels. Amongst these, one gentleman, equally remarkable for the kind and liberal tone of his criticism, the acuteness of his reasoning, and the very gentlemanlike manner in which he conducted his inquiries, displayed not only powers of accurate investigation, but a temper of mind deserving to be employed on a subject of much greater importance; and I have no doubt made converts to his opinion of almost all who thought the point worthy of consideration.*[19] Of those letters, and other attempts of the same kind, the Author could not complain, though his incognito was endangered. He had challenged the public to a game at

---

*Letters on the Author of Waverley; Rodwell and Martin, London, 1822.

bo-peep, and if he was discovered in his 'hiding-hole,' he must submit to the shame of detection.

Various reports were of course circulated in various ways; some founded on an inaccurate rehearsal of what may have been partly real, some on circumstances having no concern whatever with the subject, and others on the invention of some impatient persons, who might perhaps imagine that the readiest mode of forcing the author to disclose himself was to assign some dishonourable and discreditable cause for his silence.

It may be easily supposed that this sort of inquisition was treated with contempt by the person whom it principally re-garded; as, among all the rumours that were current, there was only one, and that as unfounded as the others, which had never-theless some alliance to probability, and indeed might have proved in some degree true.

I allude to a report which ascribed a great part, or the whole, of these Novels to the late Thomas Scott, Esq., of the 70th Regiment, then stationed in Canada.[20] Those who remember that gentleman will readily grant that, with general talents at least equal to those of his elder brother, he added a power of social humour and a deep insight into human character which rendered him an uni-versally delightful member of society, and that the habit of composition alone was wanting to render him equally successful as a writer. The Author of *Waverley* was so persuaded of the truth of this, that he warmly pressed his brother to make such an experiment, and willingly undertook all the trouble of correcting and superintending the press. Mr. Thomas Scott seemed at first very well disposed to embrace the proposal, and had even fixed on a subject and a hero. The latter was a person well known to both of us in our boyish years, from having displayed some strong traits of character. Mr. T. Scott had determined to represent his youthful acquaintance as emigrating to America, and encounter-ing the dangers and hardships of the New World, with the same dauntless spirit which he had displayed when a boy in his native country. Mr. Scott would probably have been highly successful, being familiarly acquainted with the manners of the native Indians, of the old French settlers in Canada, and of the Brulés or Woodsmen, and having the power of observing with accuracy what I have no doubt he could have sketched with force and expression. In short, the Author believes his brother would have made himself distinguished in that striking field in which, since that period, Mr. Cooper has achieved so many triumphs.[21] But Mr. T. Scott was already affected by bad health, which wholly unfitted him for literary labour, even if he could have reconciled his patience to the task. He never, I believe, wrote a single line of the projected work; and I only have the melancholy pleasure of preserving in the Appendix the simple anecdote on which he proposed to found it.

To this I may add, I can easily conceive that there may have been circumstances which gave a colour to the general report of my brother being interested in these works; and in particular that it might derive strength from my having occasion to remit to him, in consequence of certain family transactions, some considerable sums of money about that period. To which it is to be added that if any person chanced to evince particular curiosity on such a subject, my brother was likely enough to divert himself with practising on their credulity.

It may be mentioned that, while the paternity of these Novels was from time to time warmly disputed in Britain, the foreign booksellers expressed no hesitation on the matter, but affixed my name to the whole of the Novels, and to some besides to which I had no claim.

The volumes, therefore, to which the present pages form a Preface are entirely the composition of the author by whom they are now acknowledged, with the exception, always, of avowed quotations, and such unpremeditated and involuntary plagiarisms as can scarce be guarded against by any one who has read and written a great deal. The original manuscripts are all in existence, and entirely written (*horresco referens*)[22] in the Author's own hand, excepting during the years 1818 and 1819, when, being affected with severe illness, he was obliged to employ the assistance of a friendly amanuensis.[23]

The number of persons to whom the secret was necessarily entrusted, or communicated by chance, amounted, I should think, to twenty at least, to whom I am greatly obliged for the fidelity with which they observed their trust, until the derangement of the affairs of my publishers, Messrs. Constable and Co., and the exposure of their accompt books, which was the necessary consequence, rendered secrecy no longer possible. The particulars attending the avowal have been laid before the public in the Introduction to the *Chronicles of the Canongate.*

The preliminary advertisement has given a sketch of the purpose of this edition. I have some reason to fear that the notes which accompany the tales, as now published, may be thought too miscellaneous and too egotistical. It may be some apology for this, that the publication was intended to be posthumous, and still more, that old men may be permitted to speak long, because they cannot in the course of nature have long time to speak. In preparing the present edition, I have done all that I can do to explain the nature of my materials, and the use I have made of them; nor is it probable that I shall again revise or even read these Tales. I was therefore desirous rather to exceed in the portion of new and explanatory matter which is added to this edition than that the reader should have reason to complain that the information communicated was of a general and merely nominal character. It remains to be tried whether the public (like a child to whom a watch is shown) will, after having been satiated with looking at the outside, acquire some new interest in the object when it is opened and the internal machinery displayed to them.

That *Waverley* and its successors have had their day of favour and popularity must be admitted with sincere gratitude; and the Author has studied (with the prudence of a beauty whose reign has been rather long) to supply, by the assistance of art, the charms which novelty no longer affords. The publishers have endeavoured to gratify the honourable partiality of the public for the encouragement of British art, by illustrating this edition with designs by the most eminent living artists.

To my distinguished countryman, David Wilkie, to Edwin Landseer, who has exercised his talents so much on Scottish subjects and scenery, to Messrs. Leslie and Newton, my thanks are due, from a friend as well as an author. Nor am I less obliged to Messrs. Cooper, Kidd, and other artists of distinction to whom I am less personally known, for the ready zeal with which they have devoted their talents to the same purpose.[24]

Farther explanation respecting the Edition is the business of the publishers, not of the Author; and here, therefore, the latter has accomplished his task of Introduction and explanation. If, like a spoiled child, he has sometimes abused or trifled with the indulgence of the public, he feels himself entitled to full belief when he exculpates himself from the charge of having been at any time insensible of their kindness.

ABBOTSFORD, 1st *January* 1829.

GUY MANNERING

The Novel or Romance of *Waverley* made its way to the public slowly, of course, at first, but afterwards with such accumulating popularity as to encourage the Author to a second attempt. He looked about for a name and a subject; and the manner in which the novels were composed cannot be better illustrated than by reciting the simple narrative on which *Guy Mannering* was originally founded; but to which, in the progress of the work, the production ceased to bear any, even the most distant resemblance. The tale was originally told me by an old servant of my father's, an excellent old Highlander, without a fault, unless a preference to mountain dew over less potent liquors be accounted one. He believed as firmly in the story as in any part of his creed.

A grave and elderly person, according to old John Mac-Kinlay's account, while travelling in the wilder parts of Galloway, was benighted. With difficulty he found his way to a country seat, where, with the hospitality of the time and country, he was readily admitted. The owner of the house, a gentleman of good fortune, was much struck by the reverend appearance of his guest, and apologised to him for a certain degree of confusion which must unavoidably attend his reception, and could not escape his eye. The lady of the house was, he said, confined to her apartment, and on the point of making her husband a father for the first time, though they had been ten years married. At such an

103

emergency, the Laird said, he feared his guest might meet with some apparent neglect.

'Not so, sir,' said the stranger; 'my wants are few, and easily supplied, and I trust the present circumstances may even afford an opportunity of showing my gratitude for your hospitality. Let me only request that I may be informed of the exact minute of the birth; and I hope to be able to put you in possession of some particulars which may influence in an important manner the future prospects of the child now about to come into this busy and changeful world. I will not conceal from you that I am skilful in understanding and interpreting the movements of those plane-tary bodies which exert their influences on the destiny of mortals. It is a science which I do not practise, like others who call them-selves astrologers, for hire or reward; for I have a competent estate, and only use the knowledge I possess for the benefit of those in whom I feel an interest.' The Laird bowed in respect and gratitude, and the stranger was accommodated with an apart-ment which commanded an ample view of the astral regions.

The guest spent a part of the night in ascertaining the position of the heavenly bodies, and calculating their probable influence; until at length the result of his observations induced him to send for the father and conjure him in the most solemn manner to cause the assistants to retard the birth if practicable, were it but for five minutes. The answer declared this to be impossible; and almost in the instant that the message was returned the father and his guest were made acquainted with the birth of a boy.

The Astrologer on the morrow met the party who gathered around the breakfast table with looks so grave and ominous as to alarm the fears of the father, who had hitherto exulted in the prospects held out by the birth of an heir to his ancient property, failing which event it must have passed to a distant branch of the family. He hastened to draw the stranger into a private room.

'I fear from your looks,' said the father, 'that you have bad tidings to tell me of my young stranger; perhaps God will resume the blessing He has bestowed ere he attains the age of manhood, or perhaps he is destined to be unworthy of the affection which we are naturally disposed to devote to our offspring?'

'Neither the one nor the other,' answered the stranger; 'unless my judgment greatly err, the infant will survive the years of minority, and in temper and disposition will prove all that his parents can wish. But with much in his horoscope which promises many blessings, there is one evil influence strongly predominant, which threatens to subject him to an unhallowed and unhappy temptation about the time when he shall attain the age of twenty-one, which period, the constellations intimate, will be the crisis of his fate. In what shape, or with what peculiar urgency, this temptation may beset him, my art cannot discover.'

'Your knowledge, then, can afford us no defence,' said the anxious father, 'against the threatened evil?'

'Pardon me,' answered the stranger, 'it can. The influence of the constellations is powerful; but He who made the heavens is more powerful than all, if His aid be invoked in sincerity and truth. You ought to dedicate this boy to the immediate service of his Maker, with as much sincerity as Samuel was devoted to the worship in the Temple by his parents.[1] You must regard him as a being separated from the rest of the world. In childhood, in boyhood, you must surround him with the pious and virtuous, and protect him to the utmost of your power from the sight or hearing of any license in word or action. He must be educated in religious and moral principles of the strictest description. Let him not enter the world, lest he learn to partake of its follies, or perhaps of its vices. In short, preserve him as far as possible from all sin, save that of which too great a portion belongs to all the fallen race of Adam. With the approach of his twenty-first birthday comes the crisis of his fate. If he survive it, he will be happy and prosperous on earth, and a chosen vessel among those elected for heaven. But if it be otherwise—' The Astrologer stopped, and sighed deeply.

'Sir,' replied the parent, still more alarmed than before, 'your words are so kind, your advice so serious, that I will pay the deepest attention to your behests; but can you not aid me farther in this most important concern? Believe me, I will not be ungrateful.'

'I require and deserve no gratitude for doing a good action,' said the stranger, 'in especial for contributing all that lies in my power to save from an abhorred fate the harmless infant to whom, under a singular conjunction of planets, last night gave life. There is my address; you may write to me from time to time concerning the progress of the boy in religious knowledge. If he be bred up as I advise, I think it will be best that he come to my house at the time when the fatal and decisive period approaches, that is, before he has attained his twenty-first year complete. If you send him such as I desire, I humbly trust that God will protect His own through whatever strong temptation his fate may subject him to.' He then gave his host his address, which was a country seat near a post town in the south of England, and bid him an affectionate farewell.

The mysterious stranger departed, but his words remained impressed upon the mind of the anxious parent. He lost his lady while his boy was still in infancy. This calamity, I think, had been predicted by the Astrologer; and thus his confidence, which, like most people of the period, he had freely given to the science, was riveted and confirmed. The utmost care, therefore, was taken to carry into effect the severe and almost ascetic plan of education which the sage had enjoined. A tutor of the strictest principles was employed to superintend the youth's education; he was surrounded by domestics of the most established character, and closely watched and looked after by the anxious father himself.

The years of infancy, childhood, and boyhood passed as the father could have wished. A young Nazarene could not have been bred up with more rigour. All that was evil was withheld from his observation: he only heard what was pure in precept, he only witnessed what was worthy in practice.

But when the boy began to be lost in the youth, the attentive father saw cause for alarm. Shades of sadness, which gradually assumed a darker character, began to overcloud the young man's temper. Tears, which seemed involuntary, broken sleep, moonlight wanderings, and a melancholy for which he could assign no reason, seemed to threaten at once his bodily health and the stability of his mind. The Astrologer was consulted by letter, and returned for answer that this fitful state of mind was but the commencement of his trial, and that the poor youth must undergo worse and more desperate struggles with the evil that assailed him. There was no hope of remedy, save that he showed steadiness of mind in the study of the Scriptures. 'He suffers,' continued the letter of the sage, 'from the awakening of those harpies the passions, which have slept with him, as with others, till the period of life which he has now attained. Better, far better, that they torment him by ungrateful cravings than that he should have to repent having satiated them by criminal indulgence.'

The dispositions of the young man were so excellent that he combated, by reason and religion, the fits of gloom which at times overcast his mind, and it was not till he attained the commencement of his twenty-first year that they assumed a character which made his father tremble for the consequences. It seemed as if the gloomiest and most hideous of mental maladies was taking the form of religious despair. Still the youth was gentle, courteous, affectionate, and submissive to his father's will, and resisted with all his power the dark suggestions which were breathed into his mind, as it seemed by some emanation of the Evil Principle, exhorting him, like the wicked wife of Job, to curse God and die.[2]

The time at length arrived when he was to perform what was then thought a long and somewhat perilous journey, to the mansion of the early friend who had calculated his nativity. His road lay through several places of interest, and he enjoyed the amusement of travelling more than he himself thought would have been possible. Thus he did not reach the place of his destination till noon on the day preceding his birthday. It seemed as if he had been carried away with an unwonted tide of pleasurable sensation, so as to forget in some degree what his father had communicated concerning the purpose of his journey. He halted at length before a respectable but solitary old mansion, to which he was directed as the abode of his father's friend.

The servants who came to take his horse told him he had been expected for two days. He was led into a study, where the stranger, now a venerable old man, who had been his father's guest, met him with a shade of displeasure, as well as gravity, on his brow. 'Young man,' he said, 'wherefore so slow on a journey of such importance?' 'I thought,' replied the guest, blushing and looking downward, 'that there was no harm in travelling slowly and satisfying my curiosity, providing I could reach your residence by this day; for such was my father's charge.' 'You were to blame,' replied the sage, 'in lingering, considering that the avenger of blood was pressing on your footsteps. But you are come at last, and we will hope for the best, though the conflict in which you are to be engaged will be found more dreadful the longer it is postponed. But first accept of such refreshments as nature requires to satisfy, but not to pamper, the appetite.'

The old man led the way into a summer parlour, where a frugal meal was placed on the table. As they sat down to the board they were joined by a young lady about eighteen years of age, and so lovely that the sight of her carried off the feelings of the young stranger from the peculiarity and mystery of his own lot, and riveted his attention to everything she did or said. She spoke little, and it was on the most serious subjects. She played on the harpsichord at her father's command, but it was hymns with which she accompanied the instrument. At length, on a sign from the sage, she left the room, bending on the young stranger as she departed a look of inexpressible anxiety and interest.

The old man then conducted the youth to his study, and conversed with him upon the most important points of religion, to satisfy himself that he could render a reason for the faith that was in him. During the examination the youth, in spite of himself, felt his mind occasionally wander, and his recollections go in quest of the beautiful vision who had shared their meal at noon. On such occasions the Astrologer looked grave, and shook his head at this relaxation of attention; yet, on the whole, he was pleased with the youth's replies.

At sunset the young man was made to take the bath; and, having done so, he was directed to attire himself in a robe somewhat like that worn by Armenians, having his long hair combed down on his shoulders, and his neck, hands, and feet bare. In this guise he was conducted into a remote chamber totally devoid of furniture, excepting a lamp, a chair, and a table, on which lay a Bible. 'Here,' said the Astrologer, 'I must leave you alone to pass the most critical period of your life. If you can, by recollection of the great truths of which we have spoken, repel the attacks which will be made on your courage and your principles, you have nothing to apprehend. But the trial will be severe and arduous.' His features then assumed a pathetic solemnity, the tears stood in his eyes, and his voice faltered with emotion as he said, 'Dear child, at whose coming into the world I foresaw this fatal trial, may God give thee grace to support it with firmness!'

The young man was left alone; and hardly did he find himself so, when, like a swarm of demons, the recollection of all his sins of omission and commission, rendered even more terrible by the scrupulousness with which he had been educated, rushed on his mind, and, like furies armed with fiery scourges, seemed determined to drive him to despair. As he combated these horrible recollections with distracted feelings, but with a resolved mind, he became aware that his arguments were answered by the sophistry of another, and that the dispute was no longer confined to his own thoughts. The Author of Evil was present in the room with him in bodily shape, and, potent with spirits of a melancholy cast, was impressing upon him the desperation of his state, and urging suicide as the readiest mode to put an end to his sinful career. Amid his errors, the pleasure he had taken in prolonging his journey unnecessarily, and the attention which he had bestowed on the beauty of the fair female when his thoughts ought to have been dedicated to the religious discourse of her father, were set before him in the darkest colours; and he was treated as one who, having sinned against light, was therefore deservedly left a prey to the Prince of Darkness.

As the fated and influential hour rolled on, the terrors of the hateful Presence grew more confounding to the mortal senses of the victim, and the knot of the accursed sophistry became more inextricable in appearance, at least to the prey whom its meshes surrounded. He had not power to explain the assurance of pardon which he continued to assert, or to name the victorious name in which he trusted. But his faith did not abandon him, though he lacked for a time the power of expressing it. 'Say what you will,' was his answer to the Tempter; 'I know there is as much betwixt the two boards of this Book as can ensure me forgiveness for my transgressions and safety for my soul.' As he spoke, the clock, which announced the lapse of the fatal hour, was heard to strike. The speech and intellectual powers of the youth were instantly and fully restored; he burst forth into prayer, and expressed in the most glowing terms his reliance on the truth and on the Author of the Gospel. The demon retired, yelling and discomfited, and the old man, entering the apartment, with tears congratulated his guest on his victory in the fated struggle.

The young man was afterwards married to the beautiful

maiden, the first sight of whom had made such an impression on him, and they were consigned over at the close of the story to domestic happiness. So ended John Mac-Kinlay's legend.*

The Author of *Waverley* had imagined a possibility of framing an interesting, and perhaps not an unedifying, tale out of the incidents of the life of a doomed individual, whose efforts at good and virtuous conduct were to be for ever disappointed by the intervention, as it were, of some malevolent being, and who was at last to come off victorious from the fearful struggle. In short, something was meditated upon a plan resembling the imaginative tale of *Sintram and his Companions*, by Mons. Le Baron de la Motte Fouqué, although, if it then existed, the author had not seen it.[3]

The scheme projected may be traced in the three or four first chapters of the work; but farther consideration induced the author to lay his purpose aside. It appeared, on mature consideration, that astrology, though its influence was once received and admitted by Bacon himself, does not now retain influence over the general mind sufficient even to constitute the mainspring of a romance. Besides, it occurred that to do justice to such a subject would have required not only more talent than the Author could be conscious of possessing, but also involved doctrines and discussions of a nature too serious for his purpose and for the character of the narrative. In changing his plan, however, which was done in the course of printing, the early sheets retained the vestiges of the original tenor of the story, although they now hang upon it as an unnecessary and unnatural incumbrance. The cause of such vestiges occurring is now explained and apologised for.

It is here worthy of observation that, while the astrological doctrines have fallen into general contempt, and been supplanted by superstitions of a more gross and far less beautiful character, they have, even in modern days, retained some votaries.

One of the most remarkable believers in that forgotten and despised science was a late eminent professor of the art of legerdemain.[4] One would have thought that a person of this description ought, from his knowledge of the thousand ways in

---

*See Lockhart's *Life of Scott*, vol. v. pp. 5, 35, 397 (1862).

which human eyes could be deceived, to have been less than others subject to the fantasies of superstition.. Perhaps the habitual use of those abstruse calculations by which, in a manner surprising to the artist himself, many tricks upon cards, etc., are performed, induced this gentleman to study the combination of the stars and planets, with the expectation of obtaining prophetic annunciations.

He constructed a scheme of his own nativity, calculated according to such rules of art as he could collect from the best astrological authors. The result of the past he found agreeable to what had hitherto befallen him, but in the important prospect of the future a singular difficulty occurred. There were two years during the course of which he could by no means obtain any exact knowledge whether the subject of the scheme would be dead or alive. Anxious concerning so remarkable a circumstance, he gave the scheme to a brother astrologer, who was also baffled in the same manner. At one period he found the native, or subject, was certainly alive; at another that he was unquestionably dead; but a space of two years extended between these two terms, during which he could find no certainty as to his death or existence.

The astrologer marked the remarkable circumstance in his diary, and continued his exhibitions in various parts of the empire until the period was about to expire during which his existence had been warranted as actually ascertained. At last, while he was exhibiting to a numerous audience his usual tricks of legerdemain, the hands whose activity had so often baffled the closest observer suddenly lost their power, the cards dropped from them, and he sunk down a disabled paralytic. In this state the artist languished for two years, when he was at length removed by death. It is said that the diary of this modern astrologer will soon be given to the public.

The fact, if truly reported, is one of those singular coincidences which occasionally appear, differing so widely from ordinary calculation, yet without which irregularities human life would not present to mortals, looking into futurity, the abyss of impenetrable darkness which it is the pleasure of the Creator it should offer to them. Were everything to happen in the ordinary train of events, the future would be subject to the rules of arithmetic, like the chances of gaming. But extraordinary events and wonderful runs of luck defy the calculations of mankind and throw impenetrable darkness on future contingencies.

To the above anecdote, another, still more recent, may be here added. The author was lately honoured with a letter from a gentleman deeply skilled in these mysteries, who kindly undertook to calculate the nativity of the writer of Guy Mannering, who might be supposed to be friendly to the divine art which he professed. But it was impossible to supply data for the construction of a horoscope, had the native been otherwise desirous of it, since all those who could supply the minutiae of day, hour, and minute have been long removed from the mortal sphere.

Having thus given some account of the first idea, or rude sketch, of the story, which was soon departed from, the Author, in following out the plan of the present edition, has to mention the prototypes of the principal characters in *Guy Mannering*.

Some circumstances of local situation gave the Author in his youth an opportunity of seeing a little, and hearing a great deal, about that degraded class who are called gipsies;[5] who are in most cases a mixed race between the ancient Egyptians who arrived in Europe about the beginning of the fifteenth century and vagrants of European descent.

The individual gipsy upon whom the character of Meg Merrilies was founded was well known about the middle of the last century by the name of Jean Gordon, an inhabitant of the village of Kirk Yetholm, in the Cheviot Hills, adjoining to the English Border. The Author gave the public some account of this remarkable person in one of the early numbers of *Blackwood's Magazine*, to the following purpose:—

. . . .

[See Scott's account in his review of *Tales of My Landlord*, earlier in this volume.]

Nothwithstanding the failure of Jean's issue, for which

Weary fa' the waefu' wuddie,

a granddaughter survived her, whom I remember to have seen. That is, as Dr. Johnson had a shadowy recollection of Queen Anne as a stately lady in black, adorned with diamonds, so my memory is haunted by a solemn remembrance of a woman of more than female height, dressed in a long red cloak, who commenced acquaintance by giving me an apple, but whom, nevertheless, I looked on with as much awe as the future Doctor, High Church and Tory as he was doomed to be, could look upon the Queen.[6] I conceive this woman to have been Madge Gordon, of whom an impressive account is given in the same article in which her grandmother Jean is mentioned, but not by the present writer:—

. . . .

To pass to a character of a very different description, Dominie Sampson,*—the reader may easily suppose that a poor modest humble scholar who has won his way through the classics, yet has fallen to leeward in the voyage of life, is no uncommon personage in a country where a certain portion of learning is easily attained by those who are willing to suffer hunger and thirst in exchange for acquiring Greek and Latin. But there is a far more exact prototype of the worthy Dominie, upon which is founded the part which he performs in the romance, and which, for certain particular reasons, must be expressed very generally.

Such a preceptor as Mr. Sampson is supposed to have been was actually tutor in the family of a gentleman of considerable property. The young lads, his pupils, grew up and went out in the world, but the tutor continued to reside in the family, no uncommon circumstance in Scotland in former days, where food and shelter were readily afforded to humble friends and dependents. The laird's predecessors had been imprudent, he himself was passive and unfortunate. Death swept away his sons, whose success in life might have balanced his own bad luck and incapacity. Debts increased and funds diminished, until ruin came. The estate was sold; and the old man was about to remove from the house of his fathers to go he knew not whither, when, like an old piece of furniture, which, left alone in its wonted corner, may hold together for a long while, but breaks to pieces on an attempt to move it he fell down on his own threshold under a paralytic affection.

The tutor awakened as from a dream. He saw his patron dead, and that his patron's only remaining child, an elderly woman, now neither graceful nor beautiful, if she had ever been either the one or the other, had by this calamity become a homeless and

*The Rev. George Thomson, son of the minister of Melrose, who acted as tutor at Abbotsford, was supposed by his friends to have yielded the author many personal features for his fictitious character of the Dominie (*Laing*).

penniless orphan. He addressed her nearly in the words which Dominie Sampson uses to Miss Bertram, and professed his determination not to leave her. Accordingly, roused to the exercise of talents which had long slumbered, he opened a little school and supported his patron's child for the rest of her life, treating her with the same humble observance and devoted attention which he had used towards her in the days of her prosperity.

Such is the outline of Dominie Sampson's real story, in which there is neither romantic incident nor sentimental passion; but which, perhaps, from the rectitude and simplicity of character which it displays, may interest the heart and fill the eye of the reader as irresistibly as if it respected distresses of a more dignified or refined character.[7]

These preliminary notices concerning the tale of *Guy Mannering* and some of the characters introduced may save the author and reader in the present instance the trouble of writing and perusing a long string of detached notes.

ABBOTSFORD, *January* 1829.

ROB ROY

When the Author projected this further encroachment on the patience of an indulgent public, he was at some loss for a title, a good name being very nearly of as much consequence in literature as in life. The title of *Rob Roy* was suggested by the late Mr. Constable, whose sagacity and experience foresaw the germ of popularity which it included.[1]

No introduction can be more appropriate to the work than some account of the singular character whose name is given to the title-page, and who, through good report and bad report, has maintained a wonderful degree of importance in popular recollection. This cannot be ascribed to the distinction of his birth, which, though that of a gentleman, had in it nothing of high destination, and gave him little right to command in his clan. Neither, though he lived a busy, restless, and enterprising life, were his feats equal to those of other freebooters who have been less distinguished. He owed his fame in a great measure to his residing on the very verge of the Highlands, and playing such pranks in the beginning of the 18th century as are usually ascribed to Robin Hood in the middle ages, and that within forty miles of Glasgow, a great commercial city, the seat of a learned university. Thus a character like his, blending the wild virtues, the subtle policy, and unrestrained license of an American Indian, was flourishing in Scotland during the Augustan age of Queen Anne and George I. Addison, it is probable, or Pope, would have been considerably surprised if they had known that there existed in the same island with them a personage of Rob Roy's peculiar habits and profession. It is this strong contrast betwixt the civilised and cultivated mode of life on the one side of the Highland line, and the wild and lawless adventures which were habitually undertaken and achieved by one who dwelt on the opposite side of that ideal boundary, which creates the interest attached to his name. Hence it is that even yet,

> Far and near, through vale and hill,
> Are faces that attest the same,
> And kindle like a fire new stirr'd
> At sound of Rob Roy's name.[2]

. . . .

The character of Rob Roy is, of course, a mixed one. His sagacity, boldness and prudence, qualities so highly necessary to success in war, became in some degree vices from the manner in which they were employed. The circumstances of his education, however, must be admitted as some extenuation of his habitual transgressions against the law; and for his political tergiversations he might in that distracted period plead the example of men far more powerful, and less excusable in becoming the sport of circumstances, than the poor and desperate outlaw. On the other hand, he was in the constant exercise of virtues the more meritorious as they seem inconsistent with his general character. Pursuing the occupation of a predatory chieftain—in modern phrase, a captain of banditti—Rob Roy was moderate in his revenge and humane in his successes. No charge of cruelty or bloodshed, unless in battle, is brought against his memory. In like manner the formidable outlaw was the friend of the poor, and, to the utmost of his ability, the support of the widow and the orphan, kept his word when pledged, and died lamented in his own wild country, where there were hearts grateful for his beneficence, though their minds were not sufficiently instructed to appreciate his errors.

THE HEART OF MID-LOTHIAN

The Author has stated in the preface to the *Chronicles of the Canongate*, 1827, that he received from an anonymous correspondent an account of the incident upon which the following story is founded. He is now at liberty to say that the information was conveyed to him by a late amiable and ingenious lady, whose wit and power of remarking and judging of character still survive in the memory of her friends. Her maiden name was Miss Helen Lawson, of Girthhead, and she was wife of Thomas Goldie, Esq., of Craigmuie, Commissary of Dumfries.

Her communication was in these words:

'I had taken for summer lodgings a cottage near the old Abbey of Lincluden. It had formerly been inhabited by a lady who had pleasure in embellishing cottages, which she found perhaps homely and even poor enough; mine therefore possessed many marks of taste and elegance unusual in this species of habitation in Scotland, where a cottage is literally what its name declares.

'From my cottage door I had a partial view of the old Abbey before mentioned; some of the highest arches were seen over, and some through, the trees scattered along a lane which led down to the ruin, and the strange fantastic shapes of almost all those old ashes accorded wonderfully well with the building they at once shaded and ornamented.

'The Abbey itself from my door was almost on a level with the cottage; but on coming to the end of the lane, it was discovered to be situated on a high perpendicular bank, at the foot of which run the clear waters of the Cluden, where they hasten to join the sweeping Nith,

Whose distant roaring swells and fa's.

As my kitchen and parlour were not very far distant, I one day went in to purchase some chickens from a person I heard offering them for sale. It was a little, rather stout-looking woman, who seemed to be between seventy and eighty years of age; she was almost covered with a tartan plaid, and her cap had over it a black silk hood, tied under the chin, a piece of dress still much in use among elderly women of that rank of life in Scotland; her eyes were dark, and remarkably lively and intelligent. I entered into conversation with her, and began by asking how she maintained herself, etc.

'She said that in winter she footed stockings, that is, knit feet to country people's stockings, which bears about the same relation to stocking-knitting that cobbling does to shoemaking, and is of course both less profitable and less dignified; she likewise taught a few children to read, and in summer she whiles reared a few chickens.

I said I could venture to guess from her face she had never been married. She laughed heartily at this, and said, "I maun hae the queerist face that ever was seen, that ye could guess that. Now, do tell me, madam, how ye cam to think sae?" I told her it was from her cheerful disengaged countenance. She said, "Mem, have ye na far mair reason to be happy than me, wi' a gude husband and a fine family o' bairns, and plenty o' everything? For me, I'm the puirest o' a' puir bodies, and can hardly contrive to keep mysell alive in a' thae wee bits o' ways I hae tell't ye." After some more conversation, during which I was more and more pleased with the old woman's sensible conversation and the *naïveté* of her remarks, she rose to go away, when I asked her name. Her countenance suddenly clouded, and she said gravely, rather colouring, "My name is Helen Walker; but your husband kens weel about me."

'In the evening I related how much I had been pleased, and inquired what was extraordinary in the history of the poor woman. Mr. ——— said, there were perhaps few more remarkable people than Helen Walker. She had been left an orphan, with the charge of a sister considerably younger than herself, and who was educated and maintained by her exertions. Attached to her by so many ties, therefore, it will not be easy to conceive her feelings when she found that this only sister must be tried by the laws of her country for child-murder, and upon being called as principal witness against her. The counsel for the prisoner told Helen, that if she could declare that her sister had made any preparations, however slight, or had given her any intimation on the subject, such a statement would save her sister's life, as she was the principal witness against her. Helen said, "It is impossible for me to swear to a falsehood; and, whatever may be the consequence, I will give my oath according to my conscience."

'The trial came on, and the sister was found guilty and condemned; but, in Scotland, six weeks must elapse between the sentence and the execution, and Helen Walker availed herself of it. The very day of her sister's condemnation, she got a petition drawn up, stating the peculiar circumstances of the case, and that very night set out on foot to London.

'Without introduction or recommendation, with her simple, perhaps ill-expressed, petition, drawn up by some inferior clerk of the court, she presented herself, in her tartan plaid and country attire, to the late Duke of Argyle,[1] who immediately procured the pardon petitioned for, and Helen returned with it on foot, just in time to save her sister.

'I was so strongly interested by this narrative, that I determined immediately to prosecute my acquaintance with Helen Walker; but as I was to leave the country next day, I was obliged to defer it till my return in spring, when the first walk I took was to Helen Walker's cottage.

'She had died a short time before. My regret was extreme, and I endeavoured to obtain some account of Helen from an old woman who inhabited the other end of her cottage. I inquired if Helen ever spoke of her past history, her journey to London, etc. "Na," the old woman said, "Helen was a wily body, and whene'er ony o' the neebors asked anything about it, she aye turned the conversation."

'In short, every answer I received only tended to increase my regret, and raise my opinion of Helen Walker, who could unite so much prudence with so much heroic virtue.'

This narrative was inclosed in the following letter to the Author, without date or signature:—

'SIR—The occurrence just related happened to me twenty-six years ago. Helen Walker lies buried in the churchyard of Iron-gray, about six miles from Dumfries. I once proposed that a small monument should have been erected to commemorate so remarkable a character, but I now prefer leaving it to you to perpetuate her memory in a more durable manner.'

The reader is now able to judge how far the Author has improved upon, or fallen short of, the pleasing and interesting sketch of high principle and steady affection displayed by Helen Walker, the prototype of the fictitious Jeanie Deans. Mrs. Goldie was unfortunately dead before the Author had given his name to these volumes, so he lost all opportunity of thanking that lady for her highly valuable communication. But her daughter, Miss Goldie, obliged him with the following additional information:—

'Mrs. Goldie endeavoured to collect further particulars of Helen Walker, particularly concerning her journey to London, but found this nearly impossible; as the natural dignity of her character, and a high sense of family respectability, made her so indissolubly connect her sister's disgrace with her own exertions, that none of her neighbours durst ever question her upon the subject. One old woman, a distant relation of Helen's, and who is still living, says she worked an harvest with her, but that she never ventured to ask her about her sister's trial, or her journey to London. "Helen," she added, "was a lofty body, and used a high style o' language." The same old woman says that every year Helen received a cheese from her sister, who lived at Whitehaven, and that she always sent a liberal portion of it to herself or to her father's family. This fact, though trivial in itself, strongly marks the affection subsisting between the two sisters, and the complete conviction on the mind of the criminal that her sister had acted solely from high principle, not from any want of feeling, which another small but characteristic trait will further illustrate. A gentleman, a relation of Mrs. Goldie's, who happened to be travelling in the North of England, on coming to a small inn, was shown into the parlour by a female servant, who, after cautiously shutting the door, said, "Sir, I'm Nelly Walker's sister." Thus practically showing that she considered her sister as better known by her high conduct than even herself by a different kind of celebrity.

'Mrs. Goldie was extremely anxious to have a tombstone and an inscription upon it erected in Irongray churchyard; and if Sir Walter Scott will condescend to write the last, a little subscription could be easily raised in the immediate neighbourhood, and Mrs. Goldie's wish be thus fulfilled.'

It is scarcely necessary to add, that the request of Miss Goldie will be most willingly complied with, and without the necessity of any tax on the public. Nor is there much occasion to repeat how much the Author conceives himself obliged to his unknown correspondent, who thus supplied him with a theme affording such a pleasing view of the moral dignity of virtue, though unaided by birth, beauty, or talent. If the picture has suffered in the execution, it is from the failure of the Author's powers to present in detail the same simple and striking portrait exhibited in Mrs. Goldie's letter.

ABBOTSFORD, *April* 1, 1830.

THE BRIDE OF LAMMERMOOR

The Author, on a former occasion,* declined giving the real source from which he drew the tragic subject of this history, because, though occurring at a distant period, it might possibly be unpleasing to the feelings of the descendants of the parties. But as he finds an account of the circumstances given in the Notes to Law's *Memorials*,†[1] by his ingenious friend, Charles Kirkpatrick Sharpe, Esq.,[2] and also indicated in his reprint of the Rev. Mr. Symson's poems appended to the *Large Description of Galloway*, as the original of the *Bride of Lammermoor*, the Author feels himself now at liberty to tell the tale as he had it from connexions of his own, who lived very near the period, and were closely related to the family of the bride.

It is well known that the family of Dalrymple, which has produced, within the space of two centuries, as many men of talent, civil and military, and of literary, political, and professional eminence, as any house in Scotland, first rose into distinction in the person of James Dalrymple, one of the most eminent lawyers that ever lived, though the labours of his powerful mind were unhappily exercised on a subject so limited as Scottish jurisprudence, on which he has composed an admirable work.[3]

---

*See Introduction to the *Chronicles of the Canongate*.
†Law's *Memorials*, p. 226.

He married Margaret, daughter to Ross of Balneel, with whom he obtained a considerable estate. She was an able, politic, and high-minded woman, so successful in what she undertook, that the vulgar, no way partial to her husband or her family, imputed her success to necromancy. According to the popular belief, this Dame Margaret purchased the temporal prosperity of her family from the Master whom she served under a singular condition, which is thus narrated by the historian of her grandson, the great Earl of Stair:—'She lived to a great age, and at her death desired that she might not be put under ground, but that her coffin should stand upright on one end of it, promising that while she remained in that situation the Dalrymples should continue to flourish. What was the old lady's motive for the request, or whether she really made such a promise, I shall not take upon me to determine; but it's certain her coffin stands upright in the isle of the church of Kirklistown, the burial-place belonging to the family.'* The talents of this accomplished race were sufficient to have accounted for the dignities which many members of the family attained, without any supernatural assistance. But their extraordinary prosperity was attended by some equally singular family misfortunes, of which that which befell their eldest daughter was at once unaccountable and melancholy.

Miss Janet Dalrymple, daughter of the first Lord Stair and Dame Margaret Ross, had engaged herself without the knowledge of her parents to the Lord Rutherford, who was not acceptable to them either on account of his political principles or his want of fortune. The young couple broke a piece of gold together, and pledged their troth in the most solemn manner; and it is said the young lady imprecated dreadful evils on herself should she break her plighted faith. Shortly after, a suitor who was favoured by Lord Stair, and still more so by his lady, paid his addresses to Miss Dalrymple. The young lady refused the proposal, and being pressed on the subject, confessed her secret engagement. Lady Stair, a woman accustomed to universal submission, for even her husband did not dare to contradict her, treated this objection as a trifle, and insisted upon her daughter yielding her consent to marry the new suitor, David Dunbar, son

Memoirs of John Earl of Stair, by an Impartial Hand. London, printed for C. Corbett, p. 8.

and heir to David Dunbar of Baldoon, in Wigtonshire. The first lover, a man of very high spirit, then interfered by letter, and insisted on the right he had acquired by his troth plighted with the young lady. Lady Stair sent him an answer, that her daughter, sensible of her undutiful behaviour in entering into a contract unsanctioned by her parents, had retracted her unlawful vow, and now refused to fulfil her engagement with him.

The lover, in return, declined positively to receive such an answer from any one but his mistress in person; and as she had to deal with a man who was both of a most determined character and of too high condition to be trifled with, Lady Stair was obliged to consent to an interview between Lord Rutherford and her daughter. But she took care to be present in person, and argued the point with the disappointed and incensed lover with pertinacity equal to his own. She particularly insisted on the Levitical law, which declares that a woman shall be free of a vow which her parents dissent from. This is the passage of Scripture she founded on:—

'If a man vow a vow unto the Lord, or swear an oath to bind his soul with a bond; he shall not break his word, he shall do according to all that proceedeth out of his mouth.

'If a woman also vow a vow unto the Lord, and bind herself by a bond, being in her father's house in her youth;

'And her father hear her vow, and her bond wherewith she hath bound her soul, and her father shall hold his peace at her: then all her vows shall stand, and every bond wherewith she hath bound her soul shall stand.

'But if her father disallow her in the day that he heareth; not any of her vows, or of her bonds wherewith she hath bound her soul, shall stand: and the Lord shall forgive her, because her father disallowed her.'—Numbers XXX. 2–5.

While the mother insisted on these topics, the lover in vain conjured the daughter to declare her own opinion and feelings. She remained totally overwhelmed, as it seemed—mute, pale, and motionless as a statue. Only at her mother's command, sternly uttered, she summoned strength enough to restore to her plighted suitor the piece of broken gold which was the emblem of her troth. On this he burst forth into a tremendous passion, took leave of the mother with maledictions, and as he left the apartment, turned back to say to his weak, if not fickle, mistress, 'For you, madam, you will be a world's wonder'; a phrase by which some remarkable degree of calamity is usually implied. He went abroad, and returned not again. If the last Lord Rutherford was the unfortunate party, he must have been the third who bore that title, and who died in 1685.

The marriage betwixt Janet Dalrymple and David Dunbar of Baldoon now went forward, the bride showing no repugnance, but being absolutely passive in everything her mother commanded or advised. On the day of the marriage, which, as was then usual, was celebrated by a great assemblage of friends and relations, she was the same—sad, silent, and resigned, as it seemed, to her destiny. A lady, very nearly connected with the family, told the Author that she had conversed on the subject with one of the brothers of the bride, a mere lad at the time, who had ridden before his sister to church. He said her hand, which lay on his as she held her arm around his waist, was as cold and damp as marble. But, full of his new dress and the part he acted in the procession, the circumstance, which he long afterwards remembered with bitter sorrow and compunction, made no impression on him at the time.

The bridal feast was followed by dancing. The bride and bridegroom retired as usual, when of a sudden the most wild and piercing cries were heard from the nuptial chamber. It was then the custom, to prevent any coarse pleasantry which old times perhaps admitted, that the key of the nuptial chamber should be entrusted to the bridesman. He was called upon, but refused at first to give it up, till the shrieks became so hideous that he was compelled to hasten with others to learn the cause. On opening the door, they found the bridegroom lying across the threshold, dreadfully wounded, and streaming with blood. The bride was then sought for. She was found in the corner of the large chimney, having no covering save her shift, and that dabbled in gore. There she sat grinning at them, mopping and mowing, as I heard the expression used; in a word, absolutely insane. The only words she spoke were, 'Tak up your bonny bridegroom.' She survived this horrible scene little more than a fortnight, having been married on the 24th of August, and dying on the 12th of September 1669.

The unfortunate Baldoon recovered from his wounds, but sternly prohibited all inquiries respecting the manner in which he had received them. 'If a lady,' he said, 'asked him any question upon the subject, he would neither answer her nor speak to her again while he lived; if a gentleman, he would consider it as a mortal affront, and demand satisfaction as having received such.' He did not very long survive the dreadful catastrophe, having met with a fatal injury by a fall from his horse, as he rode between Leith and Holyrood House, of which he died the next day, 28th March 1682. Thus a few years removed all the principal actors in this frightful tragedy.

Various reports went abroad on this mysterious affair, many of them very inaccurate, though they could hardly be said to be exaggerated.* It was difficult at that time to become acquainted with the history of a Scottish family above the lower rank; and strange things sometimes took place there, into which even the law did not scrupulously inquire.

. . . .

It is needless to point out to the intelligent reader that the witchcraft of the mother consisted only in the ascendency of a powerful mind over a weak and melancholy one, and that the harshness with which she exercised her superiority in a case of delicacy had driven her daughter first to despair, then to frenzy. Accordingly, the Author has endeavoured to explain the tragic tale on this principle. Whatever resemblance Lady Ashton may be supposed to possess to the celebrated Dame Margaret Ross, the reader must not suppose that there was any idea of tracing the portrait of the first Lord Viscount Stair in the tricky and mean-spirited Sir William Ashton. Lord Stair, whatever might be his

---

*There appeared in the *Edinburgh Evening Post* of Oct. 10, 1840 (and afterwards in the *Lives of the Lindsays*, p. 459), a letter dated September 5th, 1823, addressed by Sir C. Horne Dalrymple Elphinstone, Bart., to the late Sir James Stewart Denham of Joltness, Bart., both descendants of Lord President Stair, from which it appears that, according to the traditional creed of the Dalrymple family, the bride's unhappy lover, Lord Rutherford, had found means to be secreted in the nuptial chamber, and that the wound of the bridegroom, Sir David Dunbar of Baldoon, was inflicted by Rutherford's hand.—J. G. LOCKHART.

moral qualities, was certainly one of the first statesmen and lawyers of his age.

The imaginary castle of Wolf's Crag has been identified by some lover of locality with that of Fast Castle. The Author is not competent to judge of the resemblance betwixt the real and imaginary scene, having never seen Fast Castle except from the sea. But fortalices of this description are found occupying, like ospreys' nests, projecting rocks, or promontories, in many parts of the eastern coast of Scotland, and the position of Fast Castle seems certainly to resemble that of Wolf's Crag as much as any other, while its vicinity to the mountain ridge of Lammermoor renders the assimilation a probable one.

We have only to add, that the death of the unfortunate bridegroom by a fall from horseback has been in the novel transferred to the no less unfortunate lover.*

---

*See the account of how this novel was composed in Lockhart's *Life of Scott*, vol. vi. p. 66 *et seq.*, ed. 1862 (*Laing*).

A LEGEND OF MONTROSE

The *Legend of Montrose* was written chiefly with a view to place before the reader the melancholy fate of John Lord Kilpont, eldest son of William Earl of Airth and Menteith, and the singular circumstances attending the birth and history of James Stewart of Ardvoirlich, by whose hand the unfortunate nobleman fell.

Our subject leads us to talk of deadly feuds, and we must begin with one still more ancient than that to which our story relates. During the reign of James IV. a great feud between the powerful families of Drummond and Murray divided Perthshire. The former, being the most numerous and powerful, cooped up eight score of the Murrays in the kirk of Monivaird and set fire to it. The wives and the children of the ill-fated men, who had also found shelter in the church, perished by the same conflagration. One man, named David Murray, escaped by the humanity of one of the Drummonds, who received him in his arms as he leaped from amongst the flames. As King James IV. ruled with more activity than most of his predecessors, this cruel deed was severely revenged, and several of the perpetrators were beheaded at Stirling. In consequence of the prosecution against his clan, the Drummond by whose assistance David Murray had escaped fled to Ireland, until, by means of the person whose life he had saved, he was permitted to return to Scotland, where he and his descendants were distinguished by the name of Drummond-Eirinich, or Ernoch, that is, Drummond of Ireland; and the same title was bestowed on their estate.

A Legend of Montrose

The Drummond-Ernoch of James VI.'s time was a king's forester in the forest of Glenartney, and chanced to be employed there in search of venison about the year 1588, or early in 1589. This forest was adjacent to the chief haunts of the MacGregors, or a particular race of them known by the title of MacEagh, or Children of the Mist. They considered the forester's hunting in their vicinity as an aggression, or perhaps they had him at feud for the apprehension or slaughter of some of their own name, or for some similar reason. This tribe of MacGregors were outlawed and persecuted, as the reader may see in the Introduction to *Rob Roy*; and every man's hand being against them, their hand was of course directed against every man. In short, they surprised and slew Drummond-Ernoch, cut off his head, and carried it with them, wrapt in the corner of one of their plaids.

In the full exultation of vengeance they stopped at the house of Ardvoirlich and demanded refreshment, which the lady, a sister of the murdered Drummond-Ernoch (her husband being absent), was afraid or unwilling to refuse. She caused bread and cheese to be placed before them, and gave directions for more substantial refreshments to be prepared. While she was absent with this hospitable intention the barbarians placed the head of her brother on the table, filling the mouth with bread and cheese, and bidding him eat, for many a merry meal he had eaten in that house.

The poor woman, returning and beholding this dreadful sight, shrieked aloud and fled into the woods, where, as described in the romance, she roamed a raving maniac, and for some time secreted herself from all living society. Some remaining instinctive feeling brought her at length to steal a glance from a distance at the maidens while they milked the cows, which being observed, her husband, Ardvoirlich, had her conveyed back to her home and detained her there till she gave birth to a child, of whom she had been pregnant; after which she was observed gradually to recover her mental faculties.

Meanwhile the outlaws had carried to the utmost their insults against the regal authority, which indeed, as exercised, they had little reason for respecting. They bore the same bloody trophy which they had so savagely exhibited to the lady of Ardvoirlich into the old church of Balquidder, nearly in the centre of their country, where the Laird of MacGregor and all his clan, being convened for the purpose, laid their hands successively on the dead man's head and swore, in heathenish and barbarous manner, to defend the author of the deed. This fierce and vindictive combination gave the Author's late and lamented friend, Sir Alexander Boswell, Bart.,[1] subject for a spirited poem, entitled *Clan-Alpin's Vow*, which was printed, but not, I believe, published,* in 1811.

The fact is ascertained by a proclamation from the Privy Council, dated 4th February 1589, directing letters of fire and sword against the MacGregors. This fearful commission was executed with uncommon fury. The late excellent John Buchanan of Cambusmore showed the Author some correspondence between his ancestor, the Laird of Buchanan, and Lord Drummond about sweeping certain valleys with their followers, on a fixed time and rendezvous, and 'taking sweet revenge for the death of their cousin, Drummond-Ernoch.' In spite of all, however, that could be done, the devoted tribe of MacGregor still bred up survivors to sustain and to inflict new cruelties and injuries.

Meanwhile young James Stewart of Ardvoirlich grew up to manhood uncommonly tall, strong, and active, with such power in the grasp of his hand in particular as could force the blood from beneath the nails of the persons who contended with him in this feat of strength. His temper was moody, fierce, and irascible; yet he must have had some ostensible good qualities, as he was greatly beloved by Lord Kilpont, the eldest son of the Earl of Airth and Menteith.

This gallant young nobleman joined Montrose in the setting up his standard in 1644, just before the decisive battle at Tippermuir, on the 1st September in that year.[2] At that time Stewart of Ardvoirlich shared the confidence of the young Lord by day and his bed by night, when, about four or five days after the battle, Ardvoirlich, either from a fit of sudden fury or deep malice long entertained against his unsuspecting friend, stabbed Lord Kilpont to the heart, and escaped from the camp of Montrose, having killed a sentinel who attempted to detain him. Bishop

---

*Printed for private circulation at Edinburgh in 1811 (*Laing*).

Guthrie gives as a reason for this villainous action, that Lord Kilpont had rejected with abhorrence a proposal of Ardvoirlich to assassinate Montrose.[3] But it does not appear that there is any authority for this charge, which rests on mere suspicion. Ardvoirlich, the assassin, certainly did fly to the Covenanters, and was employed and promoted by them. He obtained a pardon for the slaughter of Lord Kilpont, confirmed by Parliament in 1644, and was made major of Argyle's regiment in 1648. Such are the facts of the tale here given as a legend of Montrose's wars. The reader will find they are considerably altered in the fictitious narrative.

The Author has endeavoured to enliven the tragedy of the tale by the introduction of a personage proper to the time and country. In this he has been held by excellent judges to have been in some degree successful. The contempt of commerce entertained by young men having some pretence to gentility, the poverty of the country of Scotland, the national disposition to wandering and to adventure, all conduced to lead the Scots abroad into the military service of countries which were at war with each other. They were distinguished on the Continent by their bravery; but in adopting the trade of mercenary soldiers they necessarily injured their national character. The tincture of learning which most of them possessed degenerated into pedantry; their good breeding became mere ceremonial; their fear of dishonour no longer kept them aloof from that which was really unworthy, but was made to depend on certain punctilious observances totally apart from that which was in itself deserving of praise. A cavalier of honour in search of his fortune might, for example, change his service as he would his shirt, fight, like the doughty Captain Dalgetty, in one cause after another without regard to the justice of the quarrel, and might plunder the peasantry subjected to him by the fate of war with the most unrelenting rapacity; but he must beware how he sustained the slightest reproach, even from a clergyman, if it had regard to neglect on the score of duty. The following occurrence will prove the truth of what I mean:—

> 'Here I must not forget the memory of our preacher, Master William Forbesse, a preacher for soldiers, yea, and a captain in neede to lead souldiers on a good occasion, being full of courage, with discretion and good conduct beyond some captaines I have

knowne, that were not so capable as he. At this time he not onely prayed for us, but went on with us, to remarke, as I thinke, men's carriage, and having found a Sergeant neglecting his dutie and his honour at such a time (whose name I will not expresse), having chidden him, did promise to reveale him unto me, as he did after their service. The sergeant being called before me and accused, did deny his accusation, alleaging, if he were no Pastour that had alleaged it, he would not lie under the injury. The preacher offered to fight with him [in proof] that it was truth he had spoken of him; whereupon I cashiered the Sergeant, and gave his place to a worthier, called Mongo Gray, a gentleman of good worth and of much courage. The Sergeant being cashiered, never called Master William to account, for which he was evill thought of; so that he retired home, and quit the warres.'

The above quotation is taken from a work which the Author repeatedly consulted while composing the following sheets, and which is in great measure written in the humour of Captain Dugald Dalgetty. It bears the following formidable title:—

'MONRO his Expedition with the worthy Scots Regiment (called MacKeyes Regiment), levied in August 1626 by Sr. Donald MacKey, Lord Rhees, Colonell for his Majesties service of Denmark, and reduced after the battaile of Nerling to one Company, in September 1634, at Wormes, in the Palz. Discharged in severall Duties and Observations of service, first, under the magnanimous King of Denmark, during his warres against the Emperour; afterward under the invincible King of Sweden, during his Majesties lifetime; and since under the Directour-Generall, the Rex-Chancellor Oxensterne, and his Generalls. Collected and gathered together at spare hours by Colonell Robert Monro, as First Lievetenant under the said Regiment, to the Noble and worthy Captaine Thomas MacKenyee of Kildon, Brother to the noble Lord the Lord Earle of Seafort, for the use of all worthie Cavaliers favouring the laudable profession of armes. To which is annexed the Abridgement of Exercise, and divers Practicall Observations for the Younger Officer, his consideration; ending with the Souldiers Meditations going on Service.'—London, 1637.

Another worthy of the same school and nearly the same views of the military character is Sir James Turner, a soldier of fortune, who rose to considerable rank in the reign of Charles II., had a command in Galloway and Dumfriesshire for the suppression of conventicles, and was made prisoner by the insurgent Covenanters in that rising which was followed by the battle of Pentland.[4] Sir James is a person even of superior pretensions to Lieutenant-Colonel Monro, having written a military treatise on the pike-exercise, called *Pallas Armata*. Moreover, he was educated at Glasgow College, though he escaped to become an ensign in the German wars, instead of taking his degree of Master of Arts at that learned seminary.

In latter times he was author of several discourses on historical and literary subjects, from which the Bannatyne Club have extracted and printed such passages as concern his Life and Times, under the title of Sir James Turner's *Memoirs*. From this curious book I extract the following passage, as an example of how Captain Dalgetty might have recorded such an incident had he kept a journal, or, to give it a more just character, it is such as the genius of De Foe would have devised to give the minute and distinguishing features of truth to a fictitious narrative:—

'Heere I will set doun ane accident befell me; for though it was not a very strange one, yet it was a very od one in all its parts. My tuo brigads lay in a village within halfe a mile of Applebie; my oun quarter was in a gentleman's house who was a Ritmaster, and at that time with Sir Marmaduke; his wife keepd her chamber readie to be brought to bed. The castle being over, and Lambert farre enough, I resolvd to goe to bed everie night, haveing had fatigue enough before. The first night I sleepd well enough; and riseing nixt morning, I misd one linnen stockine, one halfe silke one, and one boothose, the accoustrement under a boote for one leg; neither could they be found for any search. Being provided of more of the same kind, I made myselfe reddie and rode to the headquarters. At my returne, I could heare no news of my stockins. That night I went to bed, and nixt morning found myselfe just so used; missing the three stockins for one leg onlie, the other three being left intire as they were the day before. A narrower search then the first was made, bot without successe. I had yet in reserve one paire of whole stockings, and a paire of boothose greater then the former. These I put on my legs. The third morning I found the same usage, the stockins for one leg onlie left me. It was time for me then, and my servants too, to imagine it must be rats that had shard my stockins so equallie with me; and this the mistress of the house knew well enough, but wold not tell it me. The roome, which was a low parlour, being well searchd with candles, the top of my great boothose was found at a hole, in which they had drawne all the rest. I went abroad and orderd the boards to be raised, to see how the rats had disposd of my moveables. The mistress sent a servant of her oune to be present at this action, which she knew concernd her. One board being bot a litle opend, a litle boy of mine thrust in his hand, and fetchd with him foure and tuentie old peeces of gold, and ane angell. The servant of the house affirmd it appertaind to his mistres. The boy bringing the gold to me, I went immediatlie to the gentlewoman's chamber, and told her it was probable Lambert haveing quarterd in that house, as indeed he had, some of his servants might have hid that gold; and if so, it was laufullie mine; bot if she could make it appeare it belongd to her, I sould immediatlie give it her. The poore gentlewoman told me with many teares that her husband, being none of the frugallest men (and indeed he was a spendthrift), she had hid that gold without his knowledge to make use of it as she had occasion, especiallie when she lay in; and conjurd me, as I lovd the King (for whom her husband and she had sufferd much) not to detaine her gold. She said, if there was either more or lesse then foure and tuentie whole peeces and two halfe ones, it should be none of hers; and that they were put by her in a red velvet purse. After I had given her assureance of her gold, a new search is made, the other angell is found, the velvet purse all gnawd in bits, as my stockins were, and the gold instantlie restord to the gentlewoman. I have often heard that the eating or gnauing of cloths by rats is ominous, and portends some mischance to fall on these to whom the cloths belong. I thank God I was never addicted to such divinations, or heeded them. It is true, that more misfortuns then one fell on me shortlie after; bot I am sure I could have better forseene them myselfe then rats or any such vermine, and yet did it not. I have heard indeed many fine stories told of rats, how they abandon houses and ships when the first are to be burnt and the second dround. Naturalists say they are very sagacious creatures, and I beleeve they are so; bot I shall never be of the opinion they can forsee future contingencies, which I suppose the divell himselfe can neither forknow nor fortell; these being things which the Almightie hath keepd hidden in the bosome of His divine prescience. And whither the great God hath preordained or predestinated these things, which to us are contingent, to fall out by ane uncontrollable and unavoidable necessitie, is a question not yet decided.'*

In quoting these ancient authorities, I must not forget the more modern sketch of a Scottish soldier of the old fashion, by a masterhand, in the character of Lesmahagow, since the existence of that doughty captain alone must deprive the present Author of all claim to absolute originality.[5] Still Dalgetty, as the production of his own fancy, has been so far a favourite with its parent that he has fallen into the error of assigning to the Captain too prominent a part in the story. This is the opinion of a critic[6] who encamps on the highest pinnacles of literature; and the Author is so far fortunate in having incurred his censure that it gives his modesty a decent apology for quoting the praise, which it would have ill-befitted him to bring forward in an unmingled state. The passage occurs in the *Edinburgh Review*, No. 65, containing a criticism on *Ivanhoe*:—

> 'There is too much, perhaps, of Dalgetty, or, rather, he en-grosses too great a proportion of the work, for, in himself, we think he is uniformly entertaining; and the Author has nowhere shown more affinity to that matchless spirit who could bring out his Falstaffs and his Pistols in act after act, and play after play, and exercise them every time with scenes of unbounded loquacity, without either exhausting their humour or varying a note from its characteristic tone, than in his large and reiterated specimens of the eloquence of the redoubted Rittmaster. The general idea of the character is familiar to our comic dramatists after the Restoration, and may be said in some measure to be compounded of Captain Fluellen and Bobadil; but the ludicrous combination of the *soldado* with the Divinity student of Marishal College is entirely original; and the mixture of talent, selfishness, courage, coarseness, and conceit was never so happily exemplified. Numerous as his speeches are, there is not one that is not characteristic, and, to our taste, divertingly ludicrous.'

---

*Sir James Turner's *Memoirs*, Bannatyne edition, p. 59.
†Lord Jeffrey (*Laing*).

IVANHOE

The Author of the Waverley Novels had hitherto proceeded in an unabated course of popularity, and might, in his peculiar district of literature, have been termed *l'enfant gâté*[1] of success. It was plain, however, that frequent publication must finally wear out the public favour, unless some mode could be devised to give an appearance of novelty to subsequent productions. Scottish manners, Scottish dialect, and Scottish characters of note, being those with which the Author was most intimately and familiarly acquainted, were the groundwork upon which he had hitherto relied for giving effect to his narrative. It was, however, obvious that this kind of interest must in the end occasion a degree of sameness and repetition, if exclusively resorted to, and that the reader was likely at length to adopt the language of Edwin, in Parnell's *Tale*:—

> 'Reverse the spell,' he cries,
> 'And let it fairly now suffice,
> The gambol has been shown.'[2]

Nothing can be more dangerous for the fame of a professor of the fine arts than to permit (if he can possibly prevent it) the character of a mannerist to be attached to him, or that he should be supposed capable of success only in a particular and limited style. The public are, in general, very ready to adopt the opinion that he who has pleased them in one peculiar mode of composition is, by means of that very talent, rendered incapable of venturing upon other subjects. The effect of this disinclination, on the part of the public, towards the artificers of their pleasures, when they attempt to enlarge their means of amusing, may be seen in the censures usually passed by vulgar criticism upon actors or artists who venture to change the character of their efforts, that, in so doing, they may enlarge the scale of their art.

There is some justice in this opinion, as there always is in such as attain general currency. It may often happen on the stage, that an actor, by possessing in a pre-eminent degree the external qualities necessary to give effect to comedy, may be deprived of the right to aspire to tragic excellence; and in painting or literary composition, an artist or poet may be master exclusively of modes of thought and powers of expression which confine him to a single course of subjects. But much more frequently the same capacity which carries a man to popularity in one department will obtain for him success in another, and that must be more particularly the case in literary composition than either in acting or painting, because the adventurer in that department is not impeded in his exertions by any peculiarity of features, or conformation of person, proper for particular parts, or, by any peculiar mechanical habits of using the pencil, limited to a particular class of subjects.

Whether this reasoning be correct or otherwise, the present Author felt that, in confining himself to subjects purely Scottish, he was not only likely to weary out the indulgence of his readers, but also greatly to limit his own power of affording them pleasure. In a highly polished country, where so much genius is monthly employed in catering for public amusement, a fresh topic, such as he had himself had the happiness to light upon, is the untasted spring of the desert:

Men bless their stars and call it luxury.[a]

But when men and horses, cattle, camels, and dromedaries have poached the spring into mud, it becomes loathsome to those who at first drank of it with rapture; and he who had the merit of discovering it, if he would preserve his reputation with the tribe, must display his talent by a fresh discovery of untasted fountains.

If the author, who finds himself limited to a particular class of subjects, endeavours to sustain his reputation by striving to add a novelty of attraction to themes of the same character which have been formerly successful under his management, there are manifest reasons why, after a certain point, he is likely to fail. If the mine be not wrought out, the strength and capacity of the miner become necessarily exhausted. If he closely imitates the narratives which he has before rendered successful, he is doomed to 'wonder that they please no more.' If he struggles to take a different view of the same class of subjects, he speedily discovers that what is obvious, graceful, and natural has been exhausted; and, in order to obtain the indispensable charm of novelty, he is forced upon caricature, and, to avoid being trite, must become extravagant.

It is not, perhaps, necessary to enumerate so many reasons why the Author of the Scottish Novels, as they were then exclusively termed, should be desirous to make an experiment on a subject purely English. It was his purpose, at the same time, to have rendered the experiment as complete as possible, by bringing the intended work before the public as the effort of a new candidate for their favour, in order that no degree of prejudice, whether favourable or the reverse, might attach to it, as a new production of the Author of *Waverley*; but this intention was afterwards departed from, for reasons to be hereafter mentioned.

The period of the narrative adopted was the reign of Richard I.,[4] not only as abounding with characters whose very names were sure to attract general attention, but as affording a striking contrast betwixt the Saxons, by whom the soil was cultivated, and the Normans, who still reigned in it as conquerors, reluctant to mix with the vanquished, or acknowledge themselves of the same stock. The idea of this contrast was taken from the ingenious and unfortunate Logan's tragedy of *Runnamede*,[5] in which, about the same period of history, the Author had seen the Saxon and Norman barons opposed to each other on different sides of the stage. He does not recollect that there was any attempt to contrast the two races in their habits and sentiments; and indeed it was obvious that history was violated by introducing the Saxons still existing as a high-minded and martial race of nobles.

They did, however, survive as a people, and some of the ancient Saxon families possessed wealth and power, although they were exceptions to the humble condition of the race in general. It seemed to the Author that the existence of the two races in the same country, the vanquished distinguished by their plain, homely, blunt manners, and the free spirit infused by their ancient institutions and laws; the victors, by the high spirit of military fame, personal adventure, and whatever could distinguish them as the flower of chivalry, might, intermixed with other characters belonging to the same time and country, interest the reader by the contrast, if the Author should not fail on his part.

Scotland, however, had been of late used so exclusively as the scene of what is called historical romance, that the preliminary letter of Mr. Laurence Templeton became in some measure necessary. To this, as to an Introduction, the reader is referred, as expressing the Author's purpose and opinions in undertaking this species of composition, under the necessary reservation, that he is far from thinking he has attained the point at which he aimed.

It is scarcely necessary to add, that there was no idea or wish to pass off the supposed Mr. Templeton as a real person. But a kind of continuation of the *Tales of my Landlord* had been recently attempted by a stranger,[6] and it was supposed this Dedicatory Epistle might pass for some imitation of the same kind, and thus, putting inquirers upon a false scent, induce them to believe they had before them the work of some new candidate for their favour.

After a considerable part of the work had been finished and printed, the publishers, who pretended to discern in it a germ of popularity, remonstrated strenuously against its appearing as an absolutely anonymous production, and contended that it should have the advantage of being announced as by the Author of *Waverley*. The Author did not make any obstinate opposition, for he began to be of opinion with Dr. Wheeler, in Miss Edgeworth's excellent tale of *Manoeuvring*,[7] that 'trick upon trick' might be too much for the patience of an indulgent public, and might be reasonably considered as trifling with their favour.

The book, therefore, appeared as an avowed continuation of the Waverley Novels; and it would be ungrateful not to acknowledge that it met with the same favourable reception as its predecessors.

Such annotations as may be useful to assist the reader in comprehending the characters of the Jew, the Templar, the captain of the mercenaries, or Free Companions, as they were called, and others proper to the period, are added, but with a sparing hand, since sufficient information on these subjects is to be found in general history.

An incident in the tale, which had the good fortune to find favour in the eyes of many readers, is more directly borrowed from the stores of old romance. I mean the meeting of the King with Friar Tuck at the cell of that buxom hermit. The general tone of the story belongs to all ranks and all countries, which emulate each other in describing the rambles of a disguised sovereign, who, going in search of information or amusement into the lower ranks of life, meets with adventures diverting to the reader or hearer, from the contrast betwixt the monarch's outward appearance and his real character. The Eastern tale-teller has for his theme the disguised expeditions of Haroun Alraschid with his faithful attendants, Mesrour and Giafar, through the midnight streets of Bagdad; and Scottish tradition dwells upon the similar exploits of James V., distinguished during such excursions by the travelling name of the Goodman of Ballengeich, as the Commander of the Faithful, when he desired to be incognito, was known by that of Il Bondocani. The French minstrels are not silent on so popular a theme. There must have been a Norman original of the Scottish metrical romance of *Rauf Colziar*, in which Charlemagne is introduced as the unknown guest of a charcoal-man.* It seems to have been the original of other poems of the kind.

In merry England there is no end of popular ballads on this theme. The poem of *John the Reeve*, or Steward, mentioned by Bishop Percy, in the *Reliques of English Poetry*,† is said to have turned on such an incident; and we have, besides, the *King and the Tanner of Tamworth*, the *King and the Miller of Mansfield*, and others on the same topic. But the peculiar tale of this nature to which the Author of *Ivanhoe* has to acknowledge an obligation is more ancient by two centuries than any of these last mentioned.

It was first communicated to the public in that curious record of ancient literature which has been accumulated by the combined

---

*This very curious poem, long a *desideratum* in Scottish literature, and given up as irrecoverably lost, was lately brought to light by the researches of Dr. Irvine of the Advocates' Library, and has been reprinted by Mr. David Laing, Edinburgh.

†Vol. ii. p. 167.

exertions of Sir Egerton Brydges and Mr. Hazlewood, in the periodical work entitled the *British Bibliographer*.[8] From thence it has been transferred by the Reverend Charles Henry Hartshorne, M.A., editor of a very curious volume, entitled *Ancient Metrical Tales, printed chiefly from Original Sources*, 1829. Mr. Hartshorne gives no other authority for the present fragment, except the article in the *Bibliographer*, where it is entitled the *Kyng and the Hermite*. A short abstract of its contents will show its similarity to the meeting of King Richard and Friar Tuck.

King Edward (we are not told which among the monarchs of that name, but, from his temper and habits, we may suppose Edward IV.) sets forth with his court to a gallant hunting-match in Sherwood Forest, in which, as is not unusual for princes in romance, he falls in with a deer of extraordinary size and swiftness, and pursues it closely, till he has outstripped his whole retinue, tired out hounds and horse, and finds himself alone under the gloom of an extensive forest, upon which night is descending. Under the apprehensions natural to a situation so uncomfortable, the king recollects that he has heard how poor men, when apprehensive of a bad night's lodging, pray to St. Julian, who, in the Romish calendar, stands quarter-master–general to all forlorn travellers that render him due homage. Edward puts up his orisons accordingly, and by the guidance, doubtless, of the good saint, reaches a small path, conducting him to a chapel in the forest, having a hermit's cell in its close vicinity. The king hears the reverend man, with a companion of his solitude, telling his beads within, and meekly requests of him quarters for the night. 'I have no accommodation for such a lord as ye be,' said the hermit. 'I live here in the wilderness upon roots and rinds, and may not receive into my dwelling even the poorest wretch that lives, unless it were to save his life.' The king inquires the way to the next town, and, understanding it is by a road which he cannot find without difficulty, even if he had daylight to befriend him, he declares that, with or without the hermit's consent, he is determined to be his guest that night. He is admitted accordingly, not without a hint from the recluse that, were he himself out of his priestly weeds, he would care little for his threats of using violence, and that he gives way to him not out of intimidation, but simply to avoid scandal.

The king is admitted into the cell; two bundles of straw are shaken down for his accommodation, and he comforts himself that he is now under shelter, and that

A night will soon be gone.

Other wants, however, arise. The guest becomes clamorous for supper, observing,

'For certainly, as I you say,
I ne had never so sorry a day,
   That I ne had a merry night.'

But this indication of his taste for good cheer, joined to the annunciation of his being a follower of the court, who had lost himself at the great hunting-match, cannot induce the niggard hermit to produce better fare than bread and cheese, for which his guest showed little appetite, and 'thin drink,' which was even less acceptable. At length the king presses his host on a point to which he had more than once alluded, without obtaining a satisfactory reply:

Then said the king, 'By Godys grace,
Thou wert in a merry place,
   To shoot should thou lere;
When the foresters go to rest,
Sometyme thou might have of the best,
   All of the wild deer;
I wold hold it for no scathe,
Though thou hadst bow and arrows baith,
   Althoff thou best a frere.'

The hermit, in return, expresses his apprehension that his guest means to drag him into some confession of offence against forest laws, which, being betrayed to the King, might cost him his life. Edward answers by fresh assurances of secrecy, and again urges on him the necessity of procuring some venison. The hermit replies, by once more insisting on the duties incumbent upon him as a churchman, and continues to affirm himself free from all such breaches of order:

'Many day I have here been,
And flesh-meat I eat never,
   But milk of the kye;

142

Warm thee well, and go to sleep,
And I will lap thee with my cope,
Softly to lye.'

It would seem that the manuscript is here imperfect, for we do not find the reasons which finally induce the curtal friar to amend the king's cheer. But, acknowledging his guest to be such a 'good fellow' as has seldom graced his board, the holy man at length produces the best his cell affords. Two candles are placed on a table, white bread and baked pasties are displayed by the light, besides choice of venison, both salt and fresh, from which they select collops. 'I might have eaten my bread dry,' said the king, 'had I not pressed thee on the score of archery, but now have I dined like a prince—if we had but drink enow.'

This too is afforded by the hospitable anchorite, who despatches an assistant to fetch a pot of four gallons from a secret corner near his bed, and the whole three set in to serious drinking. This amusement is superintended by the friar, according to the recurrence of certain fustian words, to be repeated by every compotator in turn before he drank—a species of high jinks, as it were, by which they regulated their potations, as toasts were given in latter times. The one toper says 'Fusty bandias,' to which the other is obliged to reply, 'Strike pantnere,' and the friar passes many jests on the king's want of memory, who sometimes forgets the words of action. The night is spent in this jolly pastime. Before his departure in the morning, the king invites his reverend host to court, promises, at least, to requite his hospitality, and expresses himself much pleased with his entertainment. The jolly hermit at length agrees to venture thither, and to inquire for Jack Fletcher, which is the name assumed by the king. After the hermit has shown Edward some feats of archery, the joyous pair separate. The king rides home, and rejoins his retinue. As the romance is imperfect, we are not acquainted how the discovery takes place; but it is probably much in the same manner as in other narratives turning on the same subject, where the host, apprehensive of death for having trespassed on the respect due to his sovereign, while incognito, is agreeably surprised by receiving honours and reward.

143

In Mr. Hartshorne's collection, there is a romance on the same foundation, called *King Edward and the Shepherd*,* which, considered as illustrating manners, is still more curious than *The King and the Hermit*; but it is foreign to the present purpose. The reader has here the original legend from which the incident in the romance is derived; and the identifying the irregular eremite with the Friar Tuck of Robin Hood's story was an obvious expedient.

The name of Ivanhoe was suggested by an old rhyme. All novelists have had occasion at some time or other to wish with Falstaff that they knew where a commodity of good names was to be had.[9] On such an occasion the Author chanced to call to memory a rhyme recording three names of the manors forfeited by the ancestor of the celebrated Hampden, for striking the Black Prince a blow with his racket, when they quarrelled at tennis:

> Tring, Wing, and Ivanhoe,
> For striking of a blow,
> Hampden did forego,
> And glad he could escape so.

The word suited the Author's purpose in two material respects— for, first, it had an ancient English sound; and secondly, it conveyed no indication whatever of the nature of the story. He presumes to hold this last quality to be of no small importance. What is called a taking title serves the direct interest of the bookseller or publisher, who by this means sometimes sells an edition while it is yet passing the press. But if the author permits an over degree of attention to be drawn to his work ere it has appeared, he places himself in the embarrassing condition of having excited a degree of expectation which, if he proves unable to satisfy, is an error fatal to his literary reputation. Besides, when we meet such a title as the Gunpowder Plot, or any other connected with general history, each reader, before he has seen the book, has formed to himself some particular idea of the sort of manner in

---

*Like the hermit, the shepherd makes havock amongst the king's game; but by means of a sling, not of a bow; like the hermit, too, he has his peculiar phrases of compotation, the sign and countersign being Passelodion and Berafriend. One can scarce conceive what humour our ancestors found in this species of gibberish; but

I warrant it proved an excuse for the glass.

which the story is to be conducted, and the nature of the amusement which he is to derive from it. In this he is probably disappointed, and in that case may be naturally disposed to visit upon the author or the work the unpleasant feelings thus excited. In such a case the literary adventurer is censured, not for having missed the mark at which he himself aimed, but for not having shot off his shaft in a direction he never thought of.

On the footing of unreserved communication which the Author has established with the reader, he may here add the trifling circumstance, that a roll of Norman warriors, occurring in the Auchinleck MS., gave him the formidable name of Front-de-Boeuf.

Ivanhoe was highly successful upon its appearance, and may be said to have procured for its Author the freedom of the rules, since he has ever since been permitted to exercise his powers of fictitious composition in England as well as Scotland.

The character of the fair Jewess* found so much favour in the eyes of some fair readers, that the writer was censured because, when arranging the fates of the characters of the drama, he had not assigned the hand of Wilfred to Rebecca, rather than the less interesting Rowena. But, not to mention that the prejudices of the age rendered such an union almost impossible, the Author may, in passing, observe, that he thinks a character of a highly virtuous and lofty stamp is degraded rather than exalted by an attempt to reward virtue with temporal prosperity. Such is not the recompense which Providence has deemed worthy of suffering merit, and it is a dangerous and fatal doctrine to teach young persons, the most common readers of romance, that rectitude of conduct and of principle are either naturally allied with or adequately rewarded by the gratification of our passions, or attainment of our wishes. In a word, if a virtuous and a self-denied character is dismissed with temporal wealth, greatness, rank, or the indulgence of such a rashly-formed or ill-assorted passion as that of Rebecca for Ivanhoe, the reader will be apt to say, 'Verily virtue has had its reward.' But a glance on the great picture of life will show that the duties of self-denial, and the sacrifice of passion to principle, are seldom thus remunerated; and that the internal consciousness of their

---

*See Lockhart's *Life of Scott*, vol. vi. p. 177, ed. 1862.

high-minded discharge of duty produces on their own reflections a more adequate recompense, in the form of that peace which the world cannot give or take away.

ABBOTSFORD, 1st September 1830.

THE MONASTERY

It would be difficult to assign any good reason why the Author of *Ivanhoe*, after using, in that work, all the art he possessed to remove the personages, action, and manners of the tale to a distance from his own country, should choose for the scene of his next attempt the celebrated ruins of Melrose, in the immediate neighbourhood of his own residence. But the reason, or caprice, which dictated his change of system has entirely escaped his recollection, nor is it worth while to attempt recalling what must be a matter of very little consequence.

The general plan of the story was to conjoin two characters in that bustling and contentious age who, thrown into situations which gave them different views on the subject of the Reformation, should, with the same sincerity and purity of intention, dedicate themselves, the one to the support of the sinking fabric of the Catholic Church, the other to the establishment of the Reformed doctrines. It was supposed that some interesting subjects for narrative might be derived from opposing two such enthusiasts to each other in the path of life, and contrasting the real worth of both with their passions and prejudices. The localities of Melrose suited well the scenery of the proposed story: the ruins themselves form a splendid theatre for any tragic incident which might be brought forward; joined to the vicinity of the fine river, with all its tributary streams, flowing through a country which has been the scene of so much fierce fighting, and is rich with so many recollections of former times, and lying almost under the immediate eye of the Author, by whom they were to be used in composition.

The situation possessed farther recommendations. On the opposite bank of the Tweed might be seen the remains of ancient inclosures, surrounded by sycamores and ash-trees of considerable size. These had once formed the crofts or arable ground of a village, now reduced to a single hut, the abode of a fisherman, who also manages a ferry. The cottages, even the church which once existed there, have sunk into vestiges hardly to be traced without visiting the spot, the inhabitants having gradually withdrawn to the more prosperous town of Galashiels, which has risen into consideration within two miles of their neighbourhood. Superstitious eld, however, has tenanted the deserted groves with aerial beings, to supply the want of the mortal tenants who have deserted it. The ruined and abandoned churchyard of Boldside has been long believed to be haunted by the fairies, and the deep broad current of the Tweed, wheeling in moonlight round the foot of the steep bank, with the number of trees originally planted for shelter round the fields of the cottagers, but now presenting the effect of scattered and detached groves, fill up the idea which one would form in imagination for a scene that Oberon and Queen Mab might love to revel in. There are evenings when the spectator might believe, with Father Chaucer, that the

> Queen of Faery,
> With harp, and pipe, and symphony,
> Were dwelling in the place.[1]

Another, and even a more familiar, refuge of the elfin race (if tradition is to be trusted) is the glen of the river, or rather brook, named the Allan, which falls into the Tweed from the northward, about a quarter of a mile above the present bridge. As the streamlet finds its way behind Lord Sommerville's hunting-seat, called the Pavilion, its valley has been popularly termed the Fairy Dean, or rather the Nameless Dean, because of the supposed ill-luck attached by the popular faith of ancient times to any one who might name or allude to the race whom our fathers distinguished as the Good Neighbours, and the Highlanders called *Daoine Shie*, or Men of Peace; rather by way of compliment than on account of any particular idea of friendship or pacific relation which either Highlander or Borderer entertained towards the irritable beings whom they thus distinguished, or supposed them to bear to humanity.

In evidence of the actual operations of the fairy people even at this time, little pieces of calcareous matter are found in the glen after a flood, which either the labours of those tiny artists or the eddies of the brook among the stones have formed into a fantastic resemblance of cups, saucers, basins, and the like, in which children who gather them pretend to discern fairy utensils.

Besides these circumstances of romantic locality, *mea paupera regna* (as Captain Dalgetty denominates his territory of Drum-thwacket)[2] are bounded by a small but deep lake, from which eyes that yet look on the light are said to have seen the waterbull ascend, and shake the hills with his roar.[3]

Indeed, the country around Melrose, if possessing less of romantic beauty than some other scenes in Scotland, is connected with so many associations of a fanciful nature, in which the imagination takes delight, as might well induce one even less attached to the spot than the Author to accommodate, after a general manner, the imaginary scenes he was framing to the localities to which he was partial. But it would be a misapprehension to suppose that, because Melrose may in general pass for Kennaquhair, or because it agrees with scenes of the *Monastery* in the circumstances of the drawbridge, the mill-dam, and other points of resemblance, that therefore an accurate or perfect local similitude is to be found in all the particulars of the picture. It was not the purpose of the Author to present a landscape copied from nature, but a piece of composition, in which a real scene, with which he is familiar, had afforded him some leading outlines. Thus the resemblance of the imaginary Glendearg with the real vale of the Allan is far from being minute, nor did the Author aim at identifying them. This must appear plain to all who know the actual character of the Glen of Allan, and have taken the trouble to read the account of the imaginary Glendearg. The stream in the latter case is described as wandering down a romantic little valley, shifting itself, after the fashion of such a brook, from one side to the other, as it can most easily find its passage, and touching nothing in its progress that gives token of cultivation. It rises near a solitary tower, the abode of a supposed church vassal, and the scene of several incidents in the Romance.

The real Allan, on the contrary, after traversing the romantic ravine called the Nameless Dean, thrown off from side to side alternately, like a billiard ball repelled by the sides of the table on which it has been played, and in that part of its course resembling the stream which pours down Glendearg, may be traced upwards into a more open country, where the banks retreat further from each other, and the vale exhibits a good deal of dry ground, which has not been neglected by the active cultivators of the district. It arrives, too, at a sort of termination, striking in itself, but totally irreconcilable with the narrative of the Romance. Instead of a single peel-house, or border tower of defence, such as Dame Glendinning is supposed to have inhabited, the head of the Allan, about five miles above its junction with the Tweed, shows three ruins of Border houses, belonging to different proprietors, and each, from the desire of mutual support so natural to troublesome times, situated at the extremity of the property of which it is the principal messuage.[4] One of these is the ruinous mansion-house of Hillslap, formerly the property of the Cairncrosses, and now of Mr. Innes of Stow; a second, the tower of Colmslie, an ancient inheritance of the Borthwick family, as is testified by their crest, the goat's head, which exists on the ruin; a third, the house of Langshaw, also ruinous, but near which the proprietor, Mr. Baillie of Jerviswood and Mellerstain, has built a small shooting-box.

All these ruins, so strangely huddled together in a very solitary spot, have recollections and traditions of their own, but none of them bear the most distant resemblance to the descriptions in the Romance of the *Monastery*; and as the Author could hardly have erred so grossly regarding a spot within a morning's ride of his own house, the inference is that no resemblance was intended. Hillslap is remembered by the humours of the last inhabitants, two or three elderly ladies, of the class of Miss Rayland, in the *Old Manor House*, though less important by birth and fortune.[5] Colmslie is commemorated in song:—

Colmslie stands on Colmslie hill,
The water it flows round Colmslie mill;

The mill and the kiln gang bonnily,
And it's up with the whippers of Colmslie!

Langshaw, although larger than the other mansions assembled at the head of the supposed Glendearg, has nothing about it more remarkable than the inscription of the present proprietor over his shooting-lodge—*Utinam hanc etiam veris impleam amicis*[6]—a modest wish, which I know no one more capable of attaining upon an extended scale than the gentleman who has expressed it upon a limited one.*

Having thus shown that I could say something of these desolated towers, which the desire of social intercourse, or the facility of mutual defence, had drawn together at the head of this glen, I need not add any further reason to show that there is no resemblance between them and the solitary habitation of Dame Elspeth Glendinning. Beyond these dwellings are some remains of natural wood, and a considerable portion of morass and bog; but I would not advise any who may be curious in localities to spend time in looking for the fountain and holly-tree of the White Lady.

While I am on the subject, I may add that Captain Clutterbuck, the imaginary editor of the *Monastery*, has no real prototype in the village of Melrose or neighbourhood that ever I saw or heard of. To give some individuality to this personage, he is described as a character which sometimes occurs in actual society—a person who, having spent his life within the necessary duties of a technical profession, from which he has been at length emancipated, finds himself without any occupation whatever, and is apt

---

*Mr. John Borthwick of Crookston, in a note to the publisher (June 14, 1843), says that Sir Walter has reversed the proprietorship of these towers—that Colmslie belonged to Mr. Innes of Stow, while Hillslap forms part of his estate of Crookston. He adds: 'In proof that the tower of Hillslap, which I have taken measures to preserve from injury, was chiefly in his head, as the tower of Glendearg, when writing the *Monastery*, I may mention that, on one of the occasions when I had the honour of being a visitor at Abbotsford, the stables then being full, I sent a pony to be put up at our tenant's at Hillslap:—"Well," said Sir Walter, "if you do that, you must trust for its not being lifted before tomorrow to the protection of Halbert Glendinning against Christie of the Clinthill." At page 258, the "winding stair" which the monk ascended is described. The winding stone stair is still to be seen in Hillslap, but not in either of the other two towers.' It is, however, probable, from the goat's head crest on Colmslie, that that tower also had been of old a possession of the Borthwicks (*Laing*).

to become the prey of *ennui*, until he discovers some petty subject of investigation commensurate to his talents, the study of which gives him employment in solitude; while the conscious possession of information peculiar to himself adds to his consequence in society. I have often observed that the lighter and trivial branches of antiquarian study are singularly useful in relieving vacuity of such a kind, and have known them serve many a Captain Clutterbuck to retreat upon; I was therefore a good deal surprised when I found the antiquarian captain identified with a neighbour and friend of my own, who could never have been confounded with him by any one who had read the book, and seen the party alluded to. This erroneous identification occurs in a work entitled, *Illustrations of the Author of Waverley, being Notices and Anecdotes of real Characters, Scenes, and Incidents, supposed to be described in his Works,* by Robert Chambers.[7] This work was, of course, liable to many errors, as any one of the kind must be, whatever may be the ingenuity of the author, which takes the task of explaining what can be only known to another person. Mistakes of place or inanimate things referred to are of very little moment; but the ingenious author ought to have been more cautious of attaching real names to fictitious characters. I think it is in the *Spectator* we read of a rustic wag who, in a copy of *The Whole Duty of Man,*[8] wrote opposite to every vice the name of some individual in the neighbourhood, and thus converted that excellent work into a libel on a whole parish.[9]

The scenery being thus ready at the Author's hand, the reminiscences of the country were equally favourable. In a land where the horses remained almost constantly saddled, and the sword seldom quitted the warrior's side; where war was the natural and constant state of the inhabitants, and peace only existed in the shape of brief and feverish truces, there could be no want of the means to complicate and extricate the incidents of his narrative at pleasure. There was a disadvantage, notwithstanding, in treading this Border district, for it had been already ransacked by the Author himself, as well as others; and unless presented under a new light, was likely to afford ground to the objection of *crambe bis cocta.*[10]

To attain the indispensable quality of novelty, something, it was thought, might be gained by contrasting the character of the vassals of the church with those of the dependants of the lay barons, by whom they were surrounded. But much advantage could not be derived from this. There were, indeed, differences betwixt the two classes, but, like tribes in the mineral and vegetable world, which, resembling each other to common eyes, can be sufficiently well discriminated by naturalists, they were yet too similar upon the whole to be placed in marked contrast with each other.

Machinery remained—the introduction of the supernatural and marvellous, the resort of distressed authors since the days of Horace, but whose privileges as a sanctuary have been disputed in the present age, and wellnigh exploded. The popular belief no longer allows the possibility of existence to the race of mysterious beings which hovered betwixt this world and that which is invisible. The fairies have abandoned their moonlight turf; the witch no longer holds her black orgies in the hemlock dell; and

> Even the last lingering phantom of the brain,
> The churchyard ghost, is now at rest again.[11]

From the discredit attached to the vulgar and more common modes in which the Scottish superstition displays itself, the Author was induced to have recourse to the beautiful, though almost forgotten, theory of astral spirits, or creatures of the elements, surpassing human beings in knowledge and power, but inferior to them as being subject, after a certain space of years, to a death which is to them annihilation, as they have no share in the promise made to the sons of Adam. These spirits are supposed to be of four distinct kinds, as the elements from which they have their origin, and are known, to those who have studied the cabalistical philosophy, by the names of Sylphs, Gnomes, Salamanders, and Naiads, as they belong to the elements of Air, Earth, Fire, or Water. The general reader will find an entertaining account of these elementary spirits in the French book entitled, *Entretiens du Compte du Gabalis*.[12] The ingenious Compte de la Motte Fouqué composed, in German, one of the most successful productions of his fertile brain, where a beautiful and even afflicting effect is produced by the introduction of a water-nymph, who loses the privilege of immortality by consenting to become accessible to human feelings, and uniting her lot with that of a mortal, who treats her with ingratitude.[13]

In imitation of an example so successful, the White Lady of Avenel was introduced into the following sheets. She is represented as connected with the family of Avenel by one of those mystic ties which, in ancient times, were supposed to exist, in certain circumstances, between the creatures of the elements and the children of men. Such instances of mysterious union are recognised in Ireland, in the real Milesian families, who are possessed of a Banshee; and they are known among the traditions of the Highlanders, which, in many cases, attached an immortal being or spirit to the service of particular families or tribes. These demons, if they are to be called so, announced good or evil fortune to the families connected with them; and though some only condescended to meddle with matters of importance, others, like the May Mollach, or Maid of the Hairy Arms, condescended to mingle in ordinary sports, and even to direct the chief how to play at draughts.

There was, therefore, no great violence in supposing such a being as this to have existed, while the elementary spirits were believed in; but it was more difficult to describe or imagine its attributes and principles of action. Shakspeare, the first of authorities in such a case, has painted Ariel, that beautiful creature of his fancy, as only approaching so near to humanity as to know the nature of that sympathy which the creatures of clay felt for each other, as we learn from the expression—'Mine would if I were human.'[14] The inferences from this are singular, but seem capable of regular deduction. A being, however superior to man in length of life, in power over the elements, in certain perceptions respecting the present, the past, and the future, yet still incapable of human passions, of sentiments of moral good and evil, of meriting future rewards or punishments, belongs rather to the class of animals than of human creatures, and must therefore be presumed to act more from temporary benevolence or caprice than from anything approaching to feeling or reasoning. Such a being's superiority in power can only be compared to that of the elephant or lion, who are greater in strength than man, though inferior in the scale of creation. The partialities which we suppose such spirits to entertain must be like those of the dog; their sudden starts of passion, or the indulgence of a frolic, or mischief, may be compared to those of the numerous varieties of the cat. All these propensities are, however, controlled by the laws which render the elementary race subordinate to the command of man—liable to be subjected by his science (so the sect of Gnostics believed, and on this turned the Rosicrucian philosophy), or to be overpowered by his superior courage and daring, when it set their illusions at defiance.

It is with reference to this idea of the supposed spirits of the elements that the White Lady of Avenel is represented as acting a varying, capricious, and inconsistent part in the pages assigned to her in the narrative; manifesting interest and attachment to the family with whom her destinies are associated, but evincing whim, and even a species of malevolence, towards other mortals, as the sacristan and the Border robber, whose incorrect life subjected them to receive petty mortifications at her hand. The White Lady is scarcely supposed, however, to have possessed either the power or the inclination to do more than inflict terror or create embarrassment, and is always subjected by those mortals who, by virtuous resolution and mental energy, could assert superiority over her. In these particulars she seems to constitute a being of a middle class, between the *esprit follet*,[15] who places its pleasure in misleading and tormenting mortals, and the benevolent fairy of the East, who uniformly guides, aids, and supports them.

Either, however, the Author executed his purpose indifferently or the public did not approve of it; for the White Lady of Avenel was far from being popular. He does not now make the present statement in the view of arguing readers into a more favourable opinion on the subject, but merely with the purpose of exculpating himself from the charge of having wantonly intruded into the narrative a being of inconsistent powers and propensities.

In the delineation of another character, the Author of the *Monastery* failed where he hoped for some success. As nothing is so successful a subject of ridicule as the fashionable follies of the time, it occurred to him that the more serious scenes of his narrative might be relieved by the humour of a cavaliero of the age of Queen Elizabeth. In every period, the attempt to gain and maintain the highest rank of society has depended on the power of assuming and supporting a certain fashionable kind of affectation, usually connected with some vivacity of talent and energy of character, but distinguished at the same time by a transcendental flight beyond sound reason and common sense; both faculties too vulgar to be admitted into the estimate of one who claims to be esteemed 'a choice spirit of the age.' These, in their different phases, constitute the gallants of the day, whose boast it is to drive the whims of fashion to extremity.

On all occasions, the manners of the sovereign, the court, and the time must give the tone to the peculiar description of qualities by which those who would attain the height of fashion must seek to distinguish themselves. The reign of Elizabeth, being that of a maiden queen, was distinguished by the decorum of the courtiers, and especially the affectation of the deepest deference to the sovereign. After the acknowledgment of the Queen's matchless perfections, the same devotion was extended to beauty as it existed among the lesser stars in her court, who sparkled, as it was the mode to say, by her reflected lustre. It is true, that gallant knights no longer vowed to Heaven, the peacock, and the ladies to perform some feat of extravagant chivalry, in which they endangered the lives of others as well as their own; but although their chivalrous displays of personal gallantry seldom went further in Elizabeth's days than the tilt-yard, where barricades, called barriers, prevented the shock of the horses, and limited the display of the cavaliers' skill to the comparatively safe encounter of their lances, the language of the lovers to their ladies was still in the exalted terms which Amadis would have addressed to Oriana, before encountering a dragon for her sake.[16] This tone of romantic gallantry found a clever but conceited author to reduce it to a species of constitution and form, and lay down the courtly manner of conversation, in a pedantic book called *Euphues and his England*.[17] Of this, a brief account is given in the text, to which it may now be proper to make some additions.

The extravagance of Euphuism, or a symbolical jargon of the same class, predominates in the romances of Calprènede and Scudéri, which were read for the amusement of the fair sex of France during the long reign of Louis XIV., and were supposed to contain the only legitimate language of love and gallantry.[18] In this reign they encountered the satire of Molière and Boileau. A similar disorder, spreading into private society, formed the ground of the affected dialogue of the *précieuses*, as they were styled, who formed the coterie of the Hôtel de Rambouillet, and afforded Molière matter for his admirable comedy, *Les Précieuses Ridicules*. In England, the humour does not seem to have long survived the accession of James I.

The Author had the vanity to think that a character, whose peculiarities should turn on extravagances which were once universally fashionable, might be read in a fictitious story with a good chance of affording amusement to the existing generation, who, fond as they are of looking back on the actions and manners of their ancestors, might be also supposed to be sensible of their absurdities. He must fairly acknowledge that he was disappointed, and that the Euphuist, far from being accounted a well-drawn and humorous character of the period, was condemned as unnatural and absurd.

It would be easy to account for this failure by supposing the defect to arise from the Author's want of skill, and probably many readers may not be inclined to look further. But, as the Author himself can scarcely be supposed willing to acquiesce in this final cause, if any other can be alleged, he has been led to suspect that, contrary to what he originally supposed, his subject was injudiciously chosen, in which, and not in his mode of treating it, lay the source of the want of success.

The manners of a rude people are always founded on nature, and therefore the feelings of a more polished generation immediately sympathise with them. We need no numerous notes, no antiquarian dissertations, to enable the most ignorant to recognise the sentiments and diction of the characters of Homer; we have but, as Lear says, to strip off our lendings[19]—to set aside the factitious principles and adornments which we have received from our comparatively artificial system of society, and our natural feelings are in unison with those of the bard of Chios and the heroes who live in his verses. It is the same with a great part of the narratives of my friend, Mr. Cooper. We sympathise with his Indian chiefs and back-woodsmen, and acknowledge, in the characters which he presents to us, the same truth of human nature by which we should feel ourselves influenced if placed in the same condition. So much is this the case that, though it is difficult, or almost impossible, to reclaim a savage, bred from his youth to war and the chase, to the restraints and the duties of civilised life, nothing is more easy or common than to find men who have been educated in all the habits and comforts of improved society willing to exchange them for the wild labours of the hunter and the fisher. The very amusements most pursued and relished by men of all ranks, whose constitutions permit active exercise, are hunting, fishing, and in some instances war, the natural and necessary business of the savage of Dryden, where his hero talks of being

As free as nature first made man,
When wild in woods the noble savage ran.[20]

But although the occupations, and even the sentiments, of human beings in a primitive state find access and interest in the minds of the more civilised part of the species, it does not therefore follow that the national tastes, opinions, and follies of one civilised period should afford either the same interest or the same amusement to those of another. These generally, when driven to extravagance, are founded not upon any natural taste proper to the species, but upon the growth of some peculiar cast of affectation, with which mankind in general, and succeeding generations in particular, feel no common interest or sympathy. The extravagances of coxcombry in manners and apparel are indeed the legitimate, and often the sucessful, objects of satire, during the time when they exist. In evidence of this, theatrical critics may observe how many dramatic *jeux d'esprit* are well received every season, because the satirist levels at some well-known or fashionable absurdity; or, in the dramatic phrase, 'shoots folly as it flies.'[21] But when the peculiar kind of folly keeps the wing no longer, it is reckoned but waste of powder to pour a discharge of ridicule on what has ceased to exist; and the pieces in which such forgotten absurdities are made the subject of ridicule fall quietly into oblivion with the follies which gave them fashion, or only continue to exist on the scene because they contain some other more permanent interest than that which connects them with manners and follies of a temporary character.

This, perhaps, affords a reason why the comedies of Ben Jonson, founded upon system, or what the age termed humours—by which was meant factitious and affected characters, superinduced on that which was common to the rest of their race—in spite of acute satire, deep scholarship, and strong sense, do not now afford general pleasure, but are confined to the closet of the antiquary, whose studies have assured him that the personages of the dramatist were once, though they are now no longer, portraits of existing nature.

Let us take another example of our hypothesis from Shakspeare himself, who, of all authors, drew his portraits for all ages. With the whole sum of the idolatry which affects us at his name, the mass of readers peruse without amusement the characters formed on the extravagances of temporary fashion; and the Euphuist Don Armado, the pedant Holofernes, even Nym and Pistol, are read with little pleasure by the mass of the public, being portraits of which we cannot recognise the humour, because the originals no longer exist. In like manner, while the distresses of Romeo and Juliet continue to interest every bosom, Mercutio, drawn as an accurate representation of the finished fine gentleman of the period, and as such received by the unanimous approbation of contemporaries, has so little to interest the present age that, stripped of all his puns and quirks of verbal wit, he only retains his place in the scene in virtue of his fine and fanciful speech upon dreaming, which belongs to no particular age, and because he is a personage whose presence is indispensable to the plot.

We have already prosecuted perhaps too far an argument the tendency of which is to prove that the introduction of an humorist, acting, like Sir Piercie Shafton, upon some forgotten and obsolete model of folly, once fashionable, is rather likely to awaken the disgust of the reader, as unnatural, than find him food for laughter. Whether owing to this theory, or whether to the more simple and probable cause of the Author's failure in the delineation of the subject he had proposed to himself, the formidable objection of *incredulus odi*[22] was applied to the Euphuist, as well as to the White Lady of Avenel; and the one was denounced as unnatural, while the other was rejected as impossible.

There was little in the story to atone for these failures in two principal points. The incidents were inartificially huddled together. There was no part of the intrigue to which deep interest was found to apply; and the conclusion was brought about, not by incidents arising out of the story itself, but in consequence of public transactions with which the narrative has little connexion, and which the reader had little opportunity to become acquainted with.

This, if not a positive fault, was yet a great defect in the Romance. It is true, that not only the practice of some great authors in this department, but even the general course of human life itself, may be quoted in favour of this more obvious, and less artificial, practice of arranging a narrative. It is seldom that the same circle of personages who have surrounded an individual at his first outset in life continue to have an interest in his career till his fate comes to a crisis. On the contrary, and more especially if the events of his life be of a varied character, and worth communicating to others, or to the world, the hero's later connexions are usually totally separated from those with whom he began the voyage, but whom the individual has outsailed, or who have drifted astray, or foundered on the passage. This hackneyed comparison holds good in another point. The numerous vessels of so many different sorts, and destined for such different purposes, which are launched in the same mighty ocean, although each endeavours to pursue its own course, are in every case more influenced by the winds and tides, which are common to the element which they all navigate, than by their own separate exertions. And it is thus in the world that, when human prudence has done its best, some general, perhaps national, event destroys the schemes of the individual, as the casual touch of a more powerful being sweeps away the web of the spider.

Many excellent romances have been composed in this view of human life, where the hero is conducted through a variety of detached scenes, in which various agents appear and disappear, without, perhaps, having any permanent influence on the progress of the story. Such is the structure of *Gil Blas*, *Roderick Random*,[23] and the lives and adventures of many other heroes, who are described as running through different stations of life, and encountering various adventures, which are only connected with each other by having happened to be witnessed by the same individual, whose identity unites them together, as the string of a necklace links the beads, which are otherwise detached.

But though such an unconnected course of adventures is what most frequently occurs in nature, yet the province of the romance writer being artificial, there is more required from him than a mere compliance with the simplicity of reality; just as we demand from the scientific gardener that he shall arrange, in curious knots and artificial parterres, the flowers which 'nature boon' distributes freely on hill and dale. Fielding, accordingly, in most of his novels, but especially in *Tom Jones*, his *chef-d'oeuvre*, has set the distinguished example of a story regularly built and consistent in all its parts, in which nothing occurs, and scarce a personage is introduced, that has not some share in tending to advance the catastrophe.

To demand equal correctness and felicity in those who may follow in the track of that illustrious novelist would be to fetter too much the power of giving pleasure, by surrounding it with penal rules; since of this sort of light literature it may be especially said, *Tout genre est permis hors le genre ennuyeux.*[24] Still, however, the more closely and happily the story is combined, and the more natural and felicitous the catastrophe, the nearer such a composition will approach the perfection of the novelist's art; nor can an author neglect this branch of his profession without incurring proportional censure.

For such censure the *Monastery* gave but too much occasion. The intrigue of the Romance, neither very interesting in itself nor very happily detailed, is at length finally disentangled by the breaking out of national hostilities between England and Scotland, and the as sudden renewal of the truce. Instances of this kind, it is true, cannot in reality have been uncommon, but the resorting to such, in order to accomplish the catastrophe, as by a *tour de force*, was objected to as inartificial, and not perfectly intelligible to the general reader.

Still, the *Monastery*, though exposed to severe and just criticism, did not fail, judging from the extent of its circulation, to have some interest for the public. And this, too, was according to the ordinary course of such matters; for it very seldom happens that literary reputation is gained by a single effort, and still more rarely is it lost by a solitary miscarriage.

The Author, therefore, had his days of grace allowed him, and time, if he pleased, to comfort himself with the burden of the old Scots song—

> If it isna weel bobbit,
> We'll bob it again.

ABBOTSFORD, 1st *November* 1830.

THE ABBOT

From what is said in the Introduction to the *Monastery*, it must necessarily be inferred that the Author considered that romance as something very like a failure. It is true, the booksellers did not complain of the sale, because, unless on very felicitous occasions, or on those which are equally the reverse, literary popularity is not gained or lost by a single publication. Leisure must be allowed for the tide both to flow and ebb. But I was conscious that, in my situation, not to advance was in some degree to recede, and being naturally unwilling to think that the principle of decay lay in myself, I was at least desirous to know of a certainty whether the degree of discountenance which I had incurred was now owing to an ill-managed story or an ill-chosen subject.

I was never, I confess, one of those who are willing to suppose the brains of an author to be a kind of milk, which will not stand above a single creaming, and who are eternally harping to young authors to husband their efforts, and to be chary of their reputation, lest it grow hackneyed in the eyes of men. Perhaps I was, and have always been, the more indifferent to the degree of estimation in which I might be held as an author because I did not put so high a value as many others upon what is termed literary reputation in the abstract, or at least upon the species of popularity which had fallen to my share; for though it were worse than affectation to deny that my vanity was satisfied at my success in the department in which chance had in some measure enlisted me, I was, nevertheless, far from thinking that the novelist or romance-writer stands high in the ranks of literature. But I spare the reader farther egotism on this subject, as I have expressed my opinion very fully in the Introductory Epistle to the *Fortunes of Nigel*, and, although it be composed in an imaginary character, it is as sincere and candid as if it had been written 'without my gown and band.'

In a word, when I considered myself as having been unsuccessful in the *Monastery*, I was tempted to try whether I could not restore, even at the risk of totally losing, my so-called reputation by a new hazard. I looked round my library, and could not but observe that, from the time of Chaucer to that of Byron, the most popular authors had been the most prolific. Even the aristarch Johnson allowed that the quality of readiness and profusion had a merit in itself, independent of the intrinsic value of the composition. Talking of Churchill, I believe, who had little merit in his prejudiced eyes, he allowed him that of fertility, with some such qualification as this—'A crab-apple can bear but crabs after all; but there is a great difference in favour of that which bears a large quantity of fruit, however indifferent, and that which produces only a few.'[1]

Looking more attentively at the patriarchs of literature, whose career was as long as it was brilliant, I thought I perceived that in the busy and prolonged course of exertion there were no doubt occasional failures, but that still those who were favourites of their age triumphed over these miscarriages. By the new efforts which they made, their errors were obliterated, they became identified with the literature of their country, and after having long received law from the critics, came in some degree to impose it. And when such a writer was at length called from the scene, his death first made the public sensible what a large share he had occupied in their attention. I recollected a passage in Grimm's *Correspondence*,[2] that, while the unexhausted Voltaire sent forth tract after tract, to the very close of a long life, the first impression made by each as it appeared was that it was inferior to its predecessors—an opinion adopted from the general idea that the Patriarch of Ferney must at last find the point from which he was to decline. But the opinion of the public finally ranked in succession the last of Voltaire's *Essays* on the same footing with those which had formerly charmed the French nation. The inference from this and similar facts seemed to me to be that new works were often judged of by the public, not so much from their own intrinsic merit, as from extrinsic ideas which readers had previously formed with regard to them, and over which a writer might hope to triumph by patience and by exertion. There is a risk in the attempt:

If he fall in, good-night, or sink or swim.[3]

But this is a chance incident to every literary attempt, and by which men of a sanguine temper are little moved.

I may illustrate what I mean by the feelings of most men in travelling. If we have found any stage particularly tedious or in an especial degree interesting, particularly short or much longer than we expected, our imaginations are so apt to exaggerate the original impression that, on repeating the journey, we usually find that we have considerably overrated the predominating quality, and the road appears to be duller or more pleasant, shorter or more tedious, than what we expected, and, consequently, than what is the actual case. It requires a third or fourth journey to enable us to form an accurate judgment of its beauty, its length, or its other attributes.

In the same manner, the public, judging of a new work, which it receives perhaps with little expectation, if surprised into applause, becomes very often ecstatic, gives a great deal more approbation than is due, and elevates the child of its immediate favour to a rank which, as it affects the author, it is equally difficult to keep and painful to lose. If, on this occasion, the author trembles at the height to which he is raised, and becomes afraid of the shadow of his own renown, he may indeed retire from the lottery with the prize which he has drawn, but, in future ages, his honour will be only in proportion to his labours. If, on the contrary, he rushes again into the lists, he is sure to be judged with severity proportioned to the former favour of the public. If he be daunted by a bad reception on this second occasion, he may again become a stranger to the arena. If, on the contrary, he can keep his ground, and stand the shuttlecock's fate, of being struck up and down, he will probably, at length, hold with some certainty the level in public opinion which he may be found to deserve; and he may perhaps boast of arresting the general attention, in the same manner as the Bachelor Samson Carrasco of fixing the weathercock La Giralda of Seville for weeks, months, or years, that is, for as long as the wind shall uniformly blow from one quarter.[4] To this degree of popularity the Author had the hardihood to aspire, while, in order to attain it, he assumed the daring resolution to keep himself in the view of the public by frequent appearances before them.

It must be added, that the Author's incognito gave him the greater courage to renew his attempts to please the public, and an advantage similar to that which Jack the Giant-killer received from his coat of darkness. In sending the *Abbot* forth so soon after the *Monastery*, he had used the well-known practice recommended by Bassanio:

> In my school-days, when I had lost one shaft,
> I shot another of the self-same flight,
> The self-same way, with more advised watch,
> To find the other forth.[5]

And, to continue the simile, his shafts, like those of the Lesser Ajax, were discharged more readily that the archer was as inaccessible to criticism, personally speaking, as the Grecian archer under his brother's sevenfold shield.[6]

Should the reader desire to know upon what principles the *Abbot* was expected to amend the fortune of the *Monastery*, I have first to request his attention to the Introductory Epistle addressed to the imaginary Captain Clutterbuck—a mode by which, like his predecessors in this walk of fiction, the real Author makes one of his *dramatis personae* the means of communicating his own sentiments to the public, somewhat more artifically than by a direct address to the readers. A pleasing French writer of fairy tales, Monsieur Pajon, author of the *History of Prince Soly*, has set a diverting example of the same machinery, where he introduces the presiding Genius of the land of Romance conversing with one of the personages of the tale.[7]

In this Introductory Epistle, the Author communicates, in confidence, to Captain Clutterbuck his sense that the White Lady had not met the taste of the times, and his reason for withdrawing her from the scene. The Author did not deem it equally necessary to be candid respecting another alteration. The *Monastery* was designed, at first, to have contained some supernatural agency, arising out of the fact that Melrose had been the place of deposit of the great Robert Bruce's heart. The writer shrunk, however, from filling up, in this particular, the sketch as it was originally traced; nor did he venture to resume, in the continuation, the subject which he had left unattempted in the original work. Thus, the incident of the discovery of the heart, which occupies the greater part of the Introduction to the *Monastery*, is a mystery unnecessarily introduced, and which remains at last very imperfectly explained. In this particular, I was happy to shroud myself by the example of the author of *Caleb Williams*,[8] who never condescends to inform us of the actual contents of that iron chest which makes such a figure in his interesting work, and gives the name to Mr. Colman's drama.[9]

The public had some claim to inquire into this matter, but it seemed indifferent policy in the Author to give the explanation. For, whatever praise may be due to the ingenuity which brings to a general combination all the loose threads of a narrative, like the knitter at the finishing of her stocking, I am greatly deceived if in many cases a superior advantage is not attained by the air of reality which the deficiency of explanation attaches to a work written on a different system. In life itself, many things befall every mortal of which the individual never knows the real cause or origin; and were we to point out the most marked distinction between a real and a fictitious narrative, we would say, that the former, in reference to the remote causes of the events it relates, is obscure, doubtful, and mysterious; whereas, in the latter case, it is a part of the author's duty to afford satisfactory details upon the causes of the separate events he has recorded, and, in a word, to account for everything. The reader, like Mungo in the *Padlock*, will not be satisfied with hearing what he is not made fully to comprehend.[10]

I omitted, therefore, in the Introduction to the *Abbot*, any attempt to explain the previous story or to apologise for unintelligibility.

Neither would it have been prudent to have endeavoured to proclaim, in the Introduction to the *Abbot*, the real spring by which I hoped it might attract a greater degree of interest than its immediate predecessor. A taking title, or the announcement of a popular subject, is a recipe for success much in favour with booksellers, but which authors will not always find efficacious. The cause is worth a moment's examination.

There occur in every country some peculiar historical characters, which are, like a spell or charm, sovereign to excite curiosity and attract attention, since every one in the slightest degree interested in the land which they belong to has heard much of them, and longs to hear more. A tale turning on the fortunes of Alfred or Elizabeth in England, or of Wallace or Bruce in Scotland, is sure by the very announcement to excite public curiosity to a considerable degree, and ensure the publisher's being relieved of the greater part of an impression, even before the contents of the work are known. This is of the last importance to the bookseller, who is at once, to use a technical phrase, 'brought home,' all his outlay being repaid. But it is a different case with the author, since it cannot be denied that we are apt to feel least satisfied with the works of which we have been induced, by titles and laudatory advertisements, to entertain exaggerated expectations. The intention of the work has been anticipated, and misconceived or misrepresented, and although the difficulty of executing the work again reminds us of Hotspur's task of 'o'erwalking a current roaring loud,'[11] yet the adventurer must look for more ridicule if he fails than applause if he executes his undertaking.

Notwithstanding a risk which should make authors pause ere they adopt a theme which, exciting general interest and curiosity, is often the preparative for disappointment, yet it would be an injudicious regulation which should deter the poet or painter from attempting to introduce historical portraits merely from the difficulty of executing the task in a satisfactory manner. Something must be trusted to the generous impulse, which often thrusts an artist upon feats of which he knows the difficulty, while he trusts courage and exertion may afford the means of surmounting it.

It is especially when he is sensible of losing ground with the public that an author may be justified in using with address such selection of subject or title as is most likely to procure a rehearing. It was with these feelings of hope and apprehension that I ventured to awaken, in a work of fiction, the memory of Queen

Mary, so interesting by her wit, her beauty, her misfortunes, and the mystery which still does, and probably always will, overhang her history. In doing so, I was aware that failure would be a conclusive disaster, so that my task was something like that of an enchanter who raises a spirit over whom he is uncertain of possessing an effectual control; and I naturally paid attention to such principles of composition as I conceived were best suited to the historical novel.

Enough has been already said to explain the purpose of composing the *Abbot*. The historical references are, as usual, explained in the notes. That which relates to Queen Mary's escape from Lochleven Castle is a more minute account of that romantic adventure than is to be found in the histories of the period.

ABBOTSFORD, 1st *January* 1831.

KENILWORTH

A certain degree of success, real or supposed, in the delineation of Queen Mary, naturally induced the Author to attempt something similar respecting 'her sister and her foe,' the celebrated Elizabeth. He will not, however, pretend to have approached the task with the same feelings; for the candid Robertson himself confesses having felt the prejudices with which a Scottishman is tempted to regard the subject;[1] and what so liberal a historian avows, a poor romance-writer dares not disown. But he hopes the influence of a prejudice almost as natural to him as his native air will not be found to have greatly affected the sketch he has attempted of England's Elizabeth. I have endeavoured to describe her as at once a high-minded sovereign and a female of passionate feelings, hesitating betwixt the sense of her rank and the duty she owed her subjects on the one hand, and on the other her attachment to a nobleman who, in external qualifications at least, amply merited her favour. The interest of the story is thrown upon that period when the sudden death of the first Countess of Leicester seemed to open to the ambition of her husband the opportunity of sharing the crown of his sovereign.

It is possible that slander, which very seldom favours the memories of persons in exalted stations, may have blackened the character of Leicester with darker shades than really belonged to it. But the almost general voice of the times attached the most foul suspicions to the death of the unfortunate countess, more especially as it took place so very opportunely for the indulgence of her lover's ambition. If we can trust Ashmole's *Antiquities of Berkshire*, there was but too much ground for the traditions which charge Leicester with the murder of his wife.[2]

. . . .

The reader will find I have borrowed several incidents as well as names* from Ashmole and the more early authorities; but my first acquaintance with the history was through the more pleasing medium of verse. There is a period in youth when the mere power of numbers has a more strong effect on ear and imagination than in more advanced life. At this season of immature taste the Author was greatly delighted with the poems of Mickle and Langhorne, poets who, though by no means deficient in the higher branches of their art, were eminent for their powers of verbal melody above most who have practised this department of poetry.[3] One of those pieces of Mickle, which the Author was particularly pleased with, is a ballad, or rather a species of elegy, on the subject of Cumnor Hall, which, with others by the same author, were to be found in Evans's *Ancient Ballads* (vol. iv. p. 130), to which work Mickle made liberal contributions. The first stanza especially had a peculiar species of enchantment for the youthful ear of the Author, the force of which is not even now entirely spent; some others are sufficiently prosaic.

. . . .

ABBOTSFORD, 1*st March* 1831.

---

*See Lockhart's *Life of Scott*, vol. vi. pp. 266, 294.

THE PIRATE

This brief preface may begin like the tale of the *Ancient Mariner*, since it was on shipboard that the Author acquired the very moderate degree of local knowledge and information, both of people and scenery, which he has endeavoured to embody in the romance of the *Pirate*.

In the summer and autumn of 1814, the Author was invited to join a party of Commissioners for the Northern Lighthouse Service, who proposed making a voyage round the coast of Scotland, and through its various groups of islands, chiefly for the purpose of seeing the condition of the many lighthouses under their direction—edifices so important whether regarding them as benevolent or political institutions. Among the commissioners who manage this important public concern, the sheriff of each county of Scotland which borders on the sea holds *ex officio* a place at the Board. These gentlemen act in every respect gratuitously, but have the use of an armed yacht, well found and fitted up, when they choose to visit the lighthouses. An excellent engineer, Mr. Robert Stevenson, is attached to the Board, to afford the benefit of his professional advice. The Author accompanied this expedition as a guest; for Selkirkshire, though it calls him sheriff, has not, like the kingdom of Bohemia in Corporal Trim's story,[1] a seaport in its circuit, nor its magistrate, of course, any place at the Board of Commissioners—a circumstance of little consequence

where all were old and intimate friends, bred to the same profession, and disposed to accommodate each other in every possible manner.

The nature of the important business which was the principal
purpose of the voyage was connected with the amusement of
visiting the leading objects of a traveller's curiosity; for the wild
cape or formidable shelve which requires to be marked out by a
lighthouse is generally at no great distance from the most
magnificent scenery of rocks, caves, and billows. Our time, too,
was at our own disposal, and, as most of us were fresh-water
sailors, we could at any time make a fair wind out of a foul one,
and run before the gale in quest of some object of curiosity which
lay under our lee.

With these purposes of public utility, and some personal
amusement, in view, we left the port of Leith on the 26th July
1814, ran along the east coast of Scotland, viewing its different
curiosities, stood over to Zetland and Orkney, where we were
some time detained by the wonders of a country which displayed
so much that was new to us; and having seen what was curious in
the Ultima Thule of the ancients, where the sun hardly thought it
worth while to go to bed, since his rising was at this season so early,
we doubled the extreme northern termination of Scotland, and
took a rapid survey of the Hebrides, where we found many
friends. There, that our little expedition might not want the
dignity of danger, we were favoured with a distant glimpse of
what was said to be an American cruiser, and had opportunity to
consider what a pretty figure we should have made had the
voyage ended in our being carried captive to the United States.
After visiting the romantic shores of Morven and the vicinity of
Oban, we made a run to the coast of Ireland and visited the
Giant's Causeway, that we might compare it with Staffa, which we
had surveyed in our course. At length, about the middle of
September, we ended our voyage in the Clyde, at the port of
Greenock.*

And thus terminated our pleasant tour, to which our equip-
ment gave unusual facilities, as the ship's company could form a
strong boat's crew, independent of those who might be left on

---

*[See Lockhart's *Life*, vol. iv. pp. 180–370.]

board the vessel, which permitted us the freedom to land wherever our curiosity carried us. Let me add, while reviewing for a moment a sunny portion of my life, that among the six or seven friends who performed this voyage together, some of them doubtless of different tastes and pursuits, and remaining for several weeks on board a small vessel, there never occurred the slightest dispute or disagreement, each seeming anxious to submit his own particular wishes to those of his friends. By this mutual accommodation all the purposes of our little expedition were attained, while for a time we might have adopted the lines of Allan Cunningham's fine sea-song,

> The world of waters was our home,
> And merry men were we![2]

But sorrow mixes her memorials with the purest remembrances of pleasure. On returning from the voyage which had proved so satisfactory, I found that fate had deprived her country most unexpectedly of a lady qualified to adorn the high rank which she held, and who had long admitted me to a share of her friendship.*[3] The subsequent loss of one of those comrades who made up the party, and he the most intimate friend I had in the world,† casts also its shade on recollections which, but for these embitterments, would be otherwise so pleasing.

I may here briefly observe, that my business in this voyage, so far as I could be said to have any, was to endeavour to discover some localities which might be useful in the *Lord of the Isles*, a poem

---

*Harriet Katherine, Duchess of Buccleuch, died 24th August 1814 (*Laing*).

†William Erskine of Kinedder, son of an Episcopal minister in Perthshire, was educated for the legal profession, and passed advocate 3d July 1790. He was appointed Sheriff-Depute of Orkney 6th June 1809, and in that capacity was accompanied by Scott in the Lighthouse voyage round the coast. He was raised to the bench, and took his seat as Lord Kinedder 29th January 1822. Unfortunately, he did not long enjoy this honour, as he died unexpectedly on the 14th of August following, to the great grief of Sir Walter, who at this very time was wholly occupied with the arrangements connected with George IV's visit to Edinburgh. Lord Kinedder, to whom Scott had from boyhood been deeply attached, was a most amiable and accomplished man.

In 1788, when the *Ode on the Popular Superstitions of the Highlands* was first published (which the Wartons thought superior to the other works of Collins, but which Dr. Johnson says, 'no search has yet found'), Mr. Erskine wrote several supplementary stanzas, intended to commemorate some Scottish superstitions omitted by Collins. These verses first appeared in the *Edinburgh Magazine* for April 1788 (*Laing*).

with which I was then threatening the public, and [which] was afterwards printed without attaining remarkable success. But as at the same time the anonymous novel of *Waverley* was making its way to popularity, I already augured the possibility of a second effort in this department of literature, and I saw much in the wild islands of the Orkneys and Zetland which I judged might be made in the highest degree interesting, should these isles ever become the scene of a narrative of fictitious events. I learned the history of Gow the pirate from an old sibyl, whose principal subsistence was by a trade in favourable winds, which she sold to mariners at Stromness. Nothing could be more interesting than the kindness and hospitality of the gentlemen of Zetland, which was to me the more affecting as several of them had been friends and correspondents of my father.

I was induced to go a generation or two farther back to find materials from which I might trace the features of the old Norwegian udaller, the Scottish gentry having in general occupied the place of that primitive race, and their language and peculiarities of manner having entirely disappeared. The only difference now to be observed betwixt the gentry of these islands and those of Scotland in general is, that the wealth and property is more equally divided among our more northern countrymen, and that there exists among the resident proprietors no men of very great wealth, whose display of its luxuries might render the others discontented with their own lot. From the same cause of general equality of fortunes, and the cheapness of living which is its natural consequence, I found the officers of a veteran regiment who had maintained the garrison at Fort Charlotte, in Lerwick, discomposed at the idea of being recalled from a country where their pay, however inadequate to the expenses of a capital, was fully adequate to their wants, and it was singular to hear natives of merry England herself regretting their approaching departure from the melancholy isles of the Ultima Thule.

Such are the trivial particulars attending the origin of that publication, which took place several years later than the agreeable journey from which it took its rise.

The state of manners which I have introduced in the romance was necessarily in a great degree imaginary, though founded in some measure on slight hints, which, showing what was, seemed to give reasonable indication of what must once have been, the tone of the society in these sequestered but interesting islands.

In one respect I was judged somewhat hastily, perhaps, when the character of Norna was pronounced by the critics a mere copy of Meg Merrilies. That I had fallen short of what I wished and desired to express is unquestionable, otherwise my object could not have been so widely mistaken; nor can I yet think that any person who will take the trouble of reading the *Pirate* with some attention can fail to trace in Norna—the victim of remorse and insanity, and the dupe of her own imposture, her mind, too, flooded with all the wild literature and extravagant superstitions of the North—something distinct from the Dumfriesshire gipsy, whose pretensions to supernatural powers are not beyond those of a Norwood Prophetess. The foundations of such a character may be perhaps traced, though it be too true that the necessary superstructure cannot have been raised upon them, otherwise these remarks would have been unnecessary. There is also great improbability in the statement of Norna's possessing power and opportunity to impress on others that belief in her supernatural gifts which distracted her own mind. Yet, amid a very credulous and ignorant population, it is astonishing what success may be attained by an imposter who is, at the same time, an enthusiast. It is such as to remind us of the couplet which assures us that

> The pleasure is as great
> In being cheated as to cheat.[4]

Indeed, as I have observed elsewhere, the professed explanation of a tale, where appearances or incidents of a supernatural character are referred to natural causes, has often, in the winding up of the story, a degree of improbability almost equal to an absolute goblin narrative. Even the genius of Mrs. Radcliffe could not always surmount this difficulty.

ABBOTSFORD, 1*st May* 1831.

THE FORTUNES OF NIGEL

But why should lordlings all our praise engross?
Rise, honest muse, and sing the Man of Ross.

POPE.[1]

Having, in the tale of the *Heart of Midlothian*, succeeded in some degree in awakening an interest in behalf of one devoid of those accomplishments which belong to a heroine almost by right, I was next tempted to choose a hero upon the same unpromising plan; and as worth of character, goodness of heart, and rectitude of principle were necessary to one who laid no claim to high birth, romantic sensibility, or any of the usual accomplishments of those who strut through the pages of this sort of composition, I made free with the name of a person who has left the most magnificent proofs of his benevolence and charity that the capital of Scotland has to display.

To the Scottish reader little more need be said than that the man alluded to is George Heriot. But for those south of the Tweed it may be necessary to add, that the person so named was a wealthy citizen of Edinburgh, and the king's goldsmith, who followed James to the English capital, and was so successful in his profession as to die, in 1624, extremely wealthy for that period. He had no children; and after making a full provision for such relations as might have claims upon him, he left the residue of his fortune to establish an hospital, in which the sons of Edinburgh freemen are gratuitously brought up and educated for the station

177

to which their talents may recommend them, and are finally enabled to enter life under respectable auspices. The hospital in which this charity is maintained is a noble quadrangle of the Gothic order, and as ornamental to the city as a building as the manner in which the youths are provided for and educated renders it useful to the community as an institution. To the honour of those who have the management (the magistrates and clergy of Edinburgh), the funds of the hospital have increased so much under their care that it now supports and educates one hundred and thirty youths annually, many of whom have done honour to their country in different situations.

The founder of such a charity as this may be reasonably supposed to have walked through life with a steady pace and an observant eye, neglecting no opportunity of assisting those who were not possessed of the experience necessary for their own guidance. In supposing his efforts directed to the benefit of a young nobleman, misguided by the aristocratic haughtiness of his own time, and the prevailing tone of selfish luxury which seems more peculiar to ours, as well as the seductions of pleasure which are predominant in all, some amusement, or even some advantage, might, I thought, be derived from the manner in which I might bring the exertions of this civic mentor to bear in his pupil's behalf. I am, I own, no great believer in the moral utility to be derived from fictitious compositions; yet, if in any case a word spoken in season may be of advantage to a young person, it must surely be when it called upon him to attend to the voice of principle and self-denial, instead of that of precipitate passion. I could not, indeed, hope or expect to represent my prudent and benevolent citizen in a point of view so interesting as that of the peasant girl, who nobly sacrificed her family affections to the integrity of her moral character. Still, however, something I hoped might be done not altogether unworthy the fame which George Heriot has secured by the lasting benefits he has bestowed on his country.

It appeared likely that, out of this simple plot, I might weave something attractive; because the reign of James I., in which George Heriot flourished, gave unbounded scope to invention in the fable, while at the same time it afforded greater variety and discrimination of character than could, with historical consistency, have been introduced, if the scene had been laid a century earlier. Lady Mary Wortley Montagu has said, with equal truth and taste, that the most romantic region of every country is that where the mountains unite themselves with the plains or lowlands.[2] For similar reasons, it may be in like manner said that the most picturesque period of history is that when the ancient rough and wild manners of a barbarous age are just becoming innovated upon and contrasted by the illumination of increased or revived learning and the instructions of renewed or reformed religion. The strong contrast produced by the opposition of ancient manners to those which are gradually subduing them affords the lights and shadows necessary to give effect to a fictitious narrative; and while such a period entitles the author to introduce incidents of a marvellous and improbable character, as arising out of the turbulent independence and ferocity, belonging to old habits of violence, still influencing the manners of a people who had been so lately in a barbarous state; yet, on the other hand, the characters and sentiments of many of the actors may, with the utmost probability, be described with great variety of shading and delineation, which belongs to the newer and more improved period, of which the world has but lately received the light.

The reign of James I. of England possessed this advantage in a peculiar degree. Some beams of chivalry, although its planet had been for some time set, continued to animate and gild the horizon, and although probably no one acted precisely on its Quixotic dictates, men and women still talked the chivalrous language of Sir Philip Sidney's *Arcadia*,[3] and the ceremonial of the tilt-yard was yet exhibited, though it now only flourished as a *place de carrousel*. Here and there a high-spirited Knight of the Bath (witness the too scrupulous Lord Herbert of Cherbury) was found devoted enough to the vows he had taken to imagine himself obliged to compel, by the sword's point, a fellow-knight or squire to restore the top-knot of ribbon which he had stolen from a fair damsel;* but yet, while men were taking each other's lives on such punctilios of honour, the hour was already arrived when Bacon

---

*See Lord Herbert of Cherbury's *Memoirs*.

was about to teach the world that they were no longer to reason from authority to fact, but to establish truth by advancing from fact to fact, till they fixed an indisputable authority, not from hypothesis, but from experiment.

The state of society in the reign of James I. was also strangely disturbed, and the license of a part of the community was perpetually giving rise to acts of blood and violence. The bravo of the Queen's day, of whom Shakspeare has given us so many varieties, as Bardolph, Nym, Pistol, Peto, and the other companions of Falstaff, men who had their humours, or their particular turn of extravaganza, had, since the commencement of the Low Country wars, given way to a race of sworders, who used the rapier and dagger instead of the far less dangerous sword and buckler; so that a historian says on this subject—

> That private quarrels were nourished, but especially between the Scots and the English, and duels in every street maintained; divers sects and particular titles passed unpunished nor regarded, as the sect of the roaring boys, bonaventors, bravadors, quarterors, and such-like, being persons prodigal and of great expense, when, having run themselves into debt, were constrained to run into factions, to defend themselves from danger of the law. These received maintenance from divers of the nobility . . . and the citizens through lasciviousness consuming their estates, it was like that their number [of these desperadoes] would rather increase than diminish; and under these pretences they entered into many desperate enterprises, and scarce any durst walk the streets after nine at night.

The same authority assures us farther that—

> Ancient gentlemen, that had left their inheritance whole and well furnished with goods and chattels (having thereupon kept good houses) unto their sons, lived to see part consumed in riot and excess, and the rest in possibility to be utterly lost; the holy state of matrimony made but a May-game, by which means divers private families have been subverted, brothel houses much frequented, and even great persons prostituting their bodies to the intent to satisfy their lusts, and consume their substance in lascivious appetites. And of all sorts, such knights or gentlemen, as either through pride or prodigality had consumed their substance, repairing to the city, and to the intent to consume their virtues also, lived dissolute lives; and many of their ladies and

daughters, to the intent to maintain themselves according to their dignity, prostitute their bodies in shameful manner; ale-houses, dicing-houses, taverns, and places of vice and iniquity beyond measure abounding in most places.*

Nor is it only in the pages of a Puritanical, perhaps a satirical, writer that we find so shocking and disgusting a picture of the coarseness of the beginning of the 17th century. On the contrary, in all the comedies of the age, the principal character for gaiety and wit is a young heir who has totally altered the establishment of the father to whom he has succeeded, and, to use the old simile, who resembles a fountain which plays off in idleness and extravagance the wealth which its careful parents painfully had assembled in hidden reservoirs.

And yet, while that spirit of general extravagance seemed at work over a whole kingdom, another and very different sort of men were gradually forming the staid and resolved characters which afterwards displayed themselves during the civil wars, and powerfully regulated and affected the character of the whole English nation, until, rushing from one extreme to another, they sunk in a gloomy fanaticism the splendid traces of the reviving fine arts.

From the quotations which I have produced, the selfish and disgusting conduct of Lord Dalgarno will not perhaps appear overstrained; nor will the scenes in Whitefriars and places of similar resort seem too highly coloured. This indeed is far from being the case. It was in James I.'s reign that vice first appeared affecting the better classes in its gross and undisguised depravity. The entertainments and amusements of Elizabeth's time had an air of that decent restraint which became the court of a maiden sovereign; and in that earlier period, to use the words of Burke, vice lost half its evil by being deprived of all its grossness.[4] In James's reign, on the contrary, the coarsest pleasures were publicly and unlimitedly indulged, since, according to Sir John Harrington, the men wallowed in beastly delights; and even ladies abandoned their delicacy and rolled about in intoxication. After a ludicrous account of a masque, in which the actors had got drunk and behaved themselves accordingly, he adds: 'I have

---

*Narrative History of the First Fourteen Years of King James's Reign, in Somers's *Tracts*, edited by Scott, vol. ii. p. 266.

much marvelled at these strange pageantries, and they do bring to my remembrance what passed of this sort in our Queen's days, of which I was sometime an humble presenter and assistant; but I never did see such lack of good order, discretion, and sobriety as I have now done . . . . The gunpowder fright is got out of all our heads, and we are going on hereabouts as if the devil was contriving every man should blow up himself by wild riot, excess, and devastation of time and temperance. The great ladies do go well masqued; and, indeed, it be the only show of their modesty to conceal their countenance; but alack, they meet with such countenance to uphold their strange doings, that I marvel not at aught that happens.'

Such being the state of the court, coarse sensuality brought along with it its ordinary companion, a brutal degree of undisguised selfishness, destructive alike of philanthropy and good-breeding; both of which, in their several spheres, depend upon the regard paid by each individual to the interest as well as the feelings of others. It is in such a time that the heartless and shameless man of wealth and power may, like the supposed Lord Dalgarno, brazen out the shame of his villainies, and affect to triumph in their consequences, so long as they were personally advantageous to his own pleasures or profit.

Alsatia is elsewhere explained as a cant name for Whitefriars, which, possessing certain privileges of sanctuary, became for that reason a nest of those mischievous characters who were generally obnoxious to the law. These privileges were derived from its having been an establishment of the Carmelites, or White Friars, founded, says Stow, in his *Survey of London*, by Sir Richard Grey, in 1241.[5] Edward I. gave them a plot of ground in Fleet Street, to build their church upon. The edifice, then erected, was rebuilt by Courtney, Earl of Devonshire, in the reign of Edward III. In the time of the Reformation the place retained its immunities as a sanctuary, and James I. confirmed and added to them by a charter in 1608. Shadwell was the first author who made some literary use of Whitefriars, in his play of the *Squire of Alsatia*, which turns upon the plot of the *Adelphi* of Terence.[6]

In this old play, two men of fortune, brothers, educate two young men, sons to the one and nephews to the other, each under his own separate system of rigour and indulgence. The elder of the subjects of this experiment, who has been very rigidly brought up, falls at once into all the vices of the town, is debauched by the cheats and bullies of Whitefriars, and, in a word, becomes the Squire of Alsatia. The poet gives, as the natural and congenial inhabitants of the place, such characters as the reader will find in Note 3 (p. 448). The play, as we learn from the dedication to the Earl of Dorset and Middlesex, was succcessful above the author's expectations, 'no comedy for these many years having filled the theatre so long together. And I had the great honour,' continues Shadwell, 'to find so many friends, that the house was never so full since it was built as upon the third day of this play, and vast numbers went away that could not be admitted.'* From the *Squire of Alsatia* the Author derived some few hints, and learned the footing on which the bullies and thieves of the sanctuary stood with their neighbours, the fiery young students of the Temple, of which some intimation is given in the dramatic piece.

Such are the materials to which the Author stands indebted for the composition of the *Fortunes of Nigel*, a novel which may be perhaps one of those that are more amusing on a second perusal than when read a first time for the sake of the story, the incidents of which are few and meagre.

The Introductory Epistle is written, in Lucio's phrase, 'according to the trick,' and would never have appeared had the writer meditated making his avowal of the work.† As it is the privilege of a masque or incognito to speak in a feigned voice and assumed character, the Author attempted, while in disguise, some liberties of the same sort; and while he continues to plead upon the various excuses which the Introduction contains, the present acknowledgment must serve as an apology for a species of 'hoity toity, whisky frisky' pertness of manner, which, in his avowed character, the Author should have considered as a departure from the rules of civility and good taste.

ABBOTSFORD, 1st *July* 1831.

---

*Dedication to the *Squire of Alsatia*. Shadwell's *Works*, vol. iv.
†[See Lockhart's *Life*, vol. vi. p. 407 and vol. vii. p. 26.]

PEVERIL OF THE PEAK

If I had valued my own reputation, as it is said I ought in prudence to have done, I might have now drawn a line, and remained for life, or (who knows?) perhaps for some years after death, the 'ingenious author of *Waverley.*' I was not, however, more desirous of this sort of immortality, which might have lasted some twenty or thirty years, than Falstaff of the embowelling which was promised him after the field of Shrewsbury, by his patron the Prince of Wales. 'Embowel'd? If you embowel me to-day, you may powder and eat me to-morrow!'[1]

If my occupation as a romancer were taken from me, I felt I should have at a late hour in life to find me out another; when I could hardly expect to acquire those new tricks which are proverbially said not to be learned by those dogs who are getting old. Besides, I had yet to learn from the public that my intrusions were disagreeable; and while I was endured with some patience, I felt I had all the reputation which I greatly coveted. My memory was well stored, both with historical, local, and traditional notices, and I had become almost as licensed a plague to the public as the well-remembered beggar of the ward, whom men distinguish by their favour, perhaps for no better reason than that they had been in the habit of giving him alms, as a part of the business of their daily promenade. The general fact is undeniable: all men grow old, all men must wear out; but men of ordinary wisdom, however aware of the general fact, are unwilling to admit in their own case any special instances of failure. Indeed, they can hardly be expected themselves to distinguish the effects of the Archbishop of Granada's apoplexy,[2] and are not unwilling to pass over in their composition, as instances of mere carelessness or bad luck, what others may consider as symptoms of mortal decay. I had no choice save that of absolutely laying aside the pen, the use of which at my time of life was become a habit, or to continue its vagaries, until the public should let me plainly understand they would no more of me—a hint which I was not unlikely to meet with, and which I was determined to take without waiting for a repetition. This hint, that the reader may plainly understand me, I was determined to take when the publication of a new Waverley novel should not be the subject of some attention in the literary world.*

An accidental circumstance decided my choice of a subject for the present work. It was now several years since my immediate younger brother, Thomas Scott, already mentioned in these notes, had resided for two or three seasons in the Isle of Man, and having access to the registers of that singular territory, had copied many of them, which he subjected to my perusal. These papers were put into my hands while my brother had thoughts of making some literary use of them, I do not well remember what; but he never came to any decision on that head, and grew tired of the task of transcription. The papers, I suppose, were lost in the course of a military man's life. The tenor of them, that is, of the most remarkable, remained engraved on the memory of the Author.

The interesting and romantic story of William Christian especially struck my fancy. I found the same individual, as well as his father, particularly noticed in some memorials of the island, preserved by the Earl of Derby, and published in Dr. Peck's *Desiderata Curiosa*.[3] This gentleman was the son of Edward, formerly governor of the island; and William himself was afterwards one of its two Dempsters, or supreme judges. Both father and son embraced the party of the islanders, and contested some feudal rights claimed by the Earl of Derby as king of the island. When the earl had suffered death at Bolton-le-Moors, Captain Christian placed himself at the head of the Roundheads, if they

---

*[See Lockhart's *Life of Scott*, vol. vii. pp. 117–126.]

might be so called, and found the means of holding communication with a fleet sent by the Parliament. The island was surrendered to the Parliament by the insurgent Manxmen. The high-spirited countess and her son were arrested and cast into prison, where they were long detained, and very indifferently treated. When the restoration took place, the countess, or by title the queen-dowager of the island, seized upon William Dhône, or Fair-haired William, as William Christian was termed, and caused him to be tried and executed, according to the laws of the island, for having dethroned his liege mistress and imprisoned her and her family. Romancers, and readers of romance, will generally allow that the fate of Christian, and the contrast of his character with that of the high-minded but vindictive Countess of Derby, famous during the civil wars for her valiant defence of Latham House, contained the essence of an interesting tale. I have, however, dwelt little either on the death of William Christian or on the manner in which Charles II. viewed that stretch of feudal power, and the heavy fine which he imposed upon the Derby estates for that stretch of jurisdiction of which the countess had been guilty. Far less have I given any opinion on the justice or guilt of that action, which is to this day judged of by the people of the island as they happen to be connected with the sufferer, or perhaps as they may look back with the eyes of favour upon the Cavaliers or Roundheads of those contentious days. I do not conceive that I have done injury to the memory of this gentleman or any of his descendants in his person; at the same time I have most willingly given his representative an opportunity of stating in this edition of the Novel what he thinks necessary for the vindication of his ancestor, and the reader will find the exposition in the Notices, for which Mr. Christian desires admission. I could do no less, considering the polite and gentlemanlike manner in which he stated feelings concerning his ancestry, to which a Scotsman can hardly be supposed to be indifferent.

In another respect, Mr. Christian with justice complains, that Edward Christian, described in the romance as the brother of the gentleman executed in consequence of the countess's arbitrary act of authority, is pourtrayed as a wretch of unbounded depravity, having only ingenuity and courage to rescue him from abhorrence, as well as hatred. Any personal allusion was entirely undesigned on the part of the Author. The Edward Christian of the tale is a mere creature of the imagination. Commentators have naturally enough identified him with a brother of William Christian, named Edward, who died in prison after being confined seven or eight years in Peel Castle, in the year 1650. Of him I had no access to know anything; and as I was not aware that such a person had existed, I could hardly be said to have traduced his character. It is sufficient for my justification that there lived at the period of my story a person named Edward Christian, 'with whom connected, or by whom begot,' I am a perfect stranger, but who we know to have been engaged in such actions as may imply his having been guilty of anything bad. The fact is, that upon the 25th June 1680, Thomas Blood, the famous crown-stealer, Edward Christian, Arthur O'Brien, and others, were found guilty of being concerned in a conspiracy for taking away the life and character of the celebrated Duke of Buckingham; but that this Edward was the same with the brother of William Christian is impossible, since that brother died in 1650; nor would I have used his christened name of Edward, had I supposed there was a chance of its being connected with any existing family. These genealogical matters are fully illustrated in the notes to the Appendix.

I ought to have mentioned in the former editions of this romance, that Charlotte de la Tremouille, Countess of Derby, represented as a Catholic, was, in fact, a French Protestant. For misrepresenting the noble dame in this manner, I have only Lucio's excuse: 'I spoke according to the trick.'[4] In a story where the greater part is avowedly fiction, the author is at liberty to introduce such variations from actual fact as his plot requires, or which are calculated to enhance it; in which predicament the religion of the Countess of Derby, during the Popish Plot, appeared to fall. If I have over-estimated a romancer's privileges and immunities, I am afraid this is not the only, nor most important, case in which I have done so. To speak big words, the heroic countess has far less grounds for an action of scandal than the memory of Virgil might be liable to for his posthumous scandal of Dido.

The character of Fenella, which, from its peculiarity, made a favourable impression on the public, was far from being original.

The fine sketch of Mignon in *Wilhelm Meister's Lehrjahre*, a celebrated work from the pen of Goethe, gave the idea of such a being.[5] But the copy will be found greatly different from my great prototype; nor can I be accused of borrowing anything, save the general idea, from an author, the honour of his own country and an example to the authors of other kingdoms, to whom all must be proud to own an obligation.

Family tradition supplied me with two circumstances, which are somewhat analogous to that in question. The first is an account of a lawsuit, taken from a Scottish report of adjudged cases, quoted in Note 16, p. 601. The other—of which the editor has no reason to doubt, having often heard it from those who were witnesses of the fact—relates to the power of a female in keeping a secret, sarcastically said to be impossible, even when that secret refers to the exercise of her tongue.

In the middle of the 18th century, a female wanderer came to the door of Mr. Robert Scott, grandfather of the present author, an opulent farmer in Roxburghshire, and made signs that she desired shelter for the night, which, according to the custom of the time, was readily granted. The next day the country was covered with snow, and the departure of the wanderer was rendered impossible. She remained for many days, her maintenance adding little to the expense of a considerable household; and by the time that the weather grew milder, she had learned to hold intercourse by signs with the household around her, and could intimate to them that she was desirous of staying where she was, and working at the wheel and other employment, to compensate for her food. This was a compact not unfrequent at that time, and the dumb woman entered upon her thrift, and proved a useful member of the patriarchal household. She was a good spinner, knitter, carder, and so forth, but her excellence lay in attending to the feeding and bringing up the domestic poultry. Her mode of whistling to call them together was so peculiarly elfish and shrill, that it was thought by those who heard it more like that of a fairy than a human being.

In this manner she lived three or four years, nor was there the slightest idea entertained in the family that she was other than the mute and deprived person she had always appeared. But in a moment of surprise she dropped the mask which she had worn so long.

It chanced upon a Sunday that the whole inhabitants of the houschold were at church excepting Dumb Lizzie, whose infirmity was supposed to render her incapable of profiting by divine service, and who therefore stayed at home to take charge of the house. It happened that, as she was sitting in the kitchen, a mischievous shepherd-boy, instead of looking after his flock on the lea, as was his duty, slunk into the house to see what he could pick up, or perhaps out of mere curiosity. Being tempted by something which was in his eyes a nicety, he put forth his hand unseen, as he conceived, to appropriate it. The dumb woman came suddenly upon him, and in the surprise forgot her part, and exclaimed, in loud Scotch and with distinct articulation, 'Ah, you little deevil's limb!' The boy, terrified more by the character of the person who rebuked him than by the mere circumstance of having been taken in the insignificant offence, fled in great dismay to the church, to carry the miraculous news that the dumb woman had found her tongue.

The family returned home in great surprise, but found that their inmate had relapsed into her usual mute condition, would communicate with them only by signs, and in that manner denied positively what the boy affirmed.

From this time confidence was broken betwixt the other inmates of the family and their dumb, or rather silent, guest. Traps were laid for the supposed imposter, all of which she skilfully eluded; firearms were often suddenly discharged near her, but never on such occasions was she seen to start. It seems probable, however, that Lizzie grew tired of all this mistrust, for she one morning disappeared as she came, without any ceremony of leave-taking.

She was seen, it is said, upon the other side of the English Border, in perfect possession of her speech. Whether this was exactly the case or not, my informers were no way anxious in inquiring, nor am I able to authenticate the fact. The shepherd-boy lived to be a man, and always averred that she had spoken distinctly to him. What could be the woman's reason for persevering so long in a disguise as unnecessary as it was severe could never be guessed, and was perhaps the consequence of a certain aberration of the mind. I can only add, that I have every reason to believe the tale to be perfectly authentic, so far as it is here given, and it may serve to parallel the supposed case of Fenella.

ABBOTSFORD, 1st July 1831.

QUENTIN DURWARD

The scene of this romance is laid in the 15th century, when the feudal system, which had been the sinews and nerves of national defence, and the spirit of chivalry, by which, as by a vivifying soul, that system was animated, began to be innovated upon and abandoned by those grosser characters who centred their sum of happiness in procuring the personal objects on which they had fixed their own exclusive attachment. The same egotism had indeed displayed itself even in more primitive ages; but it was now for the first time openly avowed as a professed principle of action. The spirit of chivalry had in it this point of excellence, that however overstrained and fantastic many of its doctrines may appear to us, they were all founded on generosity and self-denial, of which if the earth were deprived, it would be difficult to conceive the existence of virtue among the human race.

Among those who were the first to ridicule and abandon the self-denying principles in which the young knight was instructed, and to which he was so carefully trained up, Louis the Eleventh of France was the chief. That sovereign was of a character so purely selfish—so guiltless of entertaining any purpose unconnected with his ambition, covetousness, and desire of selfish enjoyment, that he almost seems an incarnation of the devil himself, permitted to do his utmost to corrupt our ideas of honour in its very source. Nor is it to be forgotten that Louis possessed to a great extent that caustic wit which can turn into ridicule all that a man does for any other person's advantage but his own, and was, therefore, peculiarly qualified to play the part of a cold-hearted and sneering fiend.

In this point of view, Goethe's conception of the character and reasoning of Mephistophiles, the tempting spirit in the singular play of *Faust*, appears to me more happy than that which has been formed by Byron,[1] and even than the Satan of Milton. These last great authors have given to the Evil Principle something which elevates and dignifies his wickedness—a sustained and unconquerable resistance against Omnipotence itself, a lofty scorn of suffering compared with submission, and all those points of attraction in the Author of Evil which have induced Burns and others to consider him as the hero of the *Paradise Lost*. The great German poet has, on the contrary, rendered his seducing spirit a being who, otherwise totally unimpassioned, seems only to have existed for the purpose of increasing, by his persuasions and temptations, the mass of moral evil, and who calls forth by his seductions those slumbering passions which otherwise might have allowed the human being who was the object of the evil spirit's operations to pass the tenor of his life in tranquillity. For this purpose Mephistophiles is, like Louis XI., endowed with an acute and depreciating spirit of caustic wit, which is employed incessantly in undervaluing and vilifying all actions the consequences of which do not lead certainly and directly to self-gratification.

Even an author of works of mere amusement may be permitted to be serious for a moment, in order to reprobate all policy, whether of a public or private character, which rests its basis upon the principles of Machiavel or the practice of Louis XI.

The cruelties, the perjuries, the suspicions of this prince were rendered more detestable, rather than amended, by the gross and debasing superstition which he constantly practised. The devotion to the Heavenly saints, of which he made such a parade, was upon the miserable principle of some petty deputy in office, who endeavours to hide or atone for the malversations of which he is conscious, by liberal gifts to those whose duty it is to observe his conduct, and endeavours to support a system of fraud by an attempt to corrupt the incorruptible. In no other light can we regard his creating the Virgin Mary a countess and colonel of his guards, or the cunning that admitted to one or two peculiar forms of oath the force of a binding obligation which he denied to all others, strictly preserving the secret, which mode of swearing he really accounted obligatory, as one of the most valuable of state mysteries.

To a total want of scruple, or, it would appear, of any sense whatever of moral obligation, Louis XI. added great natural firmness and sagacity of character, with a system of policy so highly refined, considering the times he lived in, that he sometimes overreached hmself by giving way to its dictates.

Probably there is no portrait so dark as to be without its softer shades. He understood the interests of France, and faithfully pursued them so long as he could identify them with his own. He carried the country safe through the dangerous crisis of the war termed for 'the public good'; in thus disuniting and dispersing this grand and dangerous alliance of the great crown vassals of France against the sovereign, a king of a less cautious and temporising character, and of a more bold and less crafty disposition, than Louis XI. would, in all probability, have failed. Louis had also some personal accomplishments not inconsistent with his public character. He was cheerful and witty in society; caressed his victim like the cat, which can fawn when about to deal the most bitter wound; and none was better able to sustain and extol the superiority of the coarse and selfish reasons by which he endeavoured to supply those nobler motives for exertion which his predecessors had derived from the high spirit of chivalry.

In fact that system was now becoming ancient, and had, even while in its perfection, something so overstrained and fantastic in its principles, as rendered it peculiarly the object of ridicule, whenever, like other old fashions, it began to fall out of repute, and the weapons of raillery could be employed against it, without exciting the disgust and horror with which they would have been rejected at an early period as a species of blasphemy. In the 14th century a tribe of scoffers had arisen who pretended to supply what was naturally useful in chivalry by other resources, and threw ridicule upon the extravagant and exclusive principles of honour and virtue which were openly treated as absurd, because, in fact, they were cast in a mould of perfection too lofty for the practice of fallible beings. If an ingenuous and high-spirited youth proposed to frame himself on his father's principles of honour, he was vulgarly derided as if he had brought to the field the good old knight's Durindarte or two-handed sword, ridiculous from its antique make and fashion, although its blade might be the Ebro's temper, and its ornaments of pure gold.[2]

In like manner, the principles of chivalry were cast aside, and their aid supplied by baser stimulants. Instead of the high spirit which pressed every man forward in the defence of his country, Louis XI. substituted the exertions of the ever ready mercenary soldier, and persuaded his subjects, among whom the mercantile class began to make a figure, that it was better to leave to mercenaries the risks and labours of war, and to supply the crown with the means of paying them, than to peril themselves in defence of their own substance. The merchants were easily persuaded by this reasoning. The hour did not arrive, in the days of Louis XI., when the landed gentry and nobles could be in like manner excluded from the ranks of war; but the wily monarch commenced that system, which, acted upon by his successors, at length threw the whole military defence of the state into the hands of the crown.

He was equally forward in altering the principles which were wont to regulate the intercourse of the sexes. The doctrines of chivalry had established in theory, at least, a system in which Beauty was the governing and remunerating divinity, Valour her slave, who caught his courage from her eye, and gave his life for her slightest service. It is true, the system here, as in other branches, was stretched to fantastic extravagance, and cases of scandal not unfrequently arose. Still they were generally such as those mentioned by Burke, where frailty was deprived of half its guilt by being purified from all its grossness.[3] In Louis XI.'s practice, it was far otherwise. He was a low voluptuary, seeking pleasure without sentiment, and despising the sex from whom he desired to obtain it; his mistresses were of inferior rank, as little to be compared with the elevated though faulty character of Agnes Sorel, as Louis was to his heroic father, who freed France from the threatened yoke of England. In like manner, by selecting his favourites and ministers from among the dregs of the people, Louis showed the slight regard which he paid to eminent station and high birth; and although this might be not only excusable but meritorious, where the monarch's fiat promoted obscure talent, or called forth modest worth, it was very different when the King made his favourite associates of such men as Tristan l'Hermite, the chief of his marshalsea or police; and it was evident that such a prince could no longer be, as his descendant Francis elegantly designed himself, 'the first gentleman in his dominions.'

Nor were Louis's sayings and actions, in private or public, of a kind which could redeem such gross offences against the character of a man of honour. His word, generally accounted the most sacred test of a man's character, and the least impeachment of which is a capital offence by the code of honour, was forfeited without scruple on the slightest occasion, and often accompanied by the perpetration of the most enormous crimes. If he broke his own personal and plighted faith, he did not treat that of the public with more ceremony. His sending an inferior person disguised as a herald to Edward IV. was in those days, when heralds were esteemed the sacred depositaries of public and national faith, a daring imposition, of which few save this unscrupulous prince would have been guilty.

In short, the manners, sentiments, and actions of Louis XI. were such as were inconsistent with the principles of chivalry, and his caustic wit was sufficiently disposed to ridicule a system adopted on what he considered as the most absurd of all bases, since it was founded on the principle of devoting toil, talents, and time to the accomplishment of objects from which no personal advantage could, in the nature of things, be obtained

It is more than probable that, in thus renouncing almost openly the ties of religion, honour, and morality, by which mankind at large feel themselves influenced, Louis sought to obtain great advantages in his negotiations with parties who might esteem themselves bound, while he himself enjoyed liberty. He started from the goal, he might suppose, like the racer who has got rid of the weights with which his competitors are still encumbered, and expects to succeed of course. But Providence seems always to unite the existence of peculiar danger with some circumstance which may put those exposed to the peril upon their guard. The constant suspicion attached to any public person who becomes badly eminent for breach of faith is to him what the rattle is to the poisonous serpent; and men come at last to calculate, not so much on what their antagonist says, as upon that which he is likely to do; a degree of mistrust which tends to counteract the intrigues of such a faithless character more than his freedom from the scruples of conscientious men can afford him advantage. The example of Louis XI. raised disgust and suspicion rather than a desire of imitation among other nations in Europe, and the circumstance of his outwitting more than one of his contemporaries operated to put others on their guard. Even the system of chivalry, though much less generally extended than heretofore, survived this profligate monarch's reign, who did so much to sully its lustre, and long after the death of Louis XI. it inspired the Knight without Fear and Reproach and the gallant Francis I.

Indeed, although the reign of Louis had been as successful in a political point of view as he himself could have desired, the spectacle of his death-bed might of itself be a warning-piece against the seduction of his example. Jealous of every one, but chiefly of his own son, he immured himself in his Castle of Plessis, entrusting his person exclusively to the doubtful faith of his Scottish mercenaries. He never stirred from his chamber, he admitted no one into it; and wearied Heaven and every saint with prayers, not for the forgiveness of his sins, but for the prolongation of his life. With a poverty of spirit totally inconsistent with his shrewd worldly sagacity, he importuned his physicians until they insulted as well as plundered him. In his extreme desire of life, he sent to Italy for supposed relics, and the yet more extraordinary importation of an ignorant crack-brained peasant, who, from laziness probably, had shut himself up in a cave, and renounced flesh, fish, eggs, or the produce of the dairy.[4] This man, who did not possess the slightest tincture of letters, Louis reverenced as if he had been the Pope himself, and to gain his good-will founded two cloisters.

It was not the least singular circumstance of this course of superstition that bodily health and terrestrial felicity seemed to be his only objects. Making any mention of his sins when talking on the state of his health was strictly prohibited; and when at his command a priest recited a prayer to St. Eutropius, in which he recommended the King's welfare both in body and soul, Louis caused the two last words to be omitted, saying it was not prudent to importune the blessed saint by too many requests at once.

Perhaps he thought by being silent on his crimes, he might suffer them to pass out of the recollection of the celestial patrons, whose aid he invoked for his body.

So great were the well-merited tortures of this tyrant's death-bed, that Philip des Comines enters into a regular comparison between them and the numerous cruelties inflicted on others by his order; and, considering both, comes to express an opinion, that the worldly pangs and agony suffered by Louis were such as might compensate the crimes he had committed, and that, after a reasonable quarantine in purgatory, he might in mercy be found duly qualified for the superior regions.[5]

Fénelon also has left his testimony against this prince,[6]

. . . .

The instructive but appalling scene of this tyrant's sufferings was at length closed by death, 30th August 1483.

The selection of this remarkable person as the principal character in the romance—for it will be easily comprehended that the little love intrigue of Quentin is only employed as the means of bringing out the story—afforded considerable facilities to the Author. The whole of Europe was, during the 15th century, convulsed with dissensions from such various causes, that it would have required almost a dissertation to have brought the English reader with a mind perfectly alive and prepared to admit the possibility of the strange scenes to which he was introduced.

In Louis XI.'s time, extraordinary commotions existed throughout all Europe. England's civil wars were ended rather in appearance than reality by the short-lived ascendency of the house of York. Switzerland was asserting that freedom which was afterwards so bravely defended. In the Empire and in France the great vassals of the crown were endeavouring to emancipate themselves from its control, while Charles of Burgundy by main force, and Louis more artfully by indirect means, laboured to subject them to subservience to their respective sovereignties. Louis, while with one hand he circumvented and subdued his own rebellious vassals, laboured secretly with the other to aid and encourage the large trading towns of Flanders to rebel against the Duke of Burgundy, to which their wealth and irritability naturally disposed them. In the more woodland districts of Flanders, the Duke of Gueldres, and William de la Marck, called from his ferocity the Wild Boar of Ardennes, were throwing off the habits of knights and gentlemen, to practise the violences and brutalities of common bandits.

A hundred secret combinations existed in the different provinces of France and Flanders; numerous private emissaries of the restless Louis—Bohemians, pilgrims, beggars, or agents disguised as such—were everywhere spreading the discontent which it was his policy to maintain in the dominions of Burgundy.

Amidst so great an abundance of materials, it was difficult to select such as should be most intelligible and interesting to the reader; and the Author had to regret that, though he made liberal use of the power of departing from the reality of history, he felt by no means confident of having brought his story into a pleasing, compact, and sufficiently intelligible form. The mainspring of the plot is that which all who know the least of the feudal system can easily understand, though the facts are absolutely fictitious. The right of a feudal superior was in nothing more universally acknowledged than in his power to interfere in the marriage of a female vassal. This may appear to exist as a contradiction both of the civil and canon law, which declare that marriage shall be free, while the feudal or municipal jurisprudence, in case of a fief passing to a female, acknowledges an interest in the superior of the fief to dictate the choice of her companion in marriage. This is accounted for on the principle that the superior was, by his bounty, the original grantor of the fief, and is still interested that the marriage of the vassal shall place no one there who may be inimical to his liege lord. On the other hand, it might be reasonably pleaded that this right of dictating to the vassal, to a certain extent, in the choice of a husband is only competent to the superior from whom the fief is originally derived. There is therefore no violent improbability in a vassal of Burgundy flying to the protection of the King of France, to whom the Duke of Burgandy himself was a vassal; nor is it a great stretch of probability to affirm, that Louis, unscrupulous as he was, should have formed the design of betraying the fugitive into some alliance which might prove inconvenient, if not dangerous, to his formidable kinsman and vassal of Burgundy.

I may add, that the romance of *Quentin Durward*, which acquired a popularity at home more extensive than some of its

predecessors, found also unusual success on the continent,*
where the historical allusions awakened more familiar ideas.

ABBOTSFORD, 1*st December* 1831.

---

*[See Lockhart's *Life of Scott*, vol. vii. pp. 161–167.]

ST. RONAN'S WELL

The novel which follows is upon a plan different from any other that the Author has ever written, although it is perhaps the most legitimate which relates to this kind of light literature.

It is intended, in a word, *celebrare domestica facta*[1]—to give an imitation of the shifting manners of our own time, and paint scenes the originals of which are daily passing round us, so that a minute's observation may compare the copies with the originals. It must be confessed that this style of composition was adopted by the Author rather from the tempting circumstance of its offering some novelty in his compositions, and avoiding worn-out characters and positions, than from the hope of rivalling the many formidable competitors who have already won deserved honours in this department. The ladies, in particular, gifted by nature with keen powers of observation and light satire, have been so distinguished by these works of talent that, reckoning from the authoress of *Evelina* to her of *Marriage*,[2] a catalogue might be made, including the brilliant and talented names of Edgeworth, Austen, Charlotte Smith,[3] and others, whose success seems to have appropriated this province of the novel as exclusively their own. It was therefore with a sense of temerity that the Author intruded upon a species of composition which had been of late practised with such distinguished success. This consciousness was lost, however, under the necessity of seeking for novelty, without which, it was much to be apprehended, such repeated incursions on his part would nauseate the long indulgent public at the last.

The scene chosen for the Author's little drama of modern life was a mineral spring, such as arc to bc found in both divisions of Britain, and which are supplied with the usual materials for redeeming health or driving away care. The invalid often finds relief from his complaints less from the healing virtues of the spa itself than because his system of ordinary life undergoes an entire change, in his being removed from his ledger and account-books, from his legal folios and progresses of title-deeds, from his counters and shelves, from whatever else forms the main source of his constant anxiety at home, destroys his appetite, mars the custom of his exercise, deranges the digestive powers, and clogs up the springs of life. Thither, too, comes the saunterer, anxious to get rid of that wearisome attendant *himself*, and, thither come both males and females, who, upon a different principle, desire to make themselves double.

The society of such places is regulated, by their very nature, upon a scheme much more indulgent than that which rules the world of fashion and the narrow circles of rank in the metropolis. The titles of rank, birth, and fortune are received at a watering-place without any very strict investigation, as adequate to the purpose for which they are preferred; and as the situation infers a certain degree of intimacy and sociability for the time, so to whatever heights it may have been carried, it is not understood to imply any duration beyond the length of the season. No intimacy can be supposed more close for the time, and more transitory in its endurance, than that which is attached to a watering-place acquaintance. The novelist, therefore, who fixes upon such a scene for his tale endeavours to display a species of society where the strongest contrast of humourous characters and manners may be brought to bear on and illustrate each other with less violation of probability than could be supposed to attend the same miscellaneous assemblage in any other situation.

In such scenes, too, are frequently mingled characters not merely ridiculous, but dangerous and hateful. The unprincipled gamester, the heartless fortune-hunter, all those who eke out their means of subsistence by pandering to the vices and follies of the rich and gay, who drive, by their various arts, foibles into crimes, and imprudence into acts of ruinous madness, are to be

found where their victims naturally resort, with the same certainty that eagles are gathered together at the place of slaughter.
By this the Author takes a great advantage for the management
of his story, particularly in its darker and more melancholy
passages. The impostor, the gambler, all who live loose upon the
skirts of society, or, like vermin, thrive by its corruptions, are to be
found at such retreats, when they easily, and as a matter of course,
mingle with those dupes who might otherwise have escaped their
snares. But besides those characters who are actually dangerous
to society, a well-frequented watering-place generally exhibits for
the amusement of the company, and the perplexity and amaze-
ment of the more inexperienced, a sprinkling of persons called by
the newspapers eccentric characters—individuals, namely, who,
either from some real derangement of their understanding, or,
much more frequently, from an excess of vanity, are ambitious of
distinguishing themselves by some striking peculiarity in dress or
address, conversation or manners, and perhaps in all. These
affectations are usually adopted, like Drawcansir's extravagances,
to show *they dare*;[4] and I must needs say, those who profess them
are more frequently to be found among the English than among
the natives of either of the other two divisions of the united
kingdoms. The reason probably is that the consciousness of
wealth, and a sturdy feeling of independence, which generally
pervade the English nation, are, in a few individuals, perverted
into absurdity, or at least peculiarity. The witty Irishman, on the
contrary, adapts his general behaviour to that of the best society,
or that which he thinks such; nor is it any part of the shrewd Scot's
national character unnecessarily to draw upon himself public
attention. These rules, however, are not without their exceptions;
for we find men of every country playing the eccentric at these
independent resorts of the gay and the wealthy, where every one
enjoys the license of doing what is good in his own eyes.

It scarce needed these obvious remarks to justify a novelist's
choice of a watering-place as the scene of a fictitious narrative.
Unquestionably it affords every variety of character, mixed
together in a manner which cannot, without a breach of probability, be supposed to exist elsewhere; neither can it be denied
that, in the concourse which such miscellaneous collections of

St. Ronan's Well

persons afford, events extremely different from those of the quiet routine of ordinary life may, and often do, take place.

It is not, however, sufficient that a mine be in itself rich and easily accessible; it is necessary that the engineer who explores it should himself, in mining phrase, have an accurate knowledge of the 'country,' and possess the skill necessary to work it to advantage. In this respect, the Author of *St. Ronan's Well* could not be termed fortunate. His habits of life had not led him much, of late years at least, into its general or bustling scenes, nor had he mingled often in the society which enables the observer to 'shoot folly as it flies.'[5] The consequence perhaps was, that the characters wanted that force and precision which can only be given by a writer who is familiarly acquainted with his subject.* The Author, however, had the satisfaction to chronicle his testimony against the practice of gambling, a vice which the devil has contrived to render all his own, since it is deprived of whatever pleads an apology for other vices, and is founded entirely on the cold-blooded calculation of the most exclusive selfishness. The character of the traveller, meddling, self-important, and what the ladies call fussing, but yet generous and benevolent in his purposes, was partly taken from nature. The story, being entirely modern, cannot require much explanation, after what has been here given, either in the shape of notes or a more prolix introduction.

It may be remarked that the English critics, in many instances, though none of great influence, pursued *St. Ronan's Well* with hue and cry, many of the fraternity giving it as their opinion that the Author had exhausted himself, or, as the technical phrase expresses it, 'written himself out'; and as an unusual tract of success too often provokes many persons to mark and exaggerate a slip when it does occur, the Author was publicly accused, in prose and verse, of having committed a literary suicide in this unhappy attempt. The voices, therefore, were for a time against *St. Ronan's* on the southern side of the Tweed.

In the Author's own country it was otherwise. Many of the characters were recognised as genuine Scottish portraits, and the good fortune which had hitherto attended the productions of the

*[See Lockhart's *Life of Scott*, vol. vii. pp. 206–212.]

Author of *Waverley* did not desert, notwithstanding the ominous vaticinations of its censurers, this new attempt, although out of his ordinary style.

1st February 1832.

REDGAUNTLET

The Jacobite enthusiasm of the 18th century, particularly during the rebellion of 1745, afforded a theme, perhaps the finest that could be selected for fictitious composition, founded upon real or probable incident. This civil war, and its remarkable events, were remembered by the existing generation without any degree of the bitterness of spirit which seldom fails to attend internal dissension. The Highlanders, who formed the principal strength of Charles Edward's army, were an ancient and high-spirited race, peculiar in their habits of war and of peace, brave to romance, and exhibiting a character turning upon points more adapted to poetry than to the prose of real life. Their prince, young, valiant, patient of fatigue, and despising danger, heading his army on foot in the most toilsome marches, and defeating a regular force in three battles—all these were circumstances fascinating to the imagination, and might well be supposed to seduce young and enthusiastic minds to the cause in which they were found united, although wisdom and reason frowned upon the enterprise.

The adventurous Prince, as is well known, proved to be one of those personages who distinguish themselves during some single and extraordinarily brilliant period of their lives, like the course of a shooting star, at which men wonder, as well on account of the briefness as the brilliancy of its splendour. A long trace of darkness overshadowed the subsequent life of a man who, in his youth, showed himself so capable of great undertakings; and, without the painful task of tracing his course further, we may say the latter pursuits and habits of this unhappy prince are those painfully evincing a broken heart, which seeks refuge from its own thoughts in sordid enjoyments.

Still, however, it was long ere Charles Edward appeared to be—perhaps it was long ere he altogether became—so much degraded from his original self, as he enjoyed for a time the lustre attending the progress and termination of his enterprise. Those who thought they discerned in his subsequent conduct an insensibility to the distresses of his followers, coupled with that egotistical attention to his own interests which has been often attributed to the Stuart family, and which is the natural effect of the principles of divine right in which they were brought up, were now generally considered as dissatisfied and splenetic persons, who, displeased with the issue of their adventure, and finding themselves involved in the ruins of a falling cause, indulged themselves in undeserved reproaches against their leader. Indeed, such censures were by no means frequent among those of his followers who, if what was alleged had been just, had the best right to complain. Far the greater number of those unfortunate gentlemen suffered with the most dignified patience, and were either too proud to take notice of ill treatment on the part of their prince, or so prudent as to be aware their complaints would meet with little sympathy from the world. It may be added, that the greater part of the banished Jacobites, and those of high rank and consequence, were not much within reach of the influence of the Prince's character and conduct, whether well regulated or otherwise.

In the meantime, that great Jacobite conspiracy, of which the insurrection of 1745–46 was but a small part, precipitated into action on the failure of a far more general scheme, was resumed and again put into motion by the Jacobites of England, whose force had never been broken, as they had prudently avoided bringing it into the field. The surprising effect which had been produced by small means in 1745–46 animated their hopes for more important successes, when the whole Nonjuring interest of Britain,[1] identified as it then was with great part of the landed gentlemen, should come forward to finish what had been gallantly attempted by a few Highland chiefs.

It is probable, indeed, that the Jacobites of the day were incapable of considering that the very small scale on which the effort was made was in one great measure the cause of its unexpected success. The remarkable speed with which the insurgents marched, the singularly good discipline which they preserved, the union and unanimity which for some time animated their councils, were all in a considerable degree produced by the smallness of their numbers. Notwithstanding the discomfiture of Charles Edward, the Nonjurors of the period long continued to nurse unlawful schemes, and to drink treasonable toasts, until age stole upon them. Another generation arose, who did not share the sentiments which they cherished; and at length the sparkles of disaffection, which had long smouldered, but had never been heated enough to burst into actual flame, became entirely extinguished. But in proportion as the political enthusiasm died gradually away among men of ordinary temperament, it influenced those of warm imaginations and weak understandings, and hence wild schemes were formed, as desperate as they were adventurous.

Thus a young Scotchman of rank is said to have stooped so low as to plot the surprisal of St. James's Palace, and the assassination of the royal family.[2] While these ill-digested and desperate conspiracies were agitated among the few Jacobites who still adhered with more obstinacy to their purpose, there is no question but that other plots might have been brought to an open explosion, had it not suited the policy of Sir Robert Walpole rather to prevent or disable the conspirators in their projects than to promulgate the tale of danger, which might thus have been believed to be more widely diffused than was really the case.[3]

In one instance alone this very prudential and humane line of conduct was departed from, and the event seemed to confirm the policy of the general course. Doctor Archibald Cameron, brother of the celebrated Donald Cameron of Lochiel, attainted for the rebellion of 1745, was found by a party of soldiers lurking with a comrade in the wilds of Loch Katrine, five or six years after the battle of Culloden, and was there seized. There were circumstances in his case, so far as was made known to the public, which attracted much compassion, and gave to the judicial proceedings against him an appearance of cold-blooded revenge on the part of government; and the following argument of a zealous Jacobite in his favour was received as conclusive by Dr. Johnson and other persons who might pretend to impartiality. Dr. Cameron had never borne arms, although engaged in the Rebellion, but used his medical skill for the service, indifferently, of the wounded of both parties. His return to Scotland was ascribed exclusively to family affairs. His behaviour at the bar was decent, firm, and respectful. His wife threw herself, on three different occasions, before George II. and the members of his family, was rudely repulsed from their presence, and at length placed, it was said, in the same prison with her husband, and confined with unmanly severity.

Dr. Cameron was finally executed, with all the severities of the law of treason; and his death remains in popular estimation a dark blot upon the memory of George II., being almost publicly imputed to a mean and personal hatred of Donald Cameron of Lochiel, the sufferer's heroic brother.

Yet the fact was, that whether the execution of Archibald Cameron was political or otherwise, it might certainly have been justified, had the King's ministers so pleased, upon reasons of a public nature. The unfortunate sufferer had not come to the Highlands solely upon his private affairs, as was the general belief; but it was not judged prudent by the English ministry to let it be generally known that he came to inquire about a considerable sum of money which had been remitted from France to the friends of the exiled family. He had also a commission to hold intercourse with the well-known M'Pherson of Cluny, chief of the clan Vourich, whom the Chevalier had left behind at his departure from Scotland in 1746, and who remained during ten years of proscription and danger, skulking from place to place in the Highlands, and maintaining an uninterrupted correspondence between Charles and his friends. That Dr. Cameron should have held a commission to assist this chief in raking together the dispersed embers of disaffection is in itself sufficiently natural, and, considering his political principles, in no respect dishonourable to his memory. But neither ought it to be imputed to George II. that he suffered the laws to be enforced against a person taken in the act of breaking them. When he lost his hazardous game, Dr. Cameron only paid the forfeit which he must have calculated upon. The ministers, however, thought it

proper to leave Dr. Cameron's new schemes in concealment, lest
by divulging them they had indicated the channel of communication which, it is now well known, they possessed to all the plots
of Charles Edward.But it was equally ill-advised and ungenerous
to sacrifice the character of the King to the policy of the admin-
istration. Both points might have been gained by sparing the life
of Dr. Cameron after conviction, and limiting his punishment to
perpetual exile.

These repeated and successive Jacobite plots rose and burst like
bubbles on a fountain; and one of them, at least, the Chevalier
judged of importance enough to induce him to risk himself
within the dangerous precincts of the British capital. This appears from Dr. King's *Anecdotes of his Own Times*:[4]—

> *September* 1750.—I received a note from my Lady Primrose, who
> desired to see me immediately. As soon as I waited on her, she led
> me into her dressing-room, and presented me to ———. [The
> Chevalier, doubtless.] If I was surprised to find him there, I was
> still more astonished when he acquainted me with the motives
> which had induced him to hazard a journey to England at this
> juncture. The impatience of his friends who were in exile had
> formed a scheme which was impracticable; but although it had
> been as feasible as they had represented it to him, yet no prepara-
> tion had been made, nor was anything ready to carry it into
> execution. He was soon convinced that he had been deceived;
> and, therefore, after a stay in London of five days only, he
> returned to the place from whence he came [pp. 196, 197].

Dr. King was in 1750 a keen Jacobite, as may be inferred from
the visit made by him to the Prince under such circumstances, and
from his being one of that unfortunate person's chosen correspondents. He, as well as other men of sense and observation,
began to despair of making their fortune in the party which they
had chosen. It was indeed sufficiently dangerous; for, during the
short visit just described, one of Dr. King's servants remarked the
stranger's likeness to Prince Charles, whom he recognised from
the common busts.

The occasion taken for breaking up the Stuart interest we shall
tell in Dr. King's own words:—

> When he (Charles Edward) was in Scotland, he had a mistress
> whose name is Walkenshaw, and whose sister was at that time, and
> is still, housekeeper at Leicester House. Some years after he was

released from his prison, and conducted out of France, he sent for this girl, who soon acquired such a dominion over him that she was acquainted with all his schemes, and trusted with his most secret correspondence. As soon as this was known in England, all those persons of distinction who were attached to him were greatly alarmed: they imagined that this wench had been placed in his family by the English ministers; and, considering her sister's situation, they seemed to have some ground for their suspicion; wherefore, they despatched a gentleman to Paris, where the Prince then was, who had instructions to insist that Mrs. Walkenshaw should be removed to a convent for a certain term; but her gallant absolutely refused to comply with this demand; and although Mr. M'Namara, the gentleman who was sent to him, who has a natural eloquence and an excellent understanding, urged the most cogent reasons, and used all the arts of persuasion, to induce him to part with his mistress, and even proceeded so far as to assure him, according to his instructions, that an immediate interruption of all correspondence with his most powerful friends in England, and, in short, that the ruin of his interest, which was now daily increasing, would be the infallible consequence of his refusal, yet he continued inflexible, and all M'Namara's entreaties and remonstrances were ineffectual. M'Namara staid in Paris some days beyond the time prescribed him, endeavouring to reason the Prince into a better temper; but finding him obstinately persevere in his first answer, he took his leave with concern and indignation, saying, as he passed out, 'What has your family done, sir, thus to draw down the vengeance of Heaven on every branch of it, through so many ages?' It is worthy of remark, that in all the conferences which M'Namara had with the Prince on this occasion, the latter declared that it was not a violent passion, or indeed any particular regard, which attached him to Mrs. Walkenshaw, and that he could see her removed from him without any concern; but he would not receive directions in respect to his private conduct from any man alive. When M'Namara returned to London and reported the Prince's answer to the gentlemen who had employed him, they were astonished and confounded. However, they soon resolved on the measures which they were to pursue for the future, and determined no longer to serve a man who could not be persuaded to serve himself, and chose rather to endanger the lives of his best and most faithful friends than part with an harlot whom, as he often declared, he neither loved nor esteemed [pp. 204–209].

From this anecdote, the general truth of which is indubitable, the principal fault of Charles Edward's temper is sufficiently obvious. It was a high sense of his own importance, and an obstinate adherence to what he had once determined on—qualities which, if he had succeeded in his bold attempt, gave the nation little room to hope that he would have been found free from the love of prerogative and desire of arbitrary power which characterised his unhappy grandfather. He gave a notable instance how far this was the leading feature of his character when, for no reasonable cause that can be assigned, he placed his own single will in opposition to the necessities of France, which, in order to purchase a peace become necessary to the kingdom, was reduced to gratify Britain by prohibiting the residence of Charles within any of the French dominions. It was in vain that France endeavoured to lessen the disgrace of this step by making the most flattering offers, in hopes to induce the Prince of himself to anticipate this disagreeable alternative, which, if seriously enforced, as it was likely to be, he had no means whatever of resisting, by leaving the kingdom as of his own free will. Inspired, however, by the spirit of hereditary obstinacy, Charles preferred a useless resistance to a dignified submission, and by a series of idle bravadoes laid the French court under the necessity of arresting their late ally, and sending him to close confinement in the Bastile, from which he was afterwards sent out of the French dominions, much in the manner in which a convict is transported to the place of his destination.

In addition to these repeated instances of a rash and inflexible temper, Dr. King also adds faults alleged to belong to the Prince's character of a kind less consonant with his noble birth and high pretensions. He is said by this author to have been avaricious, or parsimonious at least, to such a degree of meanness as to fail, even when he had ample means, in relieving the sufferers who had lost their fortune and sacrificed their all in his ill-fated attempt. We must receive, however, with some degree of jealousy what is said by Dr. King on this subject, recollecting that he had left at least, if he did not desert, the standard of the unfortunate prince, and was not therefore a person who was likely to form the fairest estimate of his virtues and faults. We must also remember that, if the exiled prince gave little, he had but little to give, especially considering how late he nourished the scheme of another expedition to Scotland, for which he was long endeavouring to hoard money.

The case, also, of Charles Edward must be allowed to have been a difficult one. He had to satisfy numerous persons, who, having lost their all in his cause, had, with that all, seen the extinction of hopes which they accounted nearly as good as certainties; some of these were perhaps clamorous in their applications, and certainly ill pleased with their want of success. Other parts of the Chevalier's conduct may have afforded grounds for charging him with coldness to the sufferings of his devoted followers. One of these was a sentiment which has nothing in it that is generous, but it was certainly a principle in which the young prince was trained, and which may be too probably denominated peculiar to his family, educated in all the high notions of passive obedience and non-resistance. If the unhappy prince gave implicit faith to the professions of statesmen holding such notions, which is implied by his whole conduct, it must have led to the natural, though ungracious, inference that the services of a subject could not, to whatever degree of ruin they might bring the individual, create a debt against his sovereign. Such a person could only boast that he had done his duty; nor was he entitled to be a claimant for a greater reward than it was convenient for the prince to bestow, or to hold his sovereign his debtor for losses which he had sustained through his loyalty. To a certain extent the Jacobite principles inevitably led to this cold and egotistical mode of reasoning on the part of the sovereign; nor, with all our natural pity for the situation of royalty in distress, do we feel entitled to affirm that Charles did not use this opiate to his feelings, on viewing the misery of his followers, while he certainly possessed, though in no great degree, the means of affording them more relief than he practised. His own history, after leaving France, is brief and melancholy. For a time he seems to have held the firm belief that Providence, which had borne him through so many hazards, still reserved him for some distant occasion, in which he should be empowered to vindicate the honours of his birth. But opportunity after opportunity slipt by unimproved, and the death of his father gave him the fatal proof that none of the principal powers of Europe were, after that event, likely to interest themselves in his quarrel. They refused to acknowledge him under the title of the King of England, and, on his part, he declined to be then recognised as the Prince of Wales.

Family discord came to add its sting to those of disappointed ambition; and, though a humiliating circumstance, it is generally acknowledged that Charles Edward, the adventurous, the gallant, and the handsome, the leader of a race of pristine valour, whose romantic qualities may be said to have died along with him, had, in his latter days, yielded to those humiliating habits of intoxication in which the meanest mortals seek to drown the recollection of their disappointments and miseries. Under such circumstances, the unhappy Prince lost the friendship even of those faithful followers who had most devoted themselves to his misfortunes, and was surrounded, with some honourable exceptions, by men of a lower description, regardless of the character which he was himself no longer able to protect.

It is a fact consistent with the Author's knowledge, that persons totally unentitled to, and unfitted for, such a distinction were presented to the unfortunate Prince in moments unfit for presentation of any kind. Amid these clouds was at length extinguished the torch which once shook itself over Britain with such terrific glare, and at last sunk in its own ashes, scarce remembered and scarce noted.

Meantime, while the life of Charles Edward was gradually wasting in disappointed solitude, the number of those who had shared his misfortunes and dangers had shrunk into a small handful of veterans, the heroes of a tale which had been told. Most Scottish readers who can count the number of sixty years must recollect many respected acquaintances of their youth who, as the established phrase gently worded it, had been 'out in the Forty-five.' It may be said, that their political principles and plans no longer either gained proselytes or attracted terror: those who held them had ceased to be the subjects either of fear or opposition. Jacobites were looked upon in society as men who had proved their sincerity by sacrificing their interest to their principles; and in well-regulated companies it was held a piece of ill-breeding to injure their feelings or ridicule the compromises by which they endeavoured to keep themselves abreast of the current of the day. Such, for example, was the evasion of a gentleman of fortune in Perthshire, Mr. Oliphant of Gask, who, in having the newspapers read to him, caused the King and Queen to be designated by the initial letters of 'K' and 'Q,' as if, by naming the full word, he might imply an acquiescence in the usurpation of the family of Hanover. George III., having heard of this gentleman's custom in the above and other particulars, commissioned the member for Perthshire to carry his compliments to the steady Jacobite. 'That is,' said the excellent old king, 'not the compliments of the King of England, but those of the Elector of Hanover, and tell him how much I respect him for the steadiness of his principles.'

Those who remember such old men will probably agree that the progress of time, which has withdrawn all of them from the field, has removed, at the same time, a peculiar and striking feature of ancient manners. Their love of past times, their tales of bloody battles fought against romantic odds, were all dear to the imagination, and their little idolatry of locks of hair, pictures, rings, ribbons, and other memorials of the time in which they still seemed to live, was an interesting enthusiasm; and although their political principles, had they existed in the relation of fathers, might have rendered them dangerous to the existing dynasty, yet, as we now recollect them, there could not be on the earth supposed to exist persons better qualified to sustain the capacity of innocuous and respectable grandsires.

It was while reflecting on these things that the novel of *Redgauntlet* was undertaken. But various circumstances in the composition induced the Author to alter its purport considerably as it passed through his hands, and to carry the action to that point of time when the Chevalier Charles Edward, though fallen into the sere and yellow leaf,[5] was yet meditating a second attempt, which could scarcely have been more hopeless than his first; although one to which, as we have seen, the unfortunate Prince, at least as late as 1753, still looked with hope and expectation.*

1st *April* 1832.

---

*[See Lockhart's *Life of Scott*, vol. vii. pp. 213, 214.]

THE BETROTHED

The *Tales of the Crusaders* was determined upon as the title of the following series of these novels, rather by the advice of the few friends whom death has now rendered still fewer than by the Author's own taste. Not but that he saw plainly enough the interest which might be excited by the very name of the Crusades; but he was conscious, at the same time, that that interest was of a character which it might be more easy to create than to satisfy, and that by the mention of so magnificent a subject each reader might be induced to call up to his imagination a sketch so extensive and so grand that it might not be in the power of the Author to fill it up, who would thus stand in the predicament of the dwarf bringing with him a standard to measure his own stature, and showing himself, therefore, says Sterne, 'a dwarf more ways than one.'

It is a fact, if it were worth while to examine it, that the publisher and author, however much their general interests are the same, may be said to differ so far as title-pages are concerned; and it is a secret of the tale-telling art, if it could be termed a secret worth knowing, that a taking title, as it is called, best answers the purpose of the bookseller, since it often goes far to cover his risk, and sells an edition not unfrequently before the public have well seen it. But the author ought to seek more permanent fame, and wish that his work, when its leaves are first cut open, should be at least fairly judged of. Thus many of the best novelists have been anxious to give their works such titles as render it out of the reader's power to conjecture their contents, until they should have an opportunity of reading them.

All this did not prevent the *Tales of the Crusaders* from being the title fixed on; and the celebrated year of projects (1825) being the time of publication, an introduction was prefixed according to the humour of the day.[2]

The first tale of the series was influenced in its structure rather by the wish to avoid the general expectations which might be formed from the title than to comply with any one of them, and so disappoint the rest. The story was, therefore, less an incident belonging to the Crusades than one which was occasioned by the singular cast of mind introduced and spread wide by those memorable undertakings. The confusion among families was not the least concomitant evil of the extraordinary preponderance of this superstition. It was no unusual thing for a crusader, returning from his long toils of war and pilgrimage, to find his family augmented by some young offshoot, of whom the deserted matron could give no very accurate account, or perhaps to find his marriage-bed filled, and that, instead of becoming nurse to an old man, his household dame had preferred being the lady-love of a young one. Numerous are the stories of this kind told in different parts of Europe; and the returned knight or baron, according to his temper, sat down good-naturedly contented with the account which his lady gave of a doubtful matter, or called in blood and fire to vindicate his honour, which, after all, had been endangered chiefly by his forsaking his household gods to seek adventures in Palestine.

Scottish tradition, quoted, I think, in some part of the *Border Minstrelsy*, ascribes to the clan of Tweedie, a family once stout and warlike, a descent which would not have misbecome a hero of antiquity. A baron, somewhat elderly we may suppose, had wedded a buxom young lady, and some months after their union he left her to ply the distaff alone in his old tower, among the mountains of the county of Peebles, near the sources of the Tweed. He returned after seven or eight years, no uncommon space for a pilgrimage to Palestine, and found his family had not been lonely in his absence, the lady having been cheered by the arrival of a stranger (of whose approach she could give the best

account of any one), who hung on her skirts, and called her
mammy, and was just such as the baron would have longed to call
his son, but that he could by no means make his age correspond,
according to the doctrine of civilians, with his own departure for
Palestine. He applied to his wife, therefore, for the solution of this
dilemma. The lady, after many floods of tears, which she had
reserved for the occasion, informed the honest gentleman, that,
walking one day alone by the banks of the infant river, a human
form arose from a deep eddy, still known and termed Tweed
Pool, who deigned to inform her that he was the tutelar genius of
the stream, and *bon gré mal gré*,[3] became the father of the sturdy
fellow whose appearance had so much surprised her husband.
This story, however suitable to pagan times, would have met with
full credence from few of the baron's contemporaries, but the
wife was young and beautiful, the husband old and in his dotage;
her family (the Frasers, it is believed) were powerful and warlike,
and the baron had had fighting enough in the holy wars. The
event was, that he believed, or seemed to believe, the tale, and
remained contented with the child with whom his wife and the
Tweed had generously presented him. The only circumstance
which preserved the memory of the incident was, that the youth
retained the name of Tweed or Tweedie. The baron, meanwhile,
could not, as the old Scotch song says, 'Keep the cradle rowing,'
and the Tweed apparently thought one natural son was family
enough for a decent Presbyterian lover; and so little gall had the
baron in his composition, that, having bred up the young Tweed
as his heir while he lived, he left him in that capacity when he died,
and the son of the river-god founded the family of Drummelzier
and others, from whom have flowed, in the phrase of the Ettrick
Shepherd,[4] 'many a brave fellow and many a bauld feat.'[5]

The tale of the Noble Moringer is somewhat of the same
nature;[6]

. . . .

There is also, in the rich field of German romance, another
edition of this story, which has been converted by M. Tieck
(whose labours of that kind have been so remarkable) into the
subject of one of his romantic dramas.[7] It is, however, unnecessary to detail it, as the present Author adopted his idea of the tale
chiefly from the edition preserved in the mansion of Haigh Hall,

of old the mansion-house of the family of Bradshaigh, now possessed by their descendants on the female side, the Earls of Balcarras. The story greatly resembles that of the Noble Moringer, only there is no miracle of St. Thomas to shock the belief of good Protestants.

· ·

The tradition, which the Author knew very early in life, was told to him by the late Lady Balcarras. He was so much struck with it that, being at that time profuse of legendary lore, he inserted it in the shape of a note to *Waverley*, the first of his romantic offences. Had he then known, as he now does, the value of such a story, it is likely that, as directed in the inimitable receipt for making an epic poem, preserved in *The Guardian*, he would have kept it for some future opportunity.[8]

As, however, the tale had not been completely told, and was a very interesting one, and as it was sufficiently interwoven with the crusades, the wars between the Welsh and the Norman lords of the marches were selected as a period when all freedoms might be taken with the strict truth of history without encountering any well-known fact which might render the narrative improbable.

· ·

THE TALISMAN

The Betrothed did not greatly please one or two friends, who thought that it did not well correspond to the general title of *The Crusaders*. They urged, therefore, that, without direct allusion to the manners of the Eastern tribes, and to the romantic conflicts of the period, the title of a *Tale of the Crusaders* would resemble the playbill which is said to have announced the tragedy of Hamlet, the character of the Prince of Denmark being left out. On the other hand, I felt the difficulty of giving a vivid picture of a part of the world with which I was almost totally unacquainted, unless by early recollections of the *Arabian Nights' Entertainments*; and not only did I labour under the incapacity of ignorance, in which, as far as regards Eastern manners, I was as thickly wrapped as an Egyptian in his fog; but my contemporaries were, many of them, as much enlightened upon the subject as if they had been inhabitants of the favoured land of Goshen. The love of travelling had pervaded all ranks, and carried the subject of Britain into all quarters of the world. Greece, so attractive by its remains of art, by its struggles for freedom against a Mohammedan tyrant, by its very name, where every fountain had its classical legend—Palestine, endeared to the imagination by yet more sacred remembrances, had been of late surveyed by British eyes, and described by recent travellers. Had I, therefore, attempted the difficult task of substituting manners of my own invention, instead of the genuine costume of the East, almost every traveller I met, who had extended his route beyond what was anciently called 'the grand tour,' had acquired a right, by ocular inspection, to chastise me for my presumption. Every member of the Travellers' Club, who could pretend to have thrown his shoe over Edom, was, by having done so, constituted my lawful critic and corrector. It occurred, therefore, that, where the author of *Anastasius*,[1] as well as he of *Hadji Baba*,[2] had described the manners and vices of the Eastern nations, not only with fidelity, but with the humour of Le Sage and the ludicrous power of Fielding himself, one who was a perfect stranger to the subject must necessarily produce an unfavourable contrast. The Poet Laureate also, in the charming tale of *Thalaba*,[3] had shown how extensive might be the researches of a person of acquirements and talent, by dint of investigation alone, into the ancient doctrines, history, and manners of the Eastern countries, in which we are probably to look for the cradle of mankind; Moore, in his *Lalla Rookh*, had successfully trod the same path;[4] in which, too, Byron, joining ocular experience to extensive reading, had written some of his most attractive poems. In a word, the Eastern themes had been already so successfully handled by those who were acknowledged to be masters of their craft, that I was diffident of making the attempt.

These were powerful objections, nor did they lose force when they became the subject of anxious reflection, although they did not finally prevail. The arguments on the other side were, that though I had no hope of rivalling the contemporaries whom I have mentioned, yet it occurred to me as possible to acquit myself of the task I was engaged in without entering into competition with them.

The period relating more immediately to the Crusades which I at last fixed upon was that at which the warlike character of Richard I., wild and generous, a pattern of chivalry, with all its extravagant virtues and its no less absurd errors, was opposed to that of Saladin, in which the Christian and English monarch showed all the cruelty and violence of an Eastern sultan, and Saladin, on the other hand, displayed the deep policy and prudence of a European sovereign, whilst each contended which should excel the other in the knightly qualities of bravery and generosity. This singular contrast afforded, as the Author conceived, materials for a work of fiction possessing peculiar interest.

One of the inferior characters introduced was a supposed relation of Richard Coeur-de-Lion—a violation of the truth of history which gave offence to Mr. Mills, the author of the *History of Chivalry and the Crusades*,[5] who was not, it may be presumed, aware that romantic fiction naturally includes the power of such invention, which is indeed one of the requisites of the art.

Prince David of Scotland, who was actually in the host, and was the hero of some very romantic adventures on his way home, was also pressed into my service, and constitutes one of my *dramatis personae*.

It is true I had already brought upon the field him of the Lion Heart.[6] But it was in a more private capacity than he was here to be exhibited in *The Talisman*: then as a disguised knight, now in the avowed character of a conquering monarch; so that I doubted not a name so dear to Englishmen as that of King Richard I. might contribute to their amusement for more than once.*

I had access to all which antiquity believed, whether of reality or fable, on the subject of that magnificent warrior, who was the proudest boast of Europe and their chivalry, and with whose dreadful name the Saracens, according to a historian of their own country, were wont to rebuke their startled horses. 'Do you think,' said they, 'that King Richard is on the track, that you spring so wildly from it?' The most curious register of the history of King Richard is an ancient romance, translated originally from the Norman, and at first certainly having a pretence to be termed a work of chivalry, but latterly becoming stuffed with the most astonishing and monstrous fables. There is perhaps no metrical romance upon record where, along with curious and genuine history, are mingled more absurd and exaggerated incidents. We have placed in the Appendix the passage of the romance in which Richard figures as an ogre, or literal cannibal.

A principal incident in the story is that from which the title is derived. Of all people who ever lived, the Persians were perhaps most remarkable for their unshaken credulity in amulets, spells, periapts, and similar charms, framed, it was said, under the influence of particular planets, and bestowing high medical powers, as well as the means of advancing men's fortunes in

---

*[See Lockhart, *Life of Scott*, vol. vii. p. 386.]

various manners. A story of this kind, relating to a crusader of eminence, is often told in the west of Scotland, and the relic alluded to is still in existence, and even yet held in veneration.

Sir Simon Lockhart of Lee and Cartland made a considerable figure in the reigns of Robert the Bruce and of his son David. He was one of the chief of that band of Scottish chivalry who accompanied James, the Good Lord Douglas, on his expedition to the Holy Land, with the heart of King Robert Bruce. Douglas, impatient to get at the Saracens, entered into war with those of Spain, and was killed there. Lockhart proceeded to the Holy Land with such Scottish knights as had escaped the fate of their leader, and assisted for some time in the wars against the Saracens.

The following adventure is said by tradition to have befallen him. He made prisoner in battle an emir of considerable wealth and consequence. The aged mother of the captive came to the Christian camp, to redeem her son from his state of captivity. Lockhart is said to have fixed the price at which his prisoner should ransom himself; and the lady, pulling out a large embroidered purse, proceeded to tell down the ransom, like a mother who pays little respect to gold in comparison of her son's liberty. In this operation, a pebble inserted in a coin, some say of the Lower Empire, fell out of the purse, and the Saracen matron testified so much haste to recover it as gave the Scottish knight a high idea of its value, when compared with gold or silver. 'I will not consent,' he said, 'to grant your son's liberty, unless that amulet be added to his ransom.' The lady not only consented to this, but explained to Sir Simon Lockhart the mode in which the talisman was to be used, and the uses to which it might be put. The water in which it was dipt operated as a styptic, as a febrifuge, and possessed several other properties as a medical talisman.

Sir Simon Lockhart, after much experience of the wonders which it wrought, brought it to his own country, and left it to his heirs, by whom, and by Clydesdale in general, it was, and is still distinguished by the name of the Lee Penny, from the name of his native seat of Lee.

The most remarkable part of its history, perhaps, was, that it so especially escaped condemnation when the Church of Scotland chose to impeach many other cures which savoured of the miraculous, as occasioned by sorcery, and censured the appeal to them, 'excepting only that to the amulet called the Lee Penny, to which it had pleased God to annex certain healing virtues which the Church did not presume to condemn.' It still, as has been said, exists, and its powers are sometimes resorted to. Of late they have been chiefly restricted to the cure of persons bitten by mad dogs; and as the illness in such cases frequently arises from imagination, there can be no reason for doubting that water which has been poured on the Lee Penny furnishes a congenial cure.

Such is the tradition concerning the talisman, which the Author has taken the liberty to vary in applying it to his own purposes.

Considerable liberties have also been taken with the truth of history, both with respect to Conrade of Montserrat's life as well as his death. That Conrade, however, was reckoned the enemy of Richard is agreed both in history and romance. The general opinion of the terms upon which they stood may be guessed from the proposal of the Saracens, that the Marquis of Montserrat should be invested with certain parts of Syria, which they were to yield to the Christians. Richard, according to the romance which bears his name, 'could no longer repress his fury. "The Marquis," he said, "was a traitor, who had robbed the Knights Hospitallers of sixty thousand pounds, the present of his father Henry; that he was a renegade, whose treachery had occasioned the loss of Acre"; and he concluded by a solemn oath, that he would cause him to be drawn to pieces by wild horses, if he should ever venture to pollute the Christian camp by his presence. Philip attempted to intercede in favour of the Marquis, and throwing down his glove, offered to become a pledge for his fidelity to the Christians; but his offer was rejected, and he was obliged to give way to Richard's impetuosity.'—[Ellis, *Specimens of Early English Metrical Romances*, 1805, vol. ii. p. 230.]

Conrade of Montserrat makes a considerable figure in those wars, and was at length put to death by one of the followers of the Scheik, or Old Man of the Mountain; nor did Richard remain free of the suspicion of having instigated his death.

It may be said, in general, that most of the incidents introduced in the following tale are fictitious; and that reality, where it exists, is only retained in the characters of the piece.

1st July 1832.

WOODSTOCK

The busy period of the great Civil War was one in which the character and genius of different parties were most brilliantly displayed, and, accordingly, the incidents which took place on either side were of a striking and extraordinary character, and afforded ample foundation for fictitious composition. The Author had in some measure attempted such in *Peveril of the Peak*; but the scene was in a remote part of the kingdom, and mingled with other national differences, which left him still at liberty to glean another harvest out of so ample a store.

In these circumstances, some wonderful adventures which happened at Woodstock in the year 1649 occurred to him as something he had long ago read of, although he was unable to tell where, and of which the hint appeared sufficient, although, doubtless, it might have been much better handled if the Author had not, in the lapse of time, lost everything like an accurate recollection of the real story.

It was not until about this period, namely, 1831, that the Author, being called upon to write this Introduction, obtained a general account of what really happened upon the marvellous occasion in question, in a work termed *The Everyday Book*, published by Mr. Hone, and full of curious antiquarian information concerning manners, illustrated by curious instances, rarely to be found elsewhere.* Among other matter, Mr. Hone quotes an

---

*Vol. ii. pp. 582–590, Lond. 1827 (*Laing*).

article from the *British Magazine* for 1747, in the following words, and which is probably the document which the Author of *Woodstock* had formerly perused, although he was unable to refer to the source of his information. The tract is entitled, *The Genuine History of the Good Devil of Woodstock, Famous in the World in the Year 1649, and never accounted for, or at all understood to this Time.*

The teller of this *Genuine History* proceeds verbatim as follows:

> Some original papers having lately fallen into my hands, under the name of *Authentic Memoirs of the Memorable Joseph Collins of Oxford, commonly known by the Name of Funny Joe, and now intended for the Press*, I was extremely delighted to find in them a circumstantial and unquestionable account of the most famous of all invisible agents, so well known in the year 1649, under the name of the Good Devil of Woodstock, and even adored by the people of that place, for the vexation and distress it occasioned some people they were not much pleased with. As this famous story, though related by a thousand people, and attested in all its circumstances, beyond all possibility of doubt, by people of rank, learning and reputation, of Oxford and the adjacent towns, has never yet been accounted for, or at all understood, and is perfectly explained, in a manner that can admit of no doubt, in these papers, I could not refuse my readers their share of the pleasure it gave me in reading.

There is, therefore, no doubt that, in the year 1649, a number of incidents, supposed to be supernatural, took place at the king's palace of Woodstock, which the Commissioners of Parliament were then and there endeavouring to dilapidate and destroy. The account of this by the Commissioners themselves, or under their authority, was repeatedly published, and, in particular, is inserted as Relation Sixth of *Satan's Invisible World Discovered,** by George Sinclair, Professor of Philosophy in Glasgow, an approved collector of such tales.[1]

It was the object of neither of the great political parties of that day to discredit this narrative, which gave great satisfaction both to the Cavaliers and Roundheads; the former conceiving that the license given to the demons was in consequence of the impious desecration of the king's furniture and apartments, so that the citizens of Woodstock almost adored the supposed spirits, as

---

*Originally published at Edinburgh, 1685, 12mo (*Laing*).

avengers of the cause of royalty; while the friends of the Parliament, on the other hand, imputed to the malice of the fiend the obstruction of the pious work, as they judged that which they had in hand.

At the risk of prolonging a curious quotation, I include a page or two from Mr. Hone's *Every-day Book*.
. . . .

Such is the explanation of the ghostly adventures of Woodstock, as transferred by Mr. Hone from the pages of the old tract termed the *Authentic Memoirs of the Memorable Joseph Collins of Oxford*, whose courage and loyalty were the only wizards which conjured up those strange and surprising apparitions and works of spirits which passed as so unquestionable in the eyes of the Parliamentary Commissioners, of Dr. Plot,[2] and other authors of credit. The *pulvis fulminans*, the secret principle he made use of, is now known to every apothecary's apprentice.

If my memory be not treacherous, the actor of these wonders made use of his skill in fireworks upon the following remarkable occasion. The Commissioners had not, in their zeal for the public service, overlooked their own private interests, and a deed was drawn up upon parchment, recording the share and nature of the advantages which they privately agreed to concede to each other; at the same time they were, it seems, loth to entrust to any one of their number the keeping of a document in which all were equally concerned. They hid the written agreement within a flower-pot, in which a shrub concealed it from the eyes of any chance spectator. But the rumor of the apparitions having gone abroad, curiosity drew many of the neighbours to Woodstock, and some in particular to whom the knowledge of the agreement would have afforded matter of scandal. As the Commissioners received these guests in the saloon where the flower-pot was placed, a match was suddenly set to some fireworks placed there by Sharp, the secretary. The flower-pot burst to pieces with the concussion, or was prepared so as to explode of itself, and the contract of the Commissioners, bearing testimony to their private roguery, was thrown into the midst of the visitors assembled. If I have recollected this incident accurately, for it is more than forty years since I perused the tract, it is probable that, in omitting it from the novel, I may also have passed over, from want of memory, other matters which might have made an essential addition to the story. Nothing, indeed, is more certain than that incidents which are real preserve an infinite advantage in works of this nature over such as are fictitious. The tree, however, must remain where it has fallen.

Having occasion to be in London in October 1831, I made some researches in the British Museum, and in that rich collection, with the kind assistance of the keepers, who manage it with so much credit to themselves and advantage to the public, I recovered two original pamphlets, which contain a full account of the phenomena at Woodstock in 1649. The first is a satirical poem, published in that year, which plainly shows that the legend was current among the people in the very shape in which it was afterwards made public. I have not found the explanation of Joe Collins, which, as mentioned by Mr. Hone, resolves the whole into confederacy. It might, however, be recovered by a stricter search than I had leisure for. In the meantime, it may be observed, that neither the name of Joe Collins nor Sharp occurs among the *dramatis personae* given in these tracts, published when he might have been endangered by anything which directed suspicion towards him, at least in 1649, and perhaps might have exposed him to danger even in 1660, from the malice of a powerful though defeated faction.*

1st *August* 1832.

---

*[See Lockhart, *Life of Scott*, vol. viii. pp. 353–358.]

CHRONICLES OF THE CANONGATE

Sic itur ad astra.[1]

The preceding volume* of this collection concluded the last of the pieces originally published under the *nominis umbra* of the Author of *Waverley*; and the circumstances which rendered it impossible for the writer to continue longer in the possession of his incognito were communicated, in 1827, in the Introduction to the First Series of *Chronicles of the Canongate*, consisting, besides a biographical sketch of the imaginary chronicler, of three tales, entitled *The Highland Widow, The Two Drovers,*† and *The Surgeon's Daughter.*

. . . .

I have, perhaps, said enough on former occasions of the misfortunes which led to the dropping of that mask under which I had, for a long series of years, enjoyed so large a portion of public favour. Through the success of those literary efforts I had been enabled to indulge most of the tastes which a retired person of my station might be supposed to entertain. In the pen of this nameless romancer I seemed to possess something like the secret fountain of coined gold and pearls vouchsafed to the traveller of the Eastern tale; and no doubt believed that I might venture, without silly imprudence, to extend my personal expenditure considerably beyond what I should have thought of had my means been limited to the competence which I derived from inheritance, with the moderate income of a professional situation. I bought, and built, and planted, and was considered by

---

*[*Woodstock*, according to the chronological order of original publication.]
†[Printed in the present edition along with *The Talisman*, vol. xx.]

myself, as by the rest of the world, in the safe possession of an easy fortune. My riches, however, like the other riches of this world, were liable to accidents, under which they were ultimately destined to make unto themselves wings and fly away. The year 1825, so disastrous to many branches of industry and commerce, did not spare the market of literature; and the sudden ruin that fell on so many of the booksellers could scarcely have been expected to leave unscathed one whose career had of necessity connected him deeply and extensively with the pecuniary transactions of that profession. In a word, almost without one note of premonition, I found myself involved in the sweeping catastrophe of the unhappy time, and called on to meet the demands of creditors upon commercial establishments with which my fortunes had long been bound up, to the extent of no less a sum than one hundred and twenty thousand pounds.

The Author having, however rashly, committed his pledges thus largely to the hazards of trading companies, it behoved him, of course, to abide the consequences of his conduct, and, with whatever feelings, he surrendered on the instant every shred of property which he had been accustomed to call his own. It became vested in the hands of gentlemen whose integrity, prudence, and intelligence were combined with all possible liberality and kindness of disposition, and who readily afforded every assistance towards the execution of plans in the success of which the Author contemplated the possibility of his ultimate extrication, and which were of such a nature that, had assistance of this sort been withheld, he could have had little prospect of carrying them into effect. Among other resources which occurred was the project of that complete and corrected edition of his novels and romances (whose real parentage had of necessity been disclosed at the moment of the commercial convulsions alluded to), which has now advanced with unprecedented favour nearly to its close; but as he purposed also to continue, for the behoof of those to whom he was indebted, the exercise of his pen in the same path of literature, so long as the taste of his countrymen should seem to approve of his efforts, it appeared to him that it would have been an idle piece of affectation to attempt getting up a new incognito, after his original visor had been thus dashed from his brow. Hence the personal narrative prefixed to the first work of fiction which he put forth after the paternity of the Waverley Novels had come to be publicly ascertained; and though many of the particulars originally avowed in that notice have been unavoidably adverted to in the prefaces and notes to some of the preceding volumes of the present collection, it is now reprinted as it stood at the time, because some interest is generally attached to a coin or medal struck on a special occasion, as expressing, perhaps, more faithfully than the same artist could have afterwards conveyed the feelings of the moment that gave it birth.

The Introduction to the First Series of *Chronicles of the Canongate* [1827] ran, then, in these words:

. . . .

Such was the little narrative which I thought proper to put forth in October 1827, nor have I much to add to it now. About to appear for the first time in my own name in this department of letters, it occurred to me that something in the shape of a periodical publication might carry with it a certain air of novelty, and I was willing to break, if I may so express it, the abruptness of my personal forthcoming by investing an imaginary coadjutor with at least as much distinctness of individual existence as I had ever previously thought it worth while to bestow on shadows of the same convenient tribe. Of course, it had never been in my contemplation to invite the assistance of any real person in the sustaining of my quasi-editorial character and labours. It had long been my opinion that anything like a literary picnic is likely to end in suggesting comparisons, justly termed odious, and therefore to be avoided; and, indeed, I had also had some occasion to know that promises of assistance, in efforts of that order, are apt to be more magnificent than the subsequent performance. I therefore planned a miscellany, to be dependent, after the old fashion, on my own resources alone, and although conscious enough that the moment which assigned to the Author of *Waverley* 'a local habitation and a name'[2] had seriously endangered his spell, I felt inclined to adopt the sentiment of my old hero Montrose, and to say to myself, that in literature, as in war,

> He either fears his fate too much,
>   Or his deserts are small,
> Who dares not put it to the touch,
>   To win or lose it all.[3]

To the particulars explanatory of the plan of these Chronicles, which the reader is presented with in chapter ii. by the imaginary editor, Mr. Croftangry, I have now to add, that the lady, termed in his narrative Mrs. Bethune Baliol, was designed to shadow out in its leading points the interesting character of a dear friend of mine, Mrs. Murray Keith, whose death occurring shortly before had saddened a wide circle much attached to her, as well for her genuine virtue and amiable qualities of disposition as for the extent of information which she possessed, and the delightful manner in which she was used to communicate it. In truth, the Author had, on many occasions, been indebted to her vivid memory for the *substratum* of his Scottish fictions; and she accordingly had been, from an early period, at no loss to fix the Waverley Novels on the right culprit.

In the sketch of Chrystal Croftangry's own history, the Author has been accused of introducing some not polite allusions to respectable living individuals; but he may safely, he presumes, pass over such an insinuation. The first of the narratives which Mr. Croftangry proceeds to lay before the public, *The Highland Widow*, was derived from Mrs. Murray Keith,* and is given, with the exception of a few additional circumstances—the introduction of which I am rather inclined to regret—very much as the excellent old lady used to tell the story. Neither the Highland cicerone MacTurk [MacLeish] nor the demure waiting-woman were drawn from imagination; and on re-reading my tale, after the lapse of a few years, and comparing its effect with my remembrance of my worthy friend's oral narration, which was certainly extremely affecting, I cannot but suspect myself of having marred its simplicity by some of those interpolations which, at the time when I penned them, no doubt passed with myself for embellishments.

The next tale, entitled *The Two Drovers*, I learned from another old friend, the late George Constable, Esq., of Wallace-Craigie, near Dundee, whom I have already introduced to my reader as the original Antiquary of Monkbarns. He had been present, I think, at the trial at Carlisle, and seldom mentioned the venerable judge's charge to the jury without shedding tears, which had

---

*[See Lockhart's *Life of Scott*, vol. ix. pp. 173, 174.]

peculiar pathos, as flowing down features carrying rather a sarcastic or almost a cynical expression.

This worthy gentleman's reputation for shrewd Scottish sense, knowledge of our national antiquities, and a racy humour peculiar to himself, must be still remembered. For myself, I have pride in recording that for many years we were, in Wordsworth's language,

> A pair of friends, though I was young,
> And 'George' was seventy-two.[4]

W. S.

ABBOTSFORD, *Aug.* 15, 1831.

THE FAIR MAID OF PERTH

In continuing the lucubrations of Chrystal Croftangry, it occurred that, although the press had of late years teemed with works of various descriptions concerning the Scottish Gael, no attempt had hitherto been made to sketch their manners, as these might be supposed to have existed at the period when the statute-book, as well as the page of the chronicler, begins to present constant evidence of the difficulties to which the crown was exposed, while the haughty house of Douglas all but over-balanced its authority on the Southern border, and the North was at the same time torn in pieces by the yet untamed savageness of the Highland races, and the daring loftiness to which some of the remoter chieftains still carried their pretensions. The well-authenticated fact of two powerful clans having deputed each thirty champions to fight out a quarrel of old standing, in presence of King Robert III., his brother the Duke of Albany, and the whole court of Scotland, at Perth, in the year of grace 1396, seemed to mark with equal distinctness the rancour of these mountain-feuds and the degraded condition of the general government of the country; and it was fixed upon accordingly as the point on which the main incidents of a romantic narrative might be made to hinge. The characters of Robert III., his ambitious brother, and his dissolute son seemed to offer some opportunities of interesting contrast; and the tragic fate of the heir of the throne, with its immediate consequences, might serve to complete the picture of cruelty and lawlessness.

233

Two features of the story of this barrier-battle on the Inch of Perth—the flight of one of the appointed champions, and the reckless heroism of a townsman, that voluntarily offered for a small piece of coin to supply his place in the mortal encounter—suggested the imaginary persons, on whom much of the novel is expended. The fugitive Celt might have been easily dealt with, had a ludicrous style of colouring been adopted; but it appeared to the Author that there would be more of novelty, as well as of serious interest, if he could succeed in gaining for him something of that sympathy which is incompatible with the total absence of respect. Miss Baillie had drawn a coward by nature capable of acting as a hero under the strong impulse of filial affection.[1] It seemed not impossible to conceive the case of one constitutionally weak of nerve being supported by feelings of honour and of jealousy up to a certain point, and then suddenly giving way, under circumstances to which the bravest heart could hardly refuse compassion.*

. . . .

The devotion of the young chief of Clan Quhele's foster-father and foster-brethren in the novel is a trait of clannish fidelity, of which Highland story furnishes many examples. In the battle of Inverkeithing, between the Royalists and Oliver Cromwell's troops, a foster-father and seven brave sons are known to have thus sacrificed themselves for Sir Hector Maclean of Duart; the old man, whenever one of his boys fell, thrusting forward another to fill his place at the right hand of the beloved chief, with the very words adopted in the novel—'Another for Hector!'

Nay, the feeling could outlive generations. The late much-lamented General Stewart of Garth, in his account of the battle of Killiecrankie,[2] informs us that Lochiel was attended on the field by the son of his foster-brother.

'This faithful adherent followed him like his shadow, ready to assist him with his sword, or cover him from the shot of the enemy. Suddenly the chief missed his friend from his side, and, turning round to look what had become of him, saw him lying on his back with his breast pierced by an arrow. He had hardly breath, before he expired, to tell Lochiel that, seeing an enemy, a Highlander in General Mackay's army, aiming at him with a bow and arrow, he

*[See Lockhart's *Life of Scott*, vol. ix. pp. 222–225.]

sprung behind him, and thus sheltered him from instant death. This,' observes the gallant David Stewart, 'is a species of duty not often practised, perhaps, by our aide-de-camps of the present day.'—*Sketches of the Highlanders*, vol. i. p. 65.

I have only to add, that the Second Series of *Chronicles of the Canongate*, with the chapter introductory which precedes, appeared in May 1828, and had a favourable reception.

ABBOTSFORD, *Aug.* 15, 1831.

ANNE OF GEIERSTEIN

This novel was written at a time when circumstances did not place within my reach the stores of a library tolerably rich in historical works, and especially the memoirs of the middle ages, amidst which I had been accustomed to pursue the composition of my fictitious narratives. In other words, it was chiefly the work of leisure hours in Edinburgh, not of quiet mornings in the country. In consequence of trusting to a memory strongly tenacious certainly, but not less capricious in its efforts, I have to confess on this occasion more violations of accuracy in historical details than can perhaps be alleged against others of my novels. In truth, often as I have been complimented on the strength of my memory, I have through life been entitled to adopt old Beattie of Meikledale's answer to his parish minister, when eulogising him with respect to the same faculty. 'No, doctor,' said the honest border-laird, 'I have no command of my memory: it only retains what happens to hit my fancy, and like enough, sir, if you were to preach to me for a couple of hours on end, I might be unable at the close of the discourse to remember one word of it.' Perhaps there are few men whose memory serves them with equal fidelity as to many different classes of subjects; but I am sorry to say that, while mine has rarely failed me as to any snatch of verse or trait of character that had once interested my fancy, it has generally been a frail support, not only as to names, and dates, and other minute technicalities of history, but as to many more important things.

I hope this apology will suffice for one mistake which has been pointed out to me by the descendant of one of the persons introduced in this story, and who complains with reason that I have made a peasant deputy of the ancestor of a distinguished and noble family, none of whom ever declined from the high rank to which, as far as my pen trenched on it, I now beg leave to restore them. The name of the person who figures as deputy of Soleure in these pages was always, it seems, as it is now, that of a patrician house. I am reminded by the same correspondent of another slip, probably of less consequence. The Emperor of the days my novel refers to, though the representative of that Leopold who fell in the great battle of Sempach, never set up any pretensions against the liberties of the gallant Swiss, but, on the contrary, treated with uniform prudence and forbearance such of that nation as had established their independence, and with wise, as well as generous, kindness others who still continued to acknowledge fealty to the imperial crown. Errors of this sort, however trivial, ought never, in my opinion, to be pointed out to an author without meeting with a candid and respectful acknowledgment.

With regard to a general subject of great curiosity and interest, in the eyes at least of all antiquarian students, upon which I have touched at some length in this narrative, I mean the Vehmic tribunals of Westphalia, a name so awful in men's ears during many centuries, and which, through the genius of Goethe,[1] has again been revived in public fancy with a full share of its ancient terrors, I am bound to state my opinion that a wholly new and most important light has been thrown upon this matter since *Anne of Geierstein* first appeared, by the elaborate researches of my ingenious friend, Mr. Francis Palgrave, whose proof-sheets, containing the passages I allude to, have been kindly forwarded to me, and whose complete work will be before the public ere this Introduction can pass through the press.[2]

. . . .

There are probably several other points on which I ought to have embraced this opportunity of enlarging; but the necessity of preparing for an excursion to foreign countries, in quest of health and strength, that have been for some time sinking, makes me cut short my address upon the present occasion.

Although I had never been in Switzerland, and numerous mistakes must of course have occurred in my attempts to describe the local scenery of that romantic region, I must not conclude without a statement highly gratifying to myself, that the work met with a reception of more than usual cordiality among the descendants of the Alpine heroes whose manners I had ventured to treat of; and I have in particular to express my thanks to the several Swiss gentlemen who have, since the novel was published, enriched my little collection of armour with specimens of the huge weapon that sheared the lances of the Austrian chivalry at Sempach, and was employed with equal success on the bloody days of Granson and Morat. Of the ancient double-handed *espadons* of the Switzer, I have, in this way, received, I think, not less than six, in excellent preservation, from as many different individuals, who thus testified their general approbation of these pages. They are not the less interesting, that gigantic swords of nearly the same pattern and dimensions were employed, in their conflicts with the bold knights and men-at-arms of England, by Wallace and the sturdy foot-soldiers who, under his guidance, laid the foundations of Scottish independence.

The reader who wishes to examine with attention the historical events of the period which the novel embraces, will find ample means of doing so in the valuable works of Zschokke[3] and M. de Barante—which last author's account of the Dukes of Burgundy is among the most valuable of recent accessions of European literature[4]—and in the new Parisian edition of Froissart,[5] which has not as yet attracted so much attention in this country as it well deserves to do.*

W. S.

ABBOTSFORD, *Sept.* 17, 1831.

---

*[See J. G. Lockhart, *Life of Scott*, vol. ix. pp. 321–323.]

COUNT ROBERT OF PARIS

The preface to Count Robert of Paris *is here published for the first time. Objections might be raised by admirers of Scott because of its obvious faults. But I believe it should be published for several reasons. First, Scott and Ballantyne intended to publish it. The National Library of Scotland has the manuscript, proofs, and corrected proofs of the preface. On the top of the latter, Ballantyne initials, "Correct this* instantly, *as many hands as can get about it. A new proof* must be sent out by half past 2 at latest." *For some reason—probably Scott's departure in September* 1831 *for his final trip abroad—the new proof apparently could not be gotten to Scott in time. Second, it completes the series of prefaces Scott wrote for the "Magnum Opus." In collected editions, Lockhart writes in his preface to* Count Robert *that Scott forwarded the preface to* Castle Dangerous *from Naples in February* 1832; *"but if he ever wrote one for a second edition of* Count Robert of Paris, *it has not been discovered among his papers." Third, it contains interesting information on the last of Scott's full-length novels. Fourth and most important, it testifies once again to the courage of the man. Scott's struggle against his physical and intellectual weakness disarms criticism and evokes admiration.*

The author was about to bestow some care in concluding the present romance, as being very probably the last work of fiction on which he may be again tempted to engage; but he feels that the assertion has been, for different reasons, so often solemnly made, forgot, and reiterated and again departed from, that he has very little credence to expect from the mildest of critics, who will thus take up Mrs. Quickly's reply to Falstaff, when he swears upon his honour—"Nay, you said so before."[1]

The truth however is, that a dangerous disorder, incident to the time of life which he has reached, has, for more than a twelvemonth, attacked the author, with a severity not very capable of being consistent with the works of imagination; nor is it pleasant to feel one's self discharging, with pain and toil, a task which, upon other occasions, has proved as light to himself, as it might be fairly held trifling with a view to the public. It would be too disgraceful to require the hint, extorted from the unwilling secretary of the Archbishop of Granada, and at the same time wait till a time when he himself should become incapable of profiting by it; for no writer can assure himself that the kindest criticism of the best friend might not be answered by the retort, that the Aristarch was too young to discover good from evil—that the romance which he criticised was, in fact, the best which the author had ever composed—and that the correspondence of the author's critic, if not closed by a draft upon his treasurer of a hundred ducats, or, at least, his best wishes for his admirer's prosperity, with a little more taste than it is his good fortune to enjoy at present.[2]

It must be owned, that the part played by the worthy archbishop on this occasion, is one that is by no means enviable, as considered in perspective, by any author who has ever enjoyed a considerable portion of the public favour; and the author of Waverley is determined that I will be well assured that his present composition does not smell of the apoplexy, of which I myself am perhaps no good judge, before I commit the same error in another composition. As I have always dealt upon the square with the public, I think myself obliged to do so, when producing what is probably the last of my fictitious compositions; and with this view, I will candidly explain what was my object in this last attempt, in order that he may judge fairly, whether or not it has been my good fortune to attain it.

It cannot be a matter of doubt that the purpose of an author of a work of fiction is to fix the public attention and for that purpose obtain novelty at whatever rate; nay, if he has not the fortune to unite this necessary qualification with a probable tale of a romantic nature, the public good-naturedly permits him to lay his scene in distant countries, among stranger nations, whose manners are imagined for the purpose of the story—nay, whose powers are extended beyond those of human nature, so that there are no limits within the power of a reasonably powerful enchanter, to which the fictitious author may not extend his own capacity, in despite of the limits of natural, and even moral impossibility. Whoever was the author of "Peter Wilkins," with his *glums* and his *gawries*,[3] which had the honour of suggesting to the Poet-Laureate the *Glendoveers*,[4] the most beautiful creation, perhaps, of Fancy, stepping beyond the boundaries of nature, must certainly be of opinion, that the pleasure received by the reader's imagination infinitely compensated that shock with which sober reason entertains the idea of human beings transporting themselves, with wings so ingeniously formed, through the bounds of the empyrean. A late novel, also, by the name of Frankenstein,[5] which turns upon a daring invention, supposing the discovery of a mode by which one human being is feigned to be capable of creating another, by a process hitherto unknown, has also been forgiven, because this enormous postulate being granted, gives rise to an interesting series of discussions between the person whom he has created, and he himself the creator, as he is termed, starting between them a great number of interesting situations and discussions, which could not have existed between two creatures who did not hold, with respect to each other, the impossible and extravagant relation which is here supposed.

These two celebrated instances are sufficient to prove, that almost any species of extravagance is pardoned to the author who aspires to entertain the public by the wildest flights of imagination, providing he can do so without trespassing on the rules of morality or of good breeding.

The costume of foreign nations, their habits and manners, are a very common resort upon this occasion, and the present author was of opinion, in undertaking the present task, that a more striking contrast could hardly be obtained than by setting the manners, the ultra civilization of the laws, and extreme punctiliousness of the Grecian empire towards its close, in comparison with, and in opposition to, the warlike people of the West, simple in their Arms, who came to Greece with the extraordinary intention of totally subduing the followers of Mahommed, in the kingdoms which they had gained to the faith of God and the Prophet, as the Moslem expressed it.

In comparing their people, one remarkable characteristic of the fair sex was equally contrasted with the manners of the Greek females, and those accounted decorous among the people of the East. The western ladies, in contradiction to the doctrines of Christianity, and of Nature herself, were remarkable for the slight occasions on which, transgressing the dictates of Homer, they proudly refused to leave the business of the war to men; or, in other words, mingled, without either fear or scruple, in the combats, which were the chief and constant employment of their husbands and lovers; while in other countries the female sex was contented with awarding the prize of valour, if in any respect they mixed in the field.

It is not in romances alone, that the Marphisas and Brada-mantes made themselves remarkable by deeds of manly valour, and by encountering hand to hand the strongest champions of the other sex. In history also, the wives and daughters of the western nobles showed the same courage. There cannot be found a stronger example than that of Gaeta, wife of the celebrated Robert Guiscard, thus told by Anna Comnena, whom we have so often mentioned in this history, and whose father was repeatedly at war with the celebrated Count Robert.

"The Emperor of Greece had obtained some advantage in an action of light troops with the Latins, when," the fair historian says, "they say that Gaeta, the wife of Robert, who followed her husband to the wars, and fought like a Pallas, although she was not so learned as Minerva of Athens, looked upon the fugitives of her army with an eye of anger, and raising her voice, said aloud to them, in their own language, something resembling in sense that famous line of Homer,—'How long will you fly? stop at length, and shew yourselves men.'—And since she was not so powerful as to stop the flight by the force of her voice alone, like the Pagan Goddess she pursued them with lance in hand, rallied them, and brought them back to the combat, where they defeated a fresh charge of Alexius, and killed very many of his best soldiers."— *Hist. de l'Empereur Alexius*, Chap. 5.

This heroine Gaeta is mentioned by the historian Anna Comnena, upon several other occasions, and never without commendations of her valour. It is certain, therefore, that the heroines of Europe carried into the Crusades with them their love of single combat, which must have appeared so strange to the ladies of the east. It was therefore the hope of the author to have produced some comedy from the meeting of such a heroine as Gaeta, or Brenhilda, challenging to single combat the Princess Anna Comnena, a lady of a spirit sufficiently high to despise submission to a challenge without answer, and although the defiance was of a nature to which she might hardly have thought herself amenable, yet who might be supposed rather to accept it than put up with such an affront, according to her own phrase, to a princess born in the purple chamber.

The author had not forgotten what the reader will probably remember, the ingenious allegory, namely, of the Sexes, which exists in the Spectator, and where the two nations, each pretended to count exclusively of men and women, are finally reconciled, after several ingenious events, by the force of those passions to which both men and women are naturally subject, and the contradiction of which must be, in a great measure, considered as a contradiction of the proper ends of their nature.[6]

This allegory itself, well known in its prose shape, exists also in poetry, and is, we believe, found in the earlier numbers of the Scottish Magazine.[7] The version is extremely poetical, and must be familiar to many of my readers. The real illness of Brenhilda would, indeed, have been liable to an objection which does not occur as equally applicable to supposing that at the period of the single combat her natural courage was, as physicians say usually happens, open to a train of attacks springing from the imagination, but not on that account the less certainly disabling courage, and destroying firmness of mind, upon occasions when the party would most willingly make a display of both. It happened, however, that the author did not feel himself very able to finish this part of his task with the success to which he conceived it capable of being wrought up. In the meantime, an accidental circumstance placed a part of the manuscript, without the author's knowledge, in the hands of a bookseller in America, under circumstances which permitted him to make it public, and of course rendered it impossible to refuse the actual proprietor the means of rendering available his own property for his own interest. All further anxiety with respect to the finishing of the tale was necessarily laid aside, and the romance, though perhaps the last which the Author of Waverley shall write, comes before the public like the elder Hamlet before his last Judge,

"With all its imperfections on its head."[8]

CASTLE DANGEROUS

The incidents on which the ensuing Novel mainly turns are derived from the ancient metrical chronicle of *The Bruce*, by Archdeacon Barbour,[1] and from *The History of the Houses of Douglas and Angus*, by David Hume of Godscroft;[2] and are sustained by the immemorial tradition of the western parts of Scotland. They are so much in consonance with the spirit and manners of the troubled age to which they are referred, that I can see no reason for doubting their being founded in fact: the names, indeed, of numberless localities in the vicinity of Douglas Castle appear to attest, beyond suspicion, many even of the smallest circumstances embraced in the story of Godscroft.

Among all the associates of Robert the Bruce, in his great enterprise of rescuing Scotland from the power of Edward, the first place is universally conceded to James, the eighth Lord Douglas, to this day venerated by his countrymen as 'the Good Sir James':

> And Gud Schyr James off Douglas,
> That in his time sa worthy was,
> That off his price and his bounté,
> In fer landis renownyt wes he.—BARBOUR [bk. i.].

> The Good Sir James, the dreadful blacke Douglas,
> That in his dayes so wise and worthie was,

245

Wha here, and on the infidels of Spain,
Such honour, praise, and triumphs did obtain.—GORDON.*

From the time when the King of England refused to reinstate him, on his return from France, where he had received the education of chivalry, in the extensive possessions of his family, which had been held forfeited by the exertions of his father, William the Hardy, the young knight of Douglas appears to have embraced the cause of Bruce with enthusiastic ardour, and to have adhered to the fortunes of his sovereign with unwearied fidelity and devotion. 'The Douglasse,' says Hollinshed[3] [*Historie of Scotland*, p. 215, ed. 1585], 'was joyfully received of King Robert, in whose service he faithfully continued, both in peace and war, to his life's end. Though the surname and familie of the Douglasses was in some estimation of nobilitie before those daies, yet the rising thereof to honour chanced through this James Douglasse; for, by meanes of his advancement, others of that lineage tooke occasion, by their singular manhood and noble prowess, shewed at sundrie times in defence of the realme, to grow to such height in authoritie and estimation, that their mightie puissance in mainrent, lands, and great possessions at length was, through suspicion conceived by the kings that succeeded, the cause in part of their ruinous decay.'

In every narrative of the Scottish war of independence, a considerable space is devoted to those years of perilous adventure and suffering which were spent by the illustrious friend of Bruce in harassing the English detachments successively occupying his paternal territory, and in repeated and successful attempts to wrest the formidable fortress of Douglas Castle itself from their possession. In the English as well as Scotch Chronicles, and in Rymer's *Foedera*,[4] occur frequent notices of the different officers entrusted by Edward with the keeping of this renowned stronghold; expecially Sir Robert de Clifford, ancestor of the heroic race of the Cliffords, Earls of Cumberland; his lieutenant, Sir Richard de Thurlewalle (written sometimes Thruswall), of Thirlwall Castle, on the Tipalt in Northumberland; and Sir John de Walton, the romantic story of whose love-pledge, to hold the

---

*Patrick Gordon, who published in 1615, in heroic verse, the first book of *The History of Prince Robert, surnamed the Bruce* (*Laing*).

Castle of Douglas for a year and day, or surrender all hope of
obtaining his mistress's favour, with the tragic consequences
softened in the Novel, is given at length in Godscroft, and has
often been pointed out as one of the affecting passages in the
chronicles of chivalry.*

The Author, before he had made much progress in this,
probably the last of his Novels, undertook a journey to Douglas
Dale, for the purpose of examining the remains of the famous
castle, the kirk of St. Bride of Douglas, the patron saint of that
great family, and the various localities alluded to by Godscroft in
his account of the early adventures of Good Sir James; but though
he was fortunate enough to find a zealous and well-informed
cicerone in Mr. Thomas Haddow, and had every assistance from
the kindness of Mr. Alexander Finlay, the resident chamberlain
of his friend, Lord Douglas, the state of his health at the time was
so feeble, that he found himself incapable of pursuing his
researches, as in better days he would have delighted to do, and
was obliged to be contented with such a cursory view of scenes, in
themselves most interesting, as could be snatched in a single
morning, when any bodily exertion was painful. Mr. Haddow was
attentive enough to forward subsequently some notes on the
points which the Author had seemed desirous of investigating;
but these did not reach him until, being obliged to prepare
matters for a foreign excursion in quest of health and strength, he
had been compelled to bring his work, such as it is, to a
conclusion.

The remains of the old Castle of Douglas are inconsiderable.
They consist indeed of but one ruined tower, standing at a short
distance from the modern mansion, which itself is only a fragment of the design on which the Duke of Douglas meant to
reconstruct the edifice, after its last accidental destruction by fire.
His Grace had kept in view the ancient prophecy that, as often as
Douglas Castle might be destroyed, it should rise again in
enlarged dimensions and improved splendour, and projected a
pile of building which, if it had been completed, would have much
exceeded any nobleman's residence then existing in Scotland, as

---

*The reader will find both this story and that of *Count Robert of Paris* in Sir W.
Scott's essay on 'Chivalry,' published in 1818, in the Supplement to the *Encyclopaedia Britannica* (*Lockhart*).

indeed what has been finished, amounting to about one-eighth part of the plan, is sufficiently extensive for the accommodation of a large establishment, and contains some apartments the dimensions of which are magnificent. The situation is commanding; and though the Duke's successors have allowed the mansion to continue as he left it, great expense has been lavished on the environs, which now present a vast sweep of richly undulated woodland, stretching to the borders of the Cairntable mountains, repeatedly mentioned as the favourite retreat of the great ancestor of the family in the days of his hardship and persecution. There remains at the head of the adjoining *bourg* the choir of the ancient church of St. Bride, having beneath it the vault which was used till lately as the burial-place of this princely race, and only abandoned when their stone and leaden coffins had accumulated, in the course of five or six hundred years, in such a way that it could accommodate no more. Here a silver case, containing the dust of what was once the brave heart of Good Sir James, is still pointed out; and in the dilapidated choir above appears, though in a sorely ruinous state, the once magnificent tomb of the warrior himself. After detailing the well-known circumstances of Sir James's death in Spain, 20[25]th August 1330, where he fell, assisting the King of Arragon in an expedition against the Moors, when on his way back to Scotland from Jerusalem, to which he had conveyed the heart of Bruce, the old poet Barbour tells us [bk. xiv.] that—

> Quhen his men lang had mad murnyn,
> Thai debowalyt him, and syne
> Gert scher him swa, that mycht be tane
> The flesch all haly fra the bane,
> And the carioune thar in haly place
> Erdyt, with rycht gret worschip, was.
>
> The banys haue thai with thaim tane;
> And syne ar to their schippis gane;
>
> .   .   .   .
>
> Syne towart Scotland held thair way,
> And thar ar cummyn in full gret hy.
> And the banys honorabilly
> In till the kyrk off Douglas war

Erdyt, with dule and mekill car.
Schyr Archebald his sone gert syn
Off alabastre, bath fair and fyne,
Ordane a tumbe sa richly
As it behowyt to swa worthy.

The monument is supposed to have been wantonly mutilated
and defaced by a detachment of Cromwell's troops, who, as was
their custom, converted the kirk of St. Bride of Douglas into a
stable for their horses. Enough, however, remains to identify the
resting-place of the great Sir James. The effigy, of dark stone, is
cross-legged, marking his character as one who had died after
performing the pilgrimage to the Holy Sepulchre, and in actual
conflict with the infidels of Spain; and the introduction of the
HEART, adopted as an addition to the old arms of Douglas, in
consequence of the knight's fulfilment of Bruce's dying injunc-
tion, appears, when taken in connexion with the posture of the
figure, to set the question at rest. The monument, in its original
state, must have been not inferior in any respect to the best of the
same period in Westminster Abbey; and the curious reader is
referred for farther particulars of it to *The Sepulchral Antiquities of
Great Britain*, by Edward Blore, F.S.A. (London, 1826), where
may also be found interesting details of some of the other tombs
and effigies in the cemetery of the first house of Douglas.

As considerable liberties have been taken with the historical
incidents on which this novel is founded, it is due to the reader to
place before him such extracts from Godscroft and Barbour as
may enable him to correct any mis-impression. The passages
introduced in the Appendix, from the ancient poem of *The Bruce*,
will moreover gratify those who have not in their possession a
copy of the text of Barbour, as given in the valuable quarto
edition of my learned friend Dr. Jamieson,[5] as furnishing on the
whole a favourable specimen of the style and manner of a
venerable classic who wrote when Scotland was still full of the
fame and glory of her liberators from the yoke of Plantagenet,
and especially of Sir James Douglas, 'of whom,' says Godscroft [p.
52, ed. 1644], 'we will not omit here (to shut up all) the judgment
of those times concerning him, in a rude verse indeed, yet such as
beareth witness of his true magnanimity and invincible mind in
either fortune, good or bad:—

The Late History

Good Sir James Douglas, who wise, and wight, and worthy was,
Was never overglad in no winning, nor yet oversad for no tineing;
Good fortune and evil chance he weighed both in one balance.

W. S.

NOTES

A Preface to the Prefaces

1. M. H. Macartney, "Sir Walter Scott's Use of the Preface," *Longman's Magazine* 46 (1905), rpt. in *Living Age* 247 (1905): 495.

2. Honoré de Balzac, preface to the first edition of *La Femme Supérieure* (1838), rpt. in John O. Hayden, ed., *Scott: The Critical Heritage* (New York: Barnes and Noble, 1970), p. 375.

3. George Saintsbury, *Sir Walter Scott* (Edinburgh: Oliphant, Anderson, and Ferrier, 1897), p. 69.

4. Andrew Lang, ed., *A Legend of Montrose* (Boston: Dana Estes, 1893), p. xii; R. S. Rait, "Scott as Critic and Judge," *Times Literary Supplement*, 7 November 1918, p. 509; James T. Hillhouse, *The Waverley Novels and Their Critics* (1936; rpt. New York: Octagon Books, 1968). p. 15.

5. Mary Lascelles, "Scott and the Art of Revision," *Imagined Worlds*. ed. M. Mack and I. R. Gregor (London: Methuen, 1968), pp. 139, 156.

6. For a convincing solution of the mystery, see Martin Lightfoot, "Scott's Self-Review: Manuscript and Other Evidence," *Nineteenth-Century Fiction* 23 (1968): 150–60.

7. "On a Peal of Bells," *The Roundabout Papers*, vol. 22 of *The Works of William M. Thackeray* (London: Cheltenham Society, 1904), p. 267.

8. Gustave Flaubert, letter of 12 July 1872 to George Sand, quoted in Francis Hart, "*The Fair Maid*, Manzoni's *Betrothed* and the Grounds of Waverley Criticism," *Nineteenth-Century Fiction* 18 (1963); rpt. in D. D. Devlin, ed., *Walter Scott: Modern Judgements* (Nashville: Aurora, 1970), p. 173.

Notes

9. Georg Lukács, *The Historical Novel*, trans. Hannah and Stanley Mitchell (Boston: Beacon Press, 1963 [originally published 1937]); rpt. in *Scott's Mind and Art*, ed. A. Norman Jeffares (New York: Barnes and Noble, 1970), pp. 93–131. Alexander Welsh, *The Hero of the Waverley Novels* (New Haven: Yale University Press, 1963).

10. David Masson, *British Novelists and Their Styles* (Cambridge, England: Macmillan, 1859), p. 203.

11. Mark Twain, chapter 46 of *Life on the Mississippi* (1883), rpt. in Hayden, *Scott*, p. 537.

12. Ian Jack, *English Literature: 1815–1832* (New York: Oxford University Press, 1963), p. 185.

13. *Quarterly Review* 16 (1817): 430–80.

Waverley: A Postscript

1. Heritable jurisdictions: legal rights of landowners over their tenants, abolished in 1747.

2. Thomas Douglas Selkirk (1771–1820), fifth earl of Selkirk, author of *Observations on the Present State of the Highlands of Scotland, with a View of the Causes and Probable Consequences of Emigration* (1805).

3. *Douglas*, a Scottish tragedy (1756) by the Reverend John Home (1722–1808), who also wrote *A History of the Rebellion in 1745* (1802).

4. Maria Edgeworth (1767–1849), Irish writer, whose best-known novels present a realistic picture of Irish life.

5. Elizabeth Hamilton (1758–1816), author of the novel *The Cottagers of Glenburnie* (1808).

6. Anne MacVicar Grant (1755–1838), author of *Essays on the Superstitions of the Highlanders* (1811).

7. Henry Mackenzie (1745–1831), Scottish man of letters, best known as the author of *The Man of Feeling* (1771). Colonel Caustic appears in *The Lounger* (1785–87), Umphraville in *The Mirror* (1779–80), both of which publications Mackenzie edited.

Waverley: Introductory

1. *The Mysteries of Udolpho* (1794) by Ann Radcliffe (1764–1823) was the most famous of the Gothic romances of that time. In the very first paragraph of his novelistic career, Scott is satirizing various kinds of contemporary fiction: Gothic horrors, German romances, sentimental and "silver-fork" novels. Cf. Jane Austen's satire in *Northanger Abbey*.

2. Rosicrucians and Illuminati: international secret fraternities interested in magic and the supernatural.

Notes

3. Grosvenor Square and Queen Anne Street East were fashionable addresses, the Barouche Club and the Four-in-Hand were fashionable clubs, and the Bow Street Office was the headquarters of the principal London police court and the Bow Street runners, the nearest equivalent to a modern police force.

4. Bond Street: a center for fashionable clothes.

5. Cf. Edmund Spenser, *The Shepheardes Calendar*, "Julye," l. 173.

Introduction to *The Antiquary*

1. William Wordsworth (1770–1850), in the famous preface to the second edition of *Lyrical Ballads* (1800). Scott's announced program for fiction here is remarkably like Wordsworth's for poetry.

Review of *Tales of My Landlord*

1. Cf. Terence, *Heautontimorumenos* 1. 1. 25: "Homo sum, humani nil a me alienum puto."

2. *The Rehearsal* (1671), 3. 1. Bayes is the satirical portrait of Dryden by George Villiers, second duke of Buckingham (1628–87).

3. *The Knight of the Burning Pestle*, Induction and 3. 3, Scott's conflation of two separate passages.

4. William Augustus, duke of Cumberland (1721–65), third son of King George II, and commander of the government forces in Scotland during the later stages of the campaign.

5. Scott himself, who, as a youth, was deeply impressed by Alexander Stewart's recounting of his romantic adventures.

6. Rev. Robert Law (d. 1690?), author of *Memorialls; or, The Memorable Things That Fell Out within This Island of Britain from 1638 to 1684*.

7. Paulus Pleydell, an Edinburgh advocate in *Guy Mannering* who enjoyed his "altitudes."

8. George Crabbe (1754–1832), *The Village* 1. 239.

9. Strap, an amiable, simple-hearted character from *Roderick Random* (1748).

10. Scott admits, in the introduction to *Guy Mannering*, that he himself wrote this section in the first volume of *Blackwood's Edinburgh Magazine* (1817).

11. John Emery (1777–1822), an actor famous for his impersonations of countrymen, including Dandie Dinmont.

12. *Don Quixote* 1. 32.

13. John Gay (1685–1732), author of *The Shepherd's Week in Six Pastorals* (1714). In the proeme, Gay promises a language "not only such

Notes

as in the present Times is not uttered, but was never uttered in Times past; and, if I judge aright, will never be uttered in Times future."

14. "Life of Gay" in *Prefaces, Biographical and Critical, to the Works of the English Poets* (1779–81).

15. Scott surely intended to write "inartificial," which has its nineteenth-century meaning of constructed without art or skill; inartistic.

16. *The Miller and His Men* (1813) by Isaac Pocock (1782–1835).

17. *Measure for Measure* 2. 1. Pompey actually wanted to be "supposed upon a book."

18. Thomas Scott (1774–1823), one of Scott's younger brothers, who was then in Canada. Walter Scott is, of course, indulging his own penchant for humor and mystification.

Ivanhoe: Dedicatory Epistle

1. Horn of King Ulphus, in W. R. Scott's *Antiquarian Gleanings in the North of England*: "The Horn of Ulphus is about two feet and a half in length. By means of it Ulphus, a Danish nobleman of the time of Canute, enfeoffed the church with his lands and revenues" (quoted by Andrew Lang, ed., *Ivanhoe* [Boston: Dana Estes, 1893], 1:313). But Dr. Dryasdust is, of course, a persona of Scott.

2. Epopeia: the making of epics.

3. James MacPherson (1736–96), Scottish poet and antiquarian, most famous for the production of *Fingal* (1762) and *Temora* (1763), epics purporting to be translations from the Gaelic of Ossian.

4. 2 Kings 5:12 (misquoted slightly). Kendal green was a species of green woolen cloth named after Kendal in Westmorland, its original place of manufacture.

5. Lucan (39–65), Roman poet whose chief work is the *Pharsalia*. See 6. 629–31: the witch picks out her prophet, prying into the inmost parts cold in death, till she finds the substance of the stiffened lungs unwounded and still firm, and seeking the power of utterance in a corpse (*Pharsalia*, trans. J. D. Duff [Cambridge, Mass.: Harvard University Press, 1928], p. 351).

6. Richard Henry (1718–90), author of a *History of Great Britain*; Joseph Strutt (1749–1802), artist and antiquary, author of several books on English history and a historical novel, *Queenhoo-Hall*, which was completed and arranged for publication by Scott; Sharon Turner (1768–1847), whose chief work was a *History of the Anglo-Saxons* (1799–1805).

7. Jonathan Oldbuck, the antiquary of Scott's novel of that name (1816).

Notes

8. Horace Walpole (1717–97), versatile man of letters, author of the first Gothic novel, *The Castle of Otranto* (1764).

9. George Ellis (1753–1815), poet, satirist, and friend of Scott, published *Specimens of Early English Romances in Metre* (1805).

10. William Caxton (ca. 1421–91), first English printer; Wynkyn de Worde (ca. 1457–1535), Caxton's assistant and successor.

11. Antoine Gallande (1646–1715), orientalist and translator of the *Arabian Nights* (1704–17).

12. *Faerie Queene* 4. 2. 32. 8.

13. Thomas Chatterton (1752–70), poet and antiquarian, fabricated a number of poems purporting to be the work of an imaginary fifteenth-century Bristol poet, Thomas Rowley.

14. *Merchant of Venice* 3. 1.

15. At this point, James Ballantyne, printer of Scott's work, wrote on the proof sheet, "I am so terrified for anything like the dirty rust of that hateful Queenhoo Hall, that I venture to make the needless remark, that *Shakespeare's* language is, in general, quite modern, though near 300 years old."

Scott replied, "Shakespeare I suspect is not modern—it is we who are so familiar with him that his obsolete expressions are like the square toed shoes of our grandfathers familiar to ourselves."

16. Ingulf (d. 1109), Abbot of Croyland, secretary to William the Conqueror, erroneously believed to be the chronicler of *The Croyland History*; Geoffrey de Vinsauf (fl. 1200), author of *Poëtria Nova*, a mixture of classical precept and medieval practice; Jean Froissart (ca. 1337–ca. 1410), French chronicler, whose literary artistry and chivalric spirit impressed Scott.

17. Wardour, another character from *The Antiquary* by Scott (1816). The Wardour manuscript is imaginary.

18. Arthur's Oven, an ancient building in the parish of Larbert. In *The Antiquary*, Scott satirizes antiquarian theorizing about it. As Laurence Templeton indicates here, the monument disappeared. Habitancum is a Roman fort north of Hadrian's Wall in Risingham, Northumberland.

19. Good-bye, at last; remember me.

Introductory Epistle to *The Fortunes of Nigel*

1. How good and how pleasant!

2. Cordery or Corderius, i.e., Mathurin Cordier (1478–1564), author of many grammatical works, the best known being his uninspiring *Colloquia Scholastica* (1564), still in use when Scott attended the Edinburgh High School.

Notes

3. William Collins (1721–59), "Ode on the Popular Superstitions of the Highlands of Scotland," 2. 68–69.

4. Bennaskar, in the "History of Mahoud," one of the *Tales of the Genii*.

5. Hail, great father!

6. *Faerie Queene* 7. 7. 5. 5–7.

7. Which may be allotted to males alone.

8. Cleishbotham, another persona of Scott.

9. Wanton spirit.

10. *Tempest* 4. 1. It was, in fact, a stinking pool.

11. The Cock-lane ghost and the Drummer of Tedworth were supposedly paranormal phenomena, described in Boswell's *Life of Johnson* and Joseph Glanvill's *Saducismus Triumphatus*, respectively.

12. *Midsummer Night's Dream* 1. 2.

13. *Don Quixote* 1. 20–21.

14. Henry Fielding (1707–54), author of *Tom Jones* (1749) and *Amelia* (1751).

15. Tobias Smollett (1721–71) and Alain-René Lesage (1668–1747), masters of the picaresque novel.

16. Bayes, Buckingham's satirical portrait of John Dryden in *The Rehearsal* (1671). Scott edited the works and wrote the life of Dryden, and portrayed Buckingham in *Peveril of the Peak*.

17. Junius, the pseudonymous author of a series of letters in the *Public Advertiser* (1769–71) attacking George III and important government officials. John Taylor, in *Discovery of the Author of Junius* (1813) and *The Identity of Junius* (1816), argued that Sir Philip Francis (1740–1818) was the author.

18. William Shenstone (1714–63), "Inscription to the Memory of A. L., Esquire," 2. 212–14.

19. Samuel Johnson (1709–84), to Boswell on 15 May 1783.

20. John Warburton (1682–1759), antiquary and collector of rare manuscripts. Through his carelessness and the ignorance of Betsy Baker, his servant, fifty-five manuscripts (some of them unique) were destroyed by fire.

21. Roxburghe Club: the antiquarian book club for the chief bibliophiles of the day.

22. Thomas Parnell (1679–1718), "The Hermit," ll. 171–73 (adapted freely).

23. Major Longbow, the comedian Charles Mathews (1776–1835).

24. Laberius: name of a Roman gens (the patrilinear clan forming the basic unit of the Roman tribe), the most famous member of which was D. Laberius, a knight and writer of mimes.

Notes

25. Allan Cunningham (1784–1842), the Scottish folklorist, poet, and dramatist.

26. *The Letters of Sir Walter Scott*, ed. H. J. C. Grierson et. al., 12 vols. (London: Constable, 1932–37), 6:319n. All references to the letters will be to this edition.

27. Angelica Catalani (1780–1849), the Italian diva who sang in Great Britain (1806–13). Kennaquhair means "Know-not-where."

28. Times change.

29. Robert Burns (1759–96), in "For A' That and A' That."

30. *Merry Wives of Windsor* 2. 2. Scott wrote eighteen pence; Ballantyne made the correction.

31. Edinburgh.

32. 1 *Henry IV* 2. 4 (adapted).

33. Adam Smith (1723–90), *The Wealth of Nations* (1776), pt. 2, sec. 2, chapt. 2.

34. Oliver Goldsmith (ca. 1730–74), in "The Indigent Philosopher" (1762).

35. Flappers keep the theorizing rulers of Laputa awake in the third part of *Gulliver's Travels*.

36. 1 *Henry IV* 1. 2.

37. Horace, *Odes*, 3. 30 and 1. 30: "I hope for better, not entirely to die."

38. *Faerie Queene* 3. 4. 18. 4–6.

39. Sir Richard Blackmore (ca. 1650–1729), physician to Queen Anne and writer of lengthy epics.

40. *Faerie Queene* 3. 11. 54. 1–4, 6–8 (misquoted slightly). Cf. Scott's *Letters*, 11:98.

41. Whatever it is worth.

42. Apollyon, "the angel of the bottomless pit" (Rev 9:11)

43. Cf. Scott's *Letters*, 7:178 n.

Prefatory Letter to *Peveril of the Peak*

1. By no means am I envious, I am far more astonished.

2. *Aeneid* 2. 774: "I was astounded, and my hair stood on end." But Dr. Dryasdust is wrong: it is the ghost of Creüsa that evokes this reaction from Aeneas.

3. Within the walls of a house.

4. Praise of one's self is to be despised.

5. Yielding arms to the gown.

6. To hasten into the middle of things.

7. This in jest.

8. He went off—he went forth—he broke out. Cf. Cicero's speech "Against Catiline."

9. At this point, Ballantyne wrote on the proof sheet, "*Is* such a Doctor mentioned in the H: of M. Lothian?"

Scott replied, "Yes."

10. *As You Like It* 4. 3 (misquoted).

11. Whom I—.

12. Ovid, *Metamorphoses* 6. 673: "Prominet immodicum pro longa cuspide rostrum." (Scott's version may be translated "The inordinate proboscis rises like a javelin.")

13. *Othello* 3. 3.

14. Geoffrey Crayon, a pseudonym of Washington Irving (1783–1859). See "The Stout Gentleman: A Stage-Coach Romance" in *Bracebridge Hall* (1822). Actually, the Stout Gentleman was in No. 13.

15. Shortly after the publication of *Peveril*, Scott was elected to the Roxburghe Club (see n. 21 to *The Fortunes of Nigel*, above), not in his own name, but simply as the Author of the Waverley Novels.

16. Thomas Frognall Dibdin (1776–1847), a famous bibliographer, librarian to Lord Spencer at Althorpe. Hodnet, like Althorpe, had one of the great libraries in Britain. The lord of the manor of this Shropshire estate was Richard Heber (1773–1833), a bibliomaniac and friend of Scott. Scott wrote to George Ellis: "Heber the magnificent, whose library and cellar are so superior to all others in the world" (*Letters*, 1: 264).

17. I am restoring the original word from the manuscript and corrected proof: "collar." The editor of the Dryburgh Edition substituted the meaningless "colour" because he missed the pun (admittedly not one of Scott's happiest): a *Collar of SS.*, *S's*, or *Esses* was an ornamental chain consisting of a series of *S*'s either joined together side by side or fastened in a row upon a band or ribbon, and was originally worn as a badge by the adherents of the House of Lancaster.

18. William Caxton (ca. 1421–91), the first English printer; Christopher Valdarfer (or Waldorfer) (fl. 1470s), Milanese printer, issued several important works, including the earliest edition of the *Decameron* (1471), the sale of which led to the start of the Roxburghe Club; Richard Pynson (d. 1530), London printer whose books were of a very high standard.

19. Samuel Johnson (1709–84), in Mrs. Piozzi's *Anecdotes of Samuel Johnson* (1786).

20. Evil in itself.

21. Matthew Prior (1664–1721), in "A Better Answer" (misquoted slightly).

22. Cf. Samuel Johnson, *The Rambler*, No. 4.

23. Thomas Gray (1716–71), in *The Bard* 3. 3. 3 (misquoted).

Notes

Introduction to *Chronicles of the Canongate*

1. Joseph Train (1779–1852), author of *Strains of the Mountain Muse: Poems, with Notes Illustrative of Ancient Traditions in Galloway and Ayrshire* (1814) and other historical and antiquarian works.

2. See the introduction to *The Bride of Lammermoor* for the particulars on Lord Stair and his family.

3. George Constable, as Scott revealed in the addition he made to this introduction in 1831.

4. William Erskine (1768–1822), "the only man in whose society Scott took great pleasure." See J. G. Lockhart, *Memoirs of the Life of Sir Walter Scott*, 5 vols. (Boston: Houghton Mifflin, 1902 [originally published 1837–38]), 3:587.

5. *Merry Wives of Windsor* 1. 1, or *Henry V* 2. 1.

General Preface

1. Allan Ramsay (1686–1758), Scottish poet and bookseller.

2. *Artamène, ou Le Grand Cyrus* (1649–53) by Madeleine de Scudéri (1607–1701) and *Cassandre* (1644–50) by Gauthier de Costes de la Calprenède (1614–1701) were lengthy prose romances frequently mentioned by Scott.

3. At Rosebank, a villa on the Tweed, near Kelso. It belonged to Scott's uncle, Captain Robert Scott.

4. *The Castle of Otranto* (1764), the first Gothic novel, by Horace Walpole.

5. *The Lady of the Lake* (1810), Scott's narrative poem, "shattered all records for the sale of poetry." See Edgar Johnson, *Sir Walter Scott: The Great Unknown*, 2 vols. (New York: Macmillan, 1970), 1:335.

6. William Erskine, the future Lord Kinedder, was Scott's closest friend. See n. 4 to "*Chronicles of the Canongate*," above.

7. Maria Edgeworth: see n. 4 to "*Waverley*: A Postscript," above.

8. Union of England and Ireland took place in 1801.

9. John Murray (1778–1843), the famous publisher, founder of the *Quarterly Review* in 1809.

10. Joseph Strutt: see n. 6 to "*Ivanhoe*: Dedicatory Epistle," above.

11. *The Padlock* (1768), a comic opera by the Irish playwright Isaac Bickerstaffe (d. 1812?). Mungo is a black servant.

12. Archibald Constable (1774–1827) and Robert Cadell (1788–1849), the great Edinburgh publishers.

13. James Ballantyne (1772–1833), friend and partner of Scott, printer of most of his works.

14. *Merchant of Venice* 4. 1.

Notes

15. John Leycester Adolphus (1795–1862), author of *Letters to Richard Heber, Esq. M. P., Containing Critical Remarks on the Series of Novels Beginning with Waverley and an Attempt to Ascertain Their Author* (1821).

16. Delitescency: the condition of lying hidden, concealment, seclusion.

17. Thomas Medwin (1788–1869), author of *Journal of the Conversations of Lord Byron* (1824).

18. "To the King's most gracious majesty."

19. Adolphus: see n. 15 above.

20. Thomas Scott: See n. 18 to "Review of *Tales of My Landlord*," above.

21. James Fenimore Cooper (1789–1851), the famous American novelist, whose work Scott admired.

22. *Aeneid* 2. 204: "I tremble as I tell it."

23. John Ballantyne and Will Laidlaw were Scott's amanuenses.

24. Sir David Wilkie (1785–1841), the famous Scottish artist, Scott's friend and favorite painter; Sir Edwin Landseer (1802–73), the famous English artist; Charles Robert Leslie (1794–1859); Gilbert Stuart Newton (1794–1835); Robert Cooper (d. 1836); William C. Kidd (1790–1863), all of whom contributed illustrations to the "Magnum Opus."

Guy Mannering

1. 1 Sam. 1:11.

2. Job 2:9.

3. Friedrich, baron de la Motte Fouqué (1777–1843), officer of the German cuirrassiers, one of the most prolific of German romantic writers, best remembered for the fairy tale *Undine* (1811).

4. Ingleby and Pinelli, two famous conjurors of Scott's time, are the likeliest possibilities, but the astrologer's diary does not seem to have been published. See *Guy Mannering*, ed. Andrew Lang (Boston: Dana Estes, 1892), 1:279.

5. Scott may have written the following in the composite article on Scottish gypsies in the first volume of *Blackwood's* (1817): "We well remember the peculiar feeling of curiosity and apprehension with which we sometimes encountered the formidable bands of this roaming people in our rambles among the Border hills, or when fishing for perch in the picturesque little lake at Loch Side" (p. 56).

6. Young Samuel Johnson, afflicted with the scrophula, or king's evil, was taken to Queen Anne to be touched. The regal touch, however, was without effect in this instance.

7. Cf. the introductions to *The Heart of Mid-Lothian* and *The Fortunes of Nigel* and Wordsworth's famous preface to the second edition of *Lyrical Ballads*.

Notes

Rob Roy

1. Archibald Constable (1774–1827), the great Edinburgh publisher, important for his connections with the *Edinburgh Review*, the *Encyclopaedia Britannica*, Walter Scott, and many other writers of the time.
2. William Wordsworth (1770–1850), last stanza of "Rob Roy's Grave" (misquoted).

The Heart of Mid-Lothian

1. John Campbell Argyle (1678–1743), second duke of Argyle, a prime agent in accomplishing the union of England and Scotland (1707) and preserving it in 1715. See Scott's tribute to him in *The Heart of Mid-Lothian*, 3:10.

The Bride of Lammermoor

1. Law's *Memorials: Memorialls; or, The Memorable Things That Fell Out within This Island of Brittain from 1638 to 1684*, by the Reverend Mr. Robert Law.
2. Charles Kirkpatrick Sharpe (1781–1851), poet, editor, historian, antiquarian, and connoisseur of the fine arts.
3. *The Institutions of the Law of Scotland* (1681), by James Dalrymple (1619–95), first Viscount Stair.

A Legend of Montrose

1. Sir Alexander Boswell, son of the great biographer, a poet and bibliomaniac, killed in a duel (1822).
2. James Graham Montrose (1612–50), first marquess and fifth earl of Montrose, the great royalist general in the period preceding the fall of Charles I.
3. Henry Guthrie (1600–76), bishop of Dunkeld, author of *Memoirs of Scottish Affairs, Civil and Ecclesiastical, from the Year 1637 to the Death of Charles I* (1702).
4. Pentland: the battle of Pentland Hills, near Edinburgh, on 28 November 1688, where Sir Thomas Dalzell defeated a force of Western Whigs.
5. Lieutenant Obadiah Lesmahagow, the eccentric Scottish soldier of *Humphry Clinker* (1771) by Tobias Smollett.
6. Francis Jeffrey (1773–1850), founder, editor, and chief critic of the *Edinburgh Review*. See his review of the Waverley Novels in the *Edinburgh Review* 33 (1820): 1–54.

Notes

Ivanhoe

1. The spoilt child.

2. Thomas Parnell (1679–1718), "A Fairy Tale, in the Ancient English Style," ll. 97–99 (misquoted slightly).

3. Joseph Addison (1672–1719), *Cato* 1. 4 (misquoted).

4. Richard I, "Coeur de Lion," king of England (1189–99).

5. Rev. John Logan (1748–88), a versatile but unlucky man of letters. His poems were published in 1781.

6. *Pontefract Castle* by "Jedediah Cleishbotham" in a "4th Series of *Tales of My Landlord*" was published by William Fearman in 1819.

7. "Manoeuvring" appeared in *Tales of Fashionable Life* (1809) by Maria Edgeworth.

8. Sir Samuel Egerton Brydges (1762–1837), the great bibliographer, published *The British Bibliographer* (1810–14), to which Joseph Haslewood (1769–1833) made large contributions.

9. *1 Henry IV* 1. 2.

The Monastery

1. "Tale of Sir Thopas," ll. 2004–6 (modernized).

2. Captain Dalgetty, Scott's humorous Ritt-Master from *A Legend of Montrose* (1819), a favorite character of the author.

3. The water bull, or Lowland Scottish "water-kelpie," was a fabled water spirit or demon assuming various shapes, such as that of a bullock, heifer, or horse; it was reputed to haunt lakes and rivers, and to take delight in, or even to bring about, the drowning of travelers and others.

4. Messuage: a dwelling house with its outbuildings and curtilage and the adjacent land assigned to its use.

5. *The Old Manor House* (1793) by Charlotte Smith (1749–1806). Scott said: "Old Mrs. Rayland is without a rival" (*Sir Walter Scott on Novelists and Fiction*, ed. Ioan Williams [New York: Barnes and Noble, 1968], p. 186).

6. Oh that I might fill up this house with friendly men (attributed to Socrates also).

7. Robert Chambers (1802–71), the Edinburgh publisher and author, first brought out *Illustrations of the Author of Waverley; Being Notices and Anecdotes of Real Characters, Scenes, Incidents, Etc. Presumed to Be Described in His Works* in 1822; he enlarged it in 1825.

8. *The Whole Duty of Man* (1658), a devotional work in which man's duties are discussed in detail, attributed today to Richard Allestree (1619–81), chaplain in ordinary to King Charles II and Regius professor of divinity and provost of Eton.

9. *Spectator* for Friday, 16 July 1714 (No. 568), by Addison.

10. Twice cooked cabbage.

11. George Crabbe (1754–1832), in *The Library* (1781), misquoted slightly.

12. *Le Comte de Gabalis ou entretiens sur les Sciences Secrèts* (1670) by Montfaucon de Villars (1635–73). Scott owned a copy of the 1714 London edition, *Abbé de Villars's Count de Gabalis: Being a Diverting Account of the Rosicrucian Doctrine of Spirits.*

13. *Undine* (1811), by Friedrich, baron de la Motte Fouqué.

14. *Tempest* V (misquoted slightly).

15. Wanton spirit.

16. *Amadis of Gaul*, the chivalric romance from Spain or Portugal. Scott knew the printed edition of Garcia de Montalvo (1508), but the original was probably by Joham de Lobeira (1261–1325) or Vasco de Lobeira (d. 1403).

17. *Euphues and his England* (1580), the successor to *Euphues: The Anatomy of Wit* (1578), by John Lyly (1554?–1606). As Scott indicates, *Euphues* was a very influential work.

18. Calprenède and Scudéri: see n. 2 to "General Preface," above.

19. *King Lear* 3. 4.

20. *Conquest of Granada* 1. 1.

21. Alexander Pope (1688–1744), *Essay on Man* 1. 13.

22. I detest the incredible.

23. *Gil Blas* (1715–35) by Alain-René Lesage and *Roderick Random* (1748) by Tobias Smollett are picaresque novels much admired by Scott.

24. Voltaire, preface to *L'Enfant prodigue* (1736): everything is allowed except boredom.

The Abbot

1. Johnson on 1 July 1863, in Boswell's *Life*. Charles Churchill (1731–64) was a political and social satirist.

2. Friedrich Melchior Grimm (1723–1807), and Denis Diderot (1713–84), *Mémoires historiques, etc. ou Correspondence philosophique et critique, addressee au Duc de Saxe Gotha, depuis 1753, jusqu' en 1790*, 2d ed., 7 vols. (London: 1814), 1:177.

3. *1 Henry IV* 1. 3.

4. *Don Quixote* 2. 2, 4.

5. *Merchant of Venice* 1. 1 (misquoted slightly).

6. *Iliad* 8.

7. Henri Pajon (d. 1770) published *Histoire du Prince Soly* in 1740.

8. *Caleb Williams* (1794) by William Godwin (1756–1836). Scott wrote: "We have met with few novels which excited a more powerful interest" (*Scott on Novelists and Fiction*, p. 193).

Notes

9. George Colman, the younger (1762–1836), adapted *Caleb Williams* for the stage as *The Iron Chest* (1796).

10. *The Padlock*: see n. 11 to "General Preface," above.

11. *1 Henry IV* 1. 3. Scott frequently quotes Hotspur, but this is Worcester speaking to Hotspur.

Kenilworth

1. William Robertson (1721–93), a Presbyterian minister, author of *History of Scotland during the Reigns of Queen Mary and of James VI* (1759) and other important historical works. He was the principal of Edinburgh University when Scott was a student there.

2. Elias Ashmole (1617–92), historian and astrologer, wrote and edited antiquarian and Rosicrucian works. Scott owned the 1719 edition of *Antiquities of Berkshire*.

3. William Julius Mickle (1735–88) and John Langhorne (1735–79). It was Scott's remembrance of Langhorne's "The Country Justice" that made the favorable impression upon Burns.

The Pirate

1. Corporal Trim, Uncle Toby's servant in *Tristram Shandy* (1760–67). Scott thought "Uncle Toby and his faithful squire, the most delightful characters in the work, or perhaps in any other" (*Scott on Novelists and Fiction*, p. 75). For Corporal Trim on Bohemia, see *Tristram Shandy*, 8:19. Shakespeare also gives Bohemia a seacoast.

2. "A Sea-Song" ("A Wet Sheet and a Flowing Sea"), ll. 15–16 (misquoted slightly). For Cunningham, see n. 25 to "Introductory Epistle to *The Fortunes of Nigel*," below.

3. "Of all whom I have ever seen, in whatever rank, she possessed most the power of rendering virtue lovely" (Scott, *Letters*, 3:91).

4. Samuel Butler (1612–80), *Hudibras* 3. 1–2.

The Fortunes of Nigel

1. *Moral Essays: Epistle III. To Allen Lord Bathurst*, ll. 249–50 (misquoted). The Man of Ross, who with a small estate performed many good works, was John Kyrle (1634–1724).

2. Lady Mary Wortley Montagu (1689–1762), poet and letter writer. Scott enjoyed "her inimitable *Letters*" (*Scott on Novelists and Fiction*, p. 37). For her letter above, see *The Complete Letters of Lady Mary Wortley*

Montagu, ed. Robert Halsband, 3 vols. (Oxford: Clarendon Press, 1965), 2:441.

3. *Arcadia* (1590), the important prose romance by Sir Philip Sidney (1554–86).

4. Edmund Burke (1729–97), in *Reflections on the Revolution in France* (1790). Burke is speaking specifically about the age of chivalry. See *Reflections* (London: Oxford University Press, 1907), p. 83.

5. John Stow (1525?–1605), chronicler and antiquary, producer of *A Survey of London* (1598, 1603) and several other important works.

6. *Squire of Alsatia* (1688), an interesting picture of contemporary manners by the poet and dramatist Thomas Shadwell (1642?–92).

Peveril of the Peak

1. *1 Henry IV* 5. 4 (misquoted slightly).

2. *Gil Blas* 7. 4. The archbishop's apoplexy impaired his intellect and marred his powers of composition.

3. *Desiderata Curiosa; or, A Collection of Divers Scarce and Curious Pieces, Relating Chiefly to Matters of English History; Consisting of Choice Tracts, Memoirs, Letters, Wills, Epitaphs, etc.* (1732) by Rev. Francis Peck (1692–1743).

4. *Measure for Measure* 5.

5. Mignon, the fairylike child who loves hopelessly, in *Wilhelm Meister's Apprenticeship* (1795–96).

Quentin Durward

1. Lucifer appears in Byron's *Cain* (1821), which was dedicated to Scott. Scott was much obliged: "I do not know that his muse has ever taken so lofty a flight amid her former soarings" (*Letters,* 7:37).

2. Durindana or Durandal: the sword of Roland or Orlando, which had been that of Hector of Troy. Durandarte was a knight who fell at Roncesvalles. See *Don Quixote* 2. 23, 26–29.

3. Edmund Burke, in *Reflections on the Revolution in France* (1790).

4. Robert, "the Holy Man," according to Commines.

5. Philippe de Commines or Commynes (ca. 1445–1511), critical and philosophical historian, counselor and chamberlain of the duke of Burgundy, defected to the service of Louis XI. His important *Memoirs* deal mostly with the reign of Louis XI.

6. François de Salignac de la Mothe Fénelon (1651–1715), French churchman and man of letters, author of voluminous works including the very popular *Télémaque* (1699).

Notes

St. Ronan's Well

1. Horace, *Ars Poetica* l. 287. Scott means: "to celebrate ordinary life." Cf. his review of Jane Austen's *Emma*, rpt. in *Scott on Novelists and Fiction*, pp. 225–36.

2. *Evelina* (1778) by Fanny Burney, Madame D'Arblay (1752–1840); *Marriage* (1818) by Susan Ferrier (1782–1854), a friend of Scott.

3. Maria Edgeworth (see n. 4 to "*Waverley*: A Postscript"); Jane Austen (1775–1817), whose quality Scott was one of the first to recognize; and Charlotte Smith (1749–1806).

4. Sir Alexander Drawcansir: the pseudonym under which Henry Fielding conducted *The Covent Garden Journal* (1852), a periodical containing essays on literature and manners.

5. Pope, *Essay on Man* 1. 13.

Redgauntlet

1. Nonjuring interest: those who refused to swear allegiance to the Hanoverian regime.

2. Murray of Elibank. Charles Edward Stewart refused to listen to any such assassination plot.

3. Sir Robert Walpole (1676–1745), first earl of Orford, the Whig prime minister and chancellor of the exchequer (1715–17, 1721–42).

4. *Political and Literary Anecdotes of His Own Times* (written in 1761 but not published till 1818), by Dr. William King (1685–1763).

5. *Macbeth* 5. 3.

The Betrothed

1. Laurence Sterne, in *Tristram Shandy* (1760–67), 4:25.

2. In 1825, the speculative frenzy of the recent past, especially the absurd hopes built upon the future of the South American republics, caused a serious financial panic. Scott's own ruin was involved.

3. Willy-nilly.

4. James Hogg, Ettrick Shepherd (1770–1835), versatile writer whose poetical gift was discovered and encouraged by Scott.

5. "The Fray of Elibank," l. 230: "An' mony a brave fellow, an' mony a brave feat."

6. The Noble Moringer: in an illness so severe that he dreaded the loss of his reason, Scott translated this ballad in order to confirm his mental powers.

7. Ludwig Tieck (1773–1853), German romantic poet, novelist, and dramatist, author of *Leben und Tod von Golo und Genoveva* (1800).

Notes

8. *Guardian* for Wednesday, 10 June 1713 (No. 78), the famous "Receit to Make an Epick Poem" by Alexander Pope.

The Talisman

1. *Anastasius* (1819), a picaresque romance by Thomas Hope (1770?–1831). It takes place in the East, and, in Scott's opinion, contains "deep passion and gloomy interest" (*Scott on Novelists and Fiction*, p. 359).

2. *The Adventures of Hajji Baba of Ispahan* (1824) and *The Adventures of Hajji Baba of Ispahan in England* (1828) by James Justinian Morier (1780?–1849). According to Scott, Morier "makes good what he himself affirms, . . . the single 'idea of illustrating Eastern manners by contrast with those of England' " (*Scott on Novelists and Fiction*, p. 356).

3. *Thalaba the Destroyer* (1801) by Robert Southey (1774–1843).

4. *Lalla Rookh* (1817), a series of oriental tales in verse, connected by a story in prose, by Thomas Moore (1779–1852).

5. *History of the Crusades* (1820) and *History of Chivalry; or, Knighthood, and Its Times* (1825) by Charles Mills (1788–1826). Scott wrote to Mills, patiently explaining the difference between the use of historical sources and the literary invention of sources for fictional material. See *Letters*, 9:271.

6. In *Ivanhoe*.

Woodstock

1. *Satan's Invisible World Discover'd; or, A Choice Collection of Modern Relations, Proving Evidently against the Atheists of This Present Age, That There Are Devils, Spirits, Witches, Etc. To All Which Is Added That Marvellous History of Major Weir and His Sister, the Witches of Bargarran, Pittenweem, and Calder, Etc.* (1865) by Professor George Sinclair (d. 1696).

2. Dr. Robert Plot (1640–96), antiquary, directed his attention to the systematic study of natural history and antiquities, and published *The Natural History of Oxfordshire: Being an Essay towards the Natural History of England* (1676).

Chronicles of the Canongate

1. Thus is immortality gained (Virgil).

2. *A Midsummer-Night's Dream* 5. 1.

3. James Graham (1612–50), First Marquess of Montrose, in "My Dear and Only Love" (misquoted slightly).

4. Wordsworth, in "The Fountain" (adapted).

Notes

The Fair Maid of Perth

1. Joanna Baillie (1762–1851), Scottish dramatist and poet, author of *Plays on the Passions* (1798–1836). Scott thought the character of Orra in *Fear* "exquisitely supported as well as imagined, and the language distinguished by a rich variety of fancy, which I know no instance of excepting in Shakespeare" (*Letters*, 3:35).

2. General David Stewart of Garth (1772–1829), author of *Sketches of the Highlanders of Scotland* (1822).

Anne of Geierstein

1. Goethe, *Goetz von Berlichingen* (1771), translated by Scott (1799).

2. Sir Francis Palgrave (1788–1861), author of *The Rise and Progress of the English Commonwealth* (1832) and other critical studies of medieval history.

3. Johann Heinrich Daniel Zschokké (1771–1848), author of *Des Schweizerlands Geschichten für das Schweizervolk* (1822).

4. Amable Guillaume Prosper Brugiere, baron de Barante (1782–1866), historian influenced by Scott, and author of *Histoire des Ducs de bourgogne de la Maison de Valois, 1364–1483* (1824).

5. Jean Froissart (ca. 1337–ca. 1410), French chronicler whose literary artistry and chivalric spirit impressed Scott. Scott is referring to the following edition: *Collection des Chroniques Nationales Françaises, éscrites en Langue Vulgaire, du XIII*e *au XVI*e· *siècles*, with notes and explanations by J. A. Buchon (Paris, 1824–26).

Count Robert of Paris

1. *2 Henry IV* 2. 1.

2. *Gil Blas* 7. 4. Cf. Scott's letter of 8 December 1830 to James Ballantyne in *Letters*, 11:431–32. The hint extorted from the unwilling secretary was that the archbishop's last discourse was not written with quite the overpowering eloquence and conclusive argument of his former ones.

3. Robert Paltock (1697–1767), author of *The Life and Adventures of Peter Wilkins* (1751), including "his extraordinary conveyance to the Country of the Glums and Gawrys."

4. Robert Southey (1774–1843), creator of the Glendoveers, "the loveliest race of all of heavenly birth," in *The Curse of Kehama* (1810).

5. Cf. Scott's review of *Frankenstein* in *Scott on Novelists and Fiction*, pp. 260–72.

Notes

6. *Spectator* for Thursday, 17 July 1712 (No. 433), and for Friday, 18 July 1712 (No. 434), both by Addison.

7. "The Battle of the Sexes," in the *Scots Magazine* 21 (1759): 192–96.

8. *Hamlet* 1. 5.

Castle Dangerous

1. John Barbour (1316?–95), Scottish poet and archdeacon of Aberdeen (1357), author of *The Bruce* (ca. 1375), which celebrates the war of independence and the deeds of Robert Bruce and James Douglas.

2. David Hume (1560?–1630?), of Godscroft, controversialist, historian, and poet, author of *History of the House and Race of Douglas and Angus* (1644) and other works on Scotland.

3. Raphael Holinshed (d. 1580?), planner of the famous *Chronicles* that are known by his name.

4. Thomas Rymer (1641–1713), critic and historian, remembered for his valuable collection of historical records, *Foedera, Conventiones, et cujuscunque generis Acta Publica* (1704–35).

5. See n. 1 above. Scott is referring to the following edition: *Wallace and Bruce: Barbour's Metrical History of King Robert I, and Henry the Minstrel's Life and Acts of Sir William Wallace of Ellerslie* ed. by Dr. John Jamieson (Edinburgh, 1820).